Ways of Being Roman

Discourses of Identity in the Roman West

Louise Revell

OXBOW | books
Oxford & Philadelphia

First published in the United Kingdom in 2016. Reprinted in 2021 by
OXBOW BOOKS
The Old Music Hall, 106-108 Cowley Road, Oxford, OX4 1JE

and in the United States by
OXBOW BOOKS
1950 Lawrence Road, Havertown, PA 19083

Paperback Edition: ISBN 978-1-84217-292-6
Digital Edition: ISBN 978-1-78570-188-7

A CIP record for this book is available from the British Library

Library of Congress Cataloging-in-Publication Data

Names: Revell, Louise.
Title: Ways of being Roman : discourses of identity in the Roman West / Louise Revell.
Description: Oxford : Oxbow Books, 2015. | Includes bibliographical references.
Identifiers: LCCN 2015034193 | ISBN 9781842172926 (paperback)
Subjects: LCSH: Identity (Psychology)–Social aspects–Rome–Provinces–History. | Ethnicity–Rome–Provinces–History. | Social status–Rome–Provinces–History. | Gender identity–Rome–Provinces–History. | Age groups–Rome–Provinces–History. | Roman provinces–Social conditions. | Roman provinces–Antiquities. | Social archaeology–Rome–Provinces. | Rome–History–Empire, 30 B.C.-284 A.D. | Rome–History–Empire, 284-476
Classification: LCC DG87 .R48 2015 | DDC 937/.06–dc23 LC record available at
http://lccn.loc.gov/2015034193

For a complete list of Oxbow titles, please contact:

UNITED KINGDOM
Oxbow Books
Telephone (01865) 241249
Email: oxbow@oxbowbooks.com
www.oxbowbooks.com

UNITED STATES OF AMERICA
Oxbow Books
Telephone (610) 853-9131, Fax (610) 853-9146
Email: queries@casemateacademic.com
www.casemateacademic.com/oxbow

Oxbow Books is part of the Casemate Group

Front cover: Mosaic of Medusa (MNAT 2921; photo: MNAT)
Back cover: La maison du buste en argent, Vaison-la-Romaine (photo: author)

Contents

Figures and Tables

Acknowledgements

This book has been a long time in writing. During this time, a large number of people have contributed to it either directly or indirectly through general discussions about Roman identity and social archaeology. Thanks go to Matthew Johnson for encouraging me to write this, and Stephanie Moser for support throughout the process; to Tim Champion and Yvonne Marshall for discussions about ethnicity and feminist theory respectively. Ray Laurence and Mary Harlow encouraged my interest in family and age. A great debt is owed to Natalie Kampen for reminding me that Roman archaeology is more than just 'the men talking to the men about the men', and to the remarkable group she assembled for the Getty sponsored Arts of Rome's Provinces for much discussion and debate. The book was informed by a module I taught for a number of years on Roman Identities, and I would like to thank all the students who contributed to the formation of the ideas here. At Oxbow, Clare Litt and Julie Gardiner have proved supportive throughout. Hella Eckardt, Simon Keay, Seville Archaeological Museum and the British Museum kindly granted me permission to use particular images. Lucy Elkerton, Josh Pollard, Alison Moore and Martin Millett read the full draft, and made helpful comments; any errors remain my own. Finally, I would like to thank my husband, Mike Blumenthal, for love and support and keeping me sane.

Preface

The multiple aspects which form the identity of any single person in the past intertwine to form a complex matrix of encounters and experiences. The temporal and geographical range of the Roman empire increases these exponentially, making generalisation even more difficult. And yet there are clear lines of discourse through which these identities are negotiated: ideologies and activities which take on a prominence at any one time. My intention in this book is to look at some of the structures through which various aspects of Roman identities were formed. I am not looking for the individual experience, a hypothetical paradigm of Roman-ness, but rather the ways in which it was possible to act in the past. I am not going to concentrate purely on Roman-ness, or ethnicity, but look at the multiples aspects of identity: age, gender, status, and how these intersect. It is not an exhaustive account, more an examination of the way in which various kinds of identities may have been formed, with the implicit assumption that such approaches can be used to investigate other forms of identities.

Nevertheless, there are a number of essential points which influence the approach which I shall take in this book. The first is that identity is not static: it is not fixed, but rather something which is reinforced on a daily basis through the interaction between the individual, other members of the society, and the social structures through which that society is organised. Similarly, identity can change through the progression of a person's life, not only in terms of age categories, but also the ways in which gender is understood, or professional identities created. Therefore, I am not trying to reconstruct the experience of an individual. Instead I am interested in the discourse or social structures through which any individual understood who they were and made their actions meaningful in Roman society, and the material manifestations of these discourses. However, these discourses or ideologies were not neutral or value-free. Inherent within them was a sense of inequality. Certain activities or identities were judged more acceptable, others were seen as lesser and marginalised. Implicit within this are the power relations and hierarchies within Roman society: some kinds of people were valued over others, or had greater access to resources for power. Identity and the ideology of identity came to legitimise these inequalities, making them seem natural and obvious to the members of the community.

The material which follows will be presented according to aspects of identity; nevertheless, it should be noted that these are somewhat artificial divisions and that there are some themes which cross-cut the various elements, such as the idea of *virtus* or moral standing. Similarly, the multi-vocality of material culture and social practice mean that the same activities and discourse which mediate status, for example, are also used in the mediation of gender. In any person's daily life these would overlap and interact. However, the advantage of discussing the material in this way is that it allows us to emphasis the way these themes become part of a discourse, rather than a single, unchanging entity. We can also look at the ways in which these discourses are expressed through multiple forms of material culture. This material culture not only provides our evidence for these past identities, it also formed the medium through which these identities were negotiated and expressed. As such, it is subject to distortion, not merely in terms of what we understand as bias: it is the way in which certain identities were privileged and made more visible. By looking at the discourses, we can explore the way in which certain identities were made invisible, and so begin to fill in the gaps of the possibilities of experience.

Chapter 1

Identity in Roman Archaeology

Introduction

A popular feature of many museums and archaeological sites is the cut-out of three or four people from the past. The face is cut out, and the visitor is encouraged to put their own face into the hole whilst friends and family capture the moment in a photograph. The visitor in the present becomes the person in the past, and can be photographed as part of a Roman family, or as a Roman soldier. Whilst these can add to the fun of the visit, they rely on the assumption that people in the past were just like us. In contrast, questioning the contextual specificity of identity has become an important theme within archaeology, reflecting a wider interest in the topic within the Humanities and Social Sciences. Until recently, personal identity was conceptualised as a static entity, and even an innate, essential quality. Specific aspects of identity were used as ways of describing people and were believed to be unchanging and universally applicable: to call a person a man or woman, or an adult or child was seen as self-evident and unproblematic, and similarly the criteria through which such labels were defined was also seen as universal. Because these identifiers were unproblematic they were largely ignored within archaeology: the definition of a group of people was viewed as a direct relationship to the material associated with them, or a product of their biology. The classification of the material was self-evident, and once a particular piece of material had been identified, the user or the community could then be classified in the same way. This allowed the production of an archaeological narrative of cultural groups to mirror the event-driven historical narrative produced from textual sources. Outside of the identification of cultural groups, the question of identity was of little concern.

This picture has changed completely in the last 20–30 years in both wider academia and in archaeological research. Work focussed on the question of identity arose out of an initial desire to identify so-called minority groups, such as children or women or even slaves, but it has since gone beyond that. It still takes as its fundamental starting point the recognition that there were divisions within the social group, and such marginalised groups did exist, as opposed the traditional normalisation of the experience of the elite, adult male. However, a fuller account of identity goes beyond this. There is a conceptual problem with an approach which critically explores the construction of the social identity of the marginalised, but leaves the dominant groups and the construction of their group identity unproblematised. Therefore, an archaeology of identity is concerned with looking for the ways in which all these categories of identity were made meaningful: what were the social conditions through which the identity of male or female, or even soldier, centurion and general were understood by both the individual and society overall. Further, if these conditions are not static, how might their construction change over time. The foundation of this work is sociological and philosophical theories about the nature of the self, and as such rejects the idea of common-sense assumptions of a cross-cultural universalism.

Roman archaeology has not been immune to these wider shifts. The clearest impact has the use of such theoretical approaches to rethink the question of cultural change within the provinces. The debate concerning Romanization has been reframed as the transition from one form of ethnic identity to another (or alternatively, a rejection of the imperial cultural identity). More recently, there has been an increase in the work looking at other forms of social identity, such as gender, the lifecourse, and military identities. This work on identity in the Roman world has not been confined to archaeology, and there have been parallel developments in Roman history and art history which have looked at questions of gender and status in particular.

Identity as common-sense

The idea that the question of identity is a recent innovation within the study of the Roman world may seem strange to some, since it could be argued that there is a long-standing tradition of studies of the other, whether this is women or slaves. Biographies of notable women from the ancient world, or the identification of women within the archaeological record from specific artefacts might suggest that they have formed part of our narratives of the ancient world, and raise the question of how an approach based on identity can present something new. However, this apparent visibility hides the fact that such volumes are actually few in number, and that the level of critical engagement is somewhat depressing. Eleanor Scott has demonstrated that there are a series of techniques through which marginalised groups have been excluded from serious academic study in their own right (Scott 1995: 176–9), particularly in the more grand narrative accounts of the Roman empire:

1. exclusion: women are completed ignored because the narratives of the Roman world have concentrated on male-dominated activities such as political activity within Rome and the provinces
2. pseudo-inclusion: women are included, but only appear when they are anomalous to the male norm
3. alienation: women only considered in relation to men, or when they threaten male views of 'correct' female behaviour

Whilst Scott is primarily discussing the writing out of women, these same techniques can equally be applied to the erasure of children, slaves or the poor within Roman archaeology. If we took the same three factors and substituted 'children' for 'women' and 'adult' for 'men/male', the argument would still stand. Children are excluded from the dominant adult world, except in discussions of the waning power of the paterfamilias, or in narratives of the imperial family, where they are considered in relation to the imperial succession. Similarly, studies of slavery have focussed on their economic value, and so their relationship to the production of elite wealth. The biographical tradition, which appears to rescue these excluded categories from obscurity, is more likely to provide a narrative of the events of an individual life without consideration of the social construction of their identity.

This is not to criticise the scholarship of these works or to downplay their contribution to Roman archaeology. Nevertheless, their contribution to interpretations of the social organisation of the Roman world is problematic, as the categorisation of the individual is left as a given, whether that is the more powerful free, elite man, or the 'other', the slave, child or woman. Such categorisations are taken as being self-evident and a description in themselves: we may worry about the legal definitions of slavery, but not the social definition. This was part of a wider context of social attitudes and academic research where social categories were seen as being innate and inevitable: in a world view were women were believed to be inferior to men through bodily and mental incapacity, for example, there was no need to investigate how the attributes and characteristics associated with each gender were social constructs.

There are various reasons why this incomplete account was accepted by those studying the Roman world. The first is that are various sources of evidence are not themselves value-free representations of the past, but were actively used by the Romans themselves in constructing social hierarchies. All Romanists rely heavy on the ancient writers, such as Livy or Tacitus, to provide a framework for their historical narrative. Alternatively, more specialised texts are used to provide the context for specific issues or themes, such Columella or Varro for villas, or Vitruvius for architecture. However, such sources were written by elite, adult men, who were talking about their world from their particular perspective. Until recently, they have been taken at face-value as providing an insight on how things really were, but now we are beginning to see them as part of an idealising discourse. Rather than providing a true account of the lives of children, for example, like all material culture they were part of the means through which the Romans debated the definition of childhood, the correct behaviour for children, and constructed the social boundary between child and adult. To add to this complexity, identities could be used as a metaphor: they could be used to express ideas about other aspects of society. For example, the iconography of children was used by various emperors as a way to symbolise the prosperity of their rule, most notably by Augustus on the Ara Pacis (Currie 1996).

With the problem of bias within the textual evidence, the temptation is to fall back on the archaeology as somehow conveying a more 'truthful' picture of the past, representing the lives of the non-elites and marginalised. However, this is still problematic. Post-processual archaeologists have argued that material culture is not value-free, but given symbolic meaning which is context specific (Hodder 1986, Shanks and Tilley 1992). These meanings are then drawn upon in the construction of social relationships, and as such are implicated in how people in the past maintained their positions of power within these societies. As with the textual evidence, the material culture of the Roman empire highlighted the experiences of the elite, adult male, making other groups within the society invisible. As we shall see, public architecture served to highlight the power of the elite male, writing out those marginal to the political world through which power was gained and maintained. The problem is that there has been a tendency amongst archaeologists to reconstruct this privileged experience as the norm, thus rendering the powerless invisible a second time. In this way, the writing out of certain experiences has arisen because our material record is not a direct reflection of some form of truth, but rather is implicated in the maintenance of social identity.

A second problem has arisen from what might be termed common sense assumptions, or seeing identity as something which is static and unchanging throughout human history. The result of this is that there is an approach which sees Roman identities as similar to modern experiences. Where there has been research into less privileged groups within Roman society, this has at times been uncritical and based around this Roman-modern equivalence. For example, when in 1962 Balsdon wrote about Roman women, he looked at the changes in their lifestyles within a chapter entitled 'Female emancipation', thereby directly equating it with the gender politics of the mid-20th century. His descriptions of the lives of Roman women is framed and explained through modern gender stereotypes:

> In early Rome, if she was loving and obedient to her husband, a good Hausfrau and an attentive mother, she led by Roman standards – as by the later standards of the Victorian age – a full and complete life ... By the last fifty years of the Republic, when we have plenty of contemporary evidence – for good or ill – in the smart, corrupt society of Rome itself, the New Woman has arrived. (Balsdon 1962: 45)

Balsdon equates the lives of women in the early Republic with those of the late 19th century, interpreting the changes in women's lives during the late Republic and early Imperial period with those of western women during the 20th century, and seeming to disapprove of both in equal measure. This temptation to see identity as either timeless or within a series of enduring caricatures results in a lack of critical research into identities and the way in which identities were formed in the past. There is, for example, an assumption that women had set roles within agricultural activity within the early Medieval period. However, more detailed research has demonstrated regional variability in the ways in which agricultural tasks were used to maintain the difference between men and women (Smith 2005: 122). In some areas, the production of bread is the preserve of men, in others it falls to women. Similarly, in some places harvesting the grain was allotted to men, in other estates, women were expected to participate in the harvest, sometimes through making sheaves. This warns us against assuming what constituted gender specific tasks in the past, and the allocation of domestic duties to women, and agricultural or economic activity to men.

These tendencies to project modern norms onto past behaviours have been exacerbated the privileging of the Classical world, and the way in which modern western societies have styled themselves as the successors of Classical civilization. This has impacted on how knowledge about the Roman period has been generated, both in terms of excavation priorities and assumptions implicit in the resulting interpretations. We are increasingly aware that our reconstruction of the past is fundamentally located within the context of the present, and that the politics and the social assumptions of the present impact upon our reconstruction of past societies (Shanks and Tilley 1992). Frequently cited examples of this include the imposition of a German nationalistic interpretation on prehistoric archaeology (Arnold 1990), or the appropriation of the Roman past by Mussolini under the concept of Romanità as obvious examples of the use of the past for explicitly political motives (Painter 2005). It is tempting to categorise this as a feature of extreme political regimes. However, research has gone beyond this, and looked at the more subtle appropriation of the Roman past by a number of nations and peoples from the immediate post-Roman period through to the present day. This has developed as an important theme in both archaeology and Classics (Freeman 1997, Hingley 2000), and it is not my intention here to repeat that material. Instead, I want to flag the idea that Roman material culture has been used in the creation of more recent identities, and that at times, this has impacted back on the way we have understood the meanings of specific elements of Roman material, and Roman identities themselves.

From the Renaissance onwards western societies have modelled themselves as the direct or indirect heirs of Graeco-Roman culture. The ways in which this has happened have fluctuated over time and between different countries, and I do not want to present this as a uniform phenomenon. Nevertheless, this has resulted in a mistaken familiarity with Roman culture, with the assumption that our societies functioned in similar ways and that we hold similar values (for example, Terrenato 2005). This has created a sort of feedback loop in our interpretation of Roman society. In the recent past ruling elites have modelled themselves on the Greek and Roman political elites, using the textual and material evidence to justify their position of power. In turn, this idea of social organisation has then been projected backwards to interpret the past, reinforcing this idea of similarity and familiarity, and obscuring the way in which this relationship has influenced our understanding of the Roman past. It has fed into excavation priorities, both home and abroad, with local excavations concentrating on villa sites with their wealth of mosaics, and the interest of foreign academies in the archaeology of Rome and Italy (Dyson 2008). The imbalance in the material evidence has impacted upon the narratives produced of Roman society, reinforcing the idea that the Romans were familiar and just like us.

This has continued into the models used in interpreting Roman society, both in terms of wider grand narrative and in terms of Roman Studies themselves. For example, 19th-century family history was dominated by models of social evolution, with the Graeco-Roman period seen as a pivotal period of transformation from primitive to civilised (Patterson 1998), or as bound up in debates about the difference between the oriental and the western family structures, constructed around stereotypes of patrilineality, segregation of the sexes, and endogamy/exogamy (Hajnal 1965, Pomeroy 1997). The Roman family and the roles within it have not been neutral topics of study, but, as seen from the Baldson quotation above, studied through a veil of modern assumptions about the modern, western family. This equation between Roman and modern societies is also seen in the study of the Roman army and its soldiers. Simon James has argued that Roman military studies has been influenced by desires to emulate Roman armies, and subsequently since the 18th century, active or retired soldiers have played an important role in the excavation and interpretation of military material, producing the idea of the eternal army, unaffected by their context, and fighting as a military machine. This removes the possibility that the ancient and modern armies may be different, and so the social life of the Roman soldier and the military unit has been assumed to be identical to that of the modern soldier. More recently, these assumptions have been questioned as this universal paradigm of military service has been picked apart for the Roman period. Carol van Driel-Murray, for example, has argued that that the British army structure is not the only possible model, and that the archaeological evidence of women and children attached to the Roman forts suggests an alternative analogy of the Dutch army of the 18th century, where soldiers were accompanied on campaign by their wives and children (van Driel-Murray 1995).

This questioning of assumptions about the military forms part of a wider disquiet with the 'common-sense' or essentialist approaches to social archaeology which obscured identity as a topic of research. These approaches argued that certain characteristics of gender, race, status and occupation were innate or at best only changed within a paradigm of slow-moving social evolution. This rendered the research of social structures and identity as largely inconsequential: what it was to be a woman, a Roman or a slave were inevitable and static. It was valid to see what the sources told us about specific individuals, often framed within the biographical approach, but this produced descriptive accounts based on assumptions that the Roman world being essentially the same as the modern world. However, a series of intellectual developments have led to this approach being increasingly challenged and the emergence of identity as a key question within Roman research. In the next section, I will examine some of the factors which have contributed to this.

The development of identity in Roman Studies

Since the 1970s, there has been a growing recognition that our reconstruction of past societies has centred around the construction of the normative experience as that of the adult, elite male as representative of the whole society. Concentration on the processes of the past produced a landscape curiously depopulated of humans. In contrast, the development of post-processual archaeology in the 1980s re-centred people and their identities (Trigger 1989, Johnson 1999). An important element of this was the formulation of new methods for understanding the meaning of material culture, and importantly, the rejection of the idea that it was a passive proxy for human action in the past (Hodder 1986, Shanks and Tilley 1992). Various theoretical strands influenced these approaches, and it would be erroneous to present post-processual archaeology as an homogeneous body of thought. A focus on identity came in part from Giddens' structuration theory (Giddens 1984, Barrett 1994), but other archaeologists drew on Heidegger's theory of phenomenology (Thomas 1998). A further influence was feminist theory which broadly speaking has sought to decentre the male experience, and focus attention on those who were previously marginalised, not only women, but also children and gays (Brown 1997: 13, Marshall 2008).

Within Roman archaeology, there have been two key stimuli to the emergence of identity as a theme. The first of these is a more critical investigation of the post-conquest cultural changes. Influenced by the work of Mommsen, Collingwood and Haverfield, these changes have been interpreted through a model of social evolution (Freeman 1997, Hingley 2000). This is particularly acute when dealing with the western provinces where Roman culture was valued in the present as being superior to Iron Age cultures, and so the cultural changes evident in the archaeological record were seen as inevitable in the onward march of human culture towards modern civilisation. In 1990 this was challenged by Martin Millett, who set forward a model for Romanization based upon the aspirations of the provincial elites to enter into the new networks of power (Millett 1990a, 2003/04). Although controversial and not universally accepted, Millett's work has had the effect of opening up the question of changing ethnic identity in a more explicit way and placing the question of cultural change and ethnicity centre stage. This has led to some Roman archaeologists to reinterpret their evidence through this model, and others to look for alternative theoretical explanations through which to reinterpret their archaeological evidence. One influential strand of this has been the incorporation of post-colonial theory, derived from the work of Edward Said (Said 1979, 1993, Webster 1996) and considering, amongst other elements, the idea of the subaltern and discrepant experiences of Roman imperialism (Mattingly 2004). Nevertheless, such approaches similarly have their critics (Versluys 2014), resulting in a field subject to academic contention and open to new theoretical paradigms.

The second stimulus to the development of identity studies in Roman archaeology has been the Theoretical Roman Archaeology Conference (TRAC), held annually since 1991. Eleanor Scott inaugurated the conference with the aim of offering a venue for theoretically-informed interpretations of Roman archaeology (Scott 1993). The adoption of post-processual approaches had at that time been less prominent in Roman archaeology than prehistoric archaeology, and Scott's intention was that TRAC would become a forum for their articulation, and in particular, the incorporation of gender archaeology. The annual conferences and the rapid publication of their proceedings have changed the shape of Roman archaeology in Britain at least (James and Millett 2001). The conferences have not promoted a single theoretical perspective; instead identity in the past has been approached through a range of theoretical models such as creolisation, discrepant identities and struturation theory. Whilst TRAC has succeeded in providing a forum for the discussion of new theoretical approaches, it has proved less successful in stimulating Roman archaeologists to move beyond ethnicity and consider other aspects of identity (Laurence 1999). For the first decade of TRAC, many of the papers concentrated on new approaches to Roman imperialism and ethnic identities, in part due to their concentration on the archaeology of the provinces (Hill 2001). Gradually this has begun to change and increasingly wider topics such as gender, children and the body have been considered, although with mixed success (Baker 2003, Revell 2010b). Martin Pitts has analysed publications on Roman identity over a period of ten years, and established that more than 60% of the studies focus on ethnic identity (Pitts 2007). Thus identity is now one of the core questions in Roman archaeology, although there is still a concentration on ethnic identity, with less work on status, gender and age. Furthermore, there is a notable concentration on case-studies from Roman Britain, and there is still a dearth of studies looking at aspects of identity other than ethnicity for other western provinces.

There has been a parallel development within ancient history, which has looked at aspects of social life using the textual and to a lesser extent iconographic evidence from Rome, Italy and Egypt. Within this it is possible to identify three important strands of research. The first of these is women and gender, influenced by the growth in gender studies within history and social science (Brown 1997). Following the ground-breaking work of Sarah Pomeroy (1975), a number of edited volumes were published looking at questions of women in the past (for example, Archer *et al.* 1994, Hawley and Levick 1995, Kleiner and Matheson 1996), and to a lesser extent, the question of masculinity (Foxhall and Salmon 1998b, 1998a). The second strand has been work on children and the Roman family, in part provoked by Philippe Ariès' (1962) *Centuries of Childhood*, and this has led to the rejection of the idea of the family as a universal cultural construct and assumptions of the nuclear family as the norm (Rawson 2005, Harlow and Laurence 2007). There has been extensive work looking at the construction of the Roman family, spearheaded by the work of Beryl Rawson, Suzanne Dixon and Keith Bradley, and a series of conferences dedicated to the question of the family, their focus expanding from Rome, to Italy and then to the provinces (Rawson 1986, 1991, Rawson and Weaver 1997, George 2005, Dasen and Späth 2010). This has spearheaded extensive research into the family, gendered roles within the family, and questions of infancy and childhood.

The third strand of research was provoked by the work of Michel Foucault in *The History of Sexuality*, and in particular volumes 2 and 3 in which he dealt explicitly with the classical world (Foucault 1979, 1985, 1986). His central argument was that attitudes towards body were a cultural construct, and that a discourse of power relations was located in and expressed through control of the body and sexuality. Whilst some of his interpretations have been questioned on the basis of his lack of familiarity with the classical evidence, the three volumes have had a profound influence on ancient history as a discipline. His legacy has been to challenge Classicists to deal with these questions, and consequently this has led to work focussing on the body and the question of sexuality in the past, as well as feeding into debates about gender and the role of women.

Such changing theoretical approaches within both archaeology and history have produced an intellectual context where identity is no longer seen as straightforward. We have come to see that the relationship between such classifications in the present and the meaning of them in the past as more problematic. There has been a questioning of essentialist interpretations of material culture, and running in tandem with this, we no longer see identity as having a fixed meaning; instead we have come to acknowledge that it is more dynamic and fluid. The way in which any particular aspect of identity is worked through is dependent upon the make-up of the society: what it is to be of elite rank, or to be a child, and the way in which that aspect of identity is expressed will be situational. Furthermore, the very constituent parts will also differ according to context: for example whether there are two, three or more genders, or whether there is a separate age group between child and adult (the adolescent or teenager).

The social construction of identity

As argued above, the idea of identity has become a core topic within Roman studies, as with archaeology more widely, with a dramatic increase in the number of papers and books with 'identity' in the title. This has not been without some disquiet, as I shall discuss below. As also argued above, there is no single theory of identity, and archaeological research draws upon various disciplines (anthropology, philosophy, sociology, cultural studies) and theoretical schools. It is not my intention here to provide an overview of all this literature and the various approaches; these are available elsewhere. Instead, in this section I will outline some of the key ideas which have informed the approaches presented in this book, and which are fundamental to my own research.

One common misconception is to equate identity with the individual, and the idea that researching identity is to identify the experience of an idealised person in the past. This can have the effect of producing a concentration on the individual devoid of their wider context and the social discourses through which any aspect of identity is formed. This is countered by the application of structuration theory, as outlined by Anthony Giddens (1984), and which has gained a prominent role in archaeological theory (Barrett 1988, 1995, 1997, Shanks and Tilley 1992, Gardner 2002). Neither social structures nor the individual should be considered as primary i.e. preceding the other. Instead, they exist as a duality. Each person's identity is formed within a specific socio-political context, and that context influences what is considered appropriate or normative behaviour for their gender, for example, or their social rank. However, in turn, these social structures are the products of the actions and the beliefs of the members of that society. Therefore, neither is dominant, but both exist together. This idea of a normalising discourse of identity can at first sight render the individual as a powerless pawn who bears the imprint of social stereotypes, but this is mitigated against by the idea of agency, where each person has the ability to make a difference to their situation through the resources (literal and metaphorical) allocated to them within the social structures (Johnson 1989, Dobres and Robb 2000). Furthermore, there exists an element of slippage between these discourses of identity and the individual's lived experience and their reaction to them. There will be a variety of reactions to social ideals, and the possibility of any person rejecting these norms still exists, but such rejection can only be understood within the context of the discourses themselves.

Part of this ongoing process of becoming is through the routines and encounters of daily living: the process of being within a community. A key part of how we understand our own identity is through our actions and our presentation of ourselves within any social settings. This idea of presentation or performance has been key to much of the theoretical literature on identity in general (Goffmann 1959, Bourdieu 1977, Giddens 1984, Butler 1993). We learn certain social routines as a way to go about living in the world around us, usually the mundane activities of everyday life such as work routines. These routines communicate something about who we are to other people, and allow them to understand roles and affiliations within wider society. Within an education setting, for example, there are modes of differentiating between the teacher and the student: where each stands or sits; who is allowed to speak and when; who is allowed to use associated technologies, such as the whiteboards or projection facilities; potentially who is allowed to wear specific items of clothing, jewellery or make-up.

Our actions conform to the idea of what is appropriate for specific aspects of our identity, such as our social rank, or our ethnic identity, and this idea of appropriateness is drawn from the expected social norms. In the example of the school room or the lecture theatre, there are expected modes of behaviour for both the teacher and the student, with both groups sharing in these. Access to the space at the front of the room, to the technology for communicating information, and ability to control who speaks and when all come together to help create the identity of the teacher as opposed to the student, but also emphasise to the student that the teacher possesses the authority within that particular context. Thus, our daily activities are an exercise in communication to the people around us, whether intentionally or not. They express who we are and how we fit into the wider social group.

This act of communication depends upon communally-held discourses or ideologies about what is expected from members of a particular identity group. These activities are carried out on a repetitive basis, whether that is daily or more infrequently, and so become part of the repeated routines through which we live our lives. These normative actions and roles are enforced through the sanction of other members of society, and our wish, in general, to be accepted into the overall social group, or a particular sub-group within it. We monitor our own actions as to whether they fit into what we think is expected, but at the same time, we watch the reactions of others. The approval or approbation of others becomes one of the ways in which we tailor our activities. Therefore, the teacher only has authority if the students also conform to their roles, and signs of rebellion or boredom are signals to the teacher that their authority is under threat. Again, even the subversion of the social norms relies upon the presence of an audience, although here it may be with the intention to provoke disapproval and so become the outsider or 'other'. Part of the creation of the identity of the rebellious teenager, for example, is the subversion of the norms of the schoolroom: 'talking back' to a teacher, wearing banned jewellery or make-up, or at its most extreme, non-attendence.

The power of this idea of identity as performative is that it explains how we acquire our sense of who we are within any specific society. These routines are enacted on a repetitive basis, and through this repetition, we internalise the various aspects of our identity: who we are and how we fit into our various social groups. Even the smallest actions which we carry out without thinking are at some level the product of the rules of society and contain within them aspects which conform to elements of self-identity. Rules of what we eat and rituals of dining can be specific to certain ethnic or regional groups, and shared by the group as a whole. Similarly, who is allowed to eat within formal feasting ceremonies can be a way to denote sub-groups within a certain society, whether by gender or status. Certain groups might be allocated specific seats, or others might be excluded altogether. Particular groups might be present, but take on different roles as serving staff or musicians. These moments when groups come together can form occasions when boundaries of belonging and exclusion are articulated and policed. An important element of this is the idea of difference: different groups are in contact with each other, and the boundaries between them are worked out through the actions and material culture of these groups. This process may be immediate, involving face-to-face encounters between different groups, but equally significant is the creation of metaphorical boundaries. The creation of the 'other' can revolve around the idea of a stereotypical antithesis to the expected properties of the group. This has been a focal aspect of the study of ethnicity in the ancient world (Hartog 1988, Gruen 2011), but has also formed a significant theme in feminist art history (Rodgers 1995).

A further strength of identity as performative is that it helps understand the way in which identity is internalised. The routines of daily living become the point when knowledge of expected behaviour is learnt or reaffirmed. The individual learns the ideals and expectations of the group of which they are a member, and adopt them if they self-identify with that group, for example appropriate clothing or styles of eating. On the other hand, if wishing to maintain a distance from the group, the individual will adopt different routines as a statement which can only be understood through the normative behaviours. This seems to present identity as a conscious expression of self-description, almost as though an individual is free to choose which group to identify with. This concept of identity as a conscious act has led to the suggestion that an archaeology of identity is not possible, as without a written statement of self-ascription, we can never know how a person thought of themselves. However, this is to misunderstand the nature of identity and identity-statement. Performativity is more than a presentation of identity to the external viewer: it the way in which the subject internalises their own sense of self. Through such routines, a child is socialised into the community and learns the behaviours expected of them. As the child grows, s/he will join different groups (new age-groups, professional groups etc.) and will learn the behaviours and expectations through actions. Furthermore, much of this will be subconscious, and self-ascription often only becomes important in moments when the individual is confronted by a situation where their identity is contested: a statement of "I am this; I am not that".

Material culture is bound up within the expression of identity. We use material in our everyday lives: our clothing, our eating paraphernalia, the spaces we inhabit. These are all pulled into the performance of who we are, and are used by others to 'read' that message. Material culture is filled with specific meanings: these might have a direct relationship, such as the association between military uniform and a military identity, or they might be more obscure, such as the association between pink and girls, and blue and boys in modern western cultures. Sometimes material can incorporate more abstract ideas, such as an association with tradition, or the exotic. Similarly, the spaces we inhabit are also caught up in these performances. Choices about internal and external decoration may be based upon ideas of appropriateness, but the act of dwelling in the house can also distinguish between different social groups. Some groups may be restricted to specific areas, such as the children of the house being restricted to a nursery in the elite Victorian house. Hierarchies of space may be indicated through the wealth invested in the decoration of specific areas, creating a hierarchy within those inhabiting the house. We do not necessarily identify these meanings on a daily basis, but subconsciously we are able to read them and to act in the expected manner. For example, if we enter a specific building or a room for the first time, we 'know' where to go and the expected behaviours through previous experiences in similar rooms or buildings. Nevertheless, it is important to recognise that this relationship between action and material culture on the one hand, and identity on the other is not a stable and inflexible one. There is a certain level of slippage within the relationship. In part, it is dependent upon context, and the same item of material culture can have different meanings in different settings, whether in space or time. Even within the same society, meaning can be dependent upon who is using the material, and their role within the routines. As personal identity itself is not fixed, but something which is worked through; material can be given new meanings, and used in subverting the norms of identity discourses.

Texts also form part of this material negotiation of identity. It is tempting to see them as an accurate representation of the expectations of a specific aspect of identity, but it is important to recognise that they are also being used to police the boundaries of what is expected. They become a way of talking about cultural norms and their transgressions: many of our texts from the Roman period are discussions of what it is to be an elite male and so inform us of the kinds of situations within which status or masculinity was negotiated, and the areas which were a cause of tension, rather than an accurate representation of the behaviour of every member of the elite. Similarly, we can use the tendency towards idealisation within iconography to understand the discourse, rather than taking such images as a photographic snapshot of reality. These various forms of material evidence all formed different aspects of the same discourse, for example the use of adorning or caring for the body as part of the way in which gender differences were articulated. In Ovid's *Ars Amatoria* the poet gives advice to men and women about the care of the body (Wyke 1994). Although Ovid's advice is aimed at those who wanted to seduce a member of the opposite sex, it points to a difference in the relationship between bodily adornment and the two genders. Women were to visibly alter (improve) their bodies, creating an artifice through cosmetics, arranging their hair, and removing unwanted body hair, whilst men were to scorn such care as effeminate, and groom their natural good looks. Similar stereotypes are recorded in funerary iconography and in particular the familiar style of funerary relief depicting a seated woman attended by one or more slave tending her hair, often with a mirror included in the scene, whilst such intimate scenes are never included in male funerary reliefs. Finally, a similar discourse can be identified in Roman Britain, where mirrors and combs are associated with women in grave assemblages, and the same may be the case for glass unguent bottles (Swift 2011: 208). None of these media constitutes a true picture of gender identities, but rather part of a negotiation of the ideals of identity: the way in which individuals adopted a response to the expectations of a specific gender. These responses could broadly be identified as sharing a common identity, but at the same time they allowed a certain level of individuality due to the particular circumstances of any individual person's life.

Nevertheless, there is temptation to see identity is as being a stable category or an identifier with some form of essential component, but an important element of poststructuralist approaches has been to destabilise essentialist categories of identity. As Judith Butler (1999) argues, gender, for example, is a term in process. Taking de Beauvoir's statement that one becomes a woman rather than being born one, she argues: "it follows that *woman* itself is a term in process, a becoming, a constructing that cannot be said to originate or to end" (*ibid.*: 45). Gender and all other aspects of identity are about continually becoming, and less about being. It is a project of ongoing maintenance, being worked at through the moments of social practice and social interaction. These practices become solidified or 'congealed' to give the impression of stability, however, this can be disrupted, reinterpreted and reinvented. We can learn new ways of being, interacting with different groups and internalising new forms of behaviours and ideals. To add to this instability of identity, any individual's personal identity will be formed from multiple aspects of different elements. Butler's own work deals with the intersection of gender and sexuality, and how this challenges a normative gender discourse. Similarly, Bhabha (1994) argues against singular aspects of identity as the subject of enquiry, and argues that instead, research should focus on the moments when differences in identity are expressed, and so the discourses of identity performed.

There is a move towards acknowledging something of this complexity for the Roman world. Within Roman archaeology, this has largely been how other aspects of identity intersect with ethnic identity, to critique the assumed homogeneity of Romanization. Hingley has discussed how the adoption of Roman material differed between the elite and the non-elite, thus arguing for an intersection between ethnic and status identities (Hingley 2005). Similarly, Gardner has argued that within the Roman empire, identities operate on different scales: the macro-scale of ethnic and military identities, as opposed to the more community-based identities such as gender, status and profession (Gardner 2002). Most influential has been Mattingly's argument for discrepant identities (Mattingly 2004). Mattingly draws on Said's idea of discrepant experiences of imperialism (Said 1993: in particular 35–50), in which Said argues that there are different interpretations of the imperial experience, and offers alternatives to the western-centric reading of modern western imperialisms. Mattingly then argues that this idea of discrepant experience can be expanded into discrepant identity. His approach is to look for differences in use of material culture, and then assess whether they can be attributed to the expression of distinct identities. Using the specific example of the tombstone Regina from the Roman fort of South Shields (RIB 1065), he charts how multiple factors can be recognized as forming part of her life experience which would have had an impact on her identity: status, wealth, location, employment, religion, origin, links to the Roman state, legal jurisdiction, language and literacy, gender, and age (Mattingly 2004: table 3). However, these factors never move beyond the level of descriptor, and lack the rigour with which Maureen Carroll interrogated them for the same inscription (Carroll 2012), in which, for example, she examined the dress Regina was depicted as wearing as a way to understand how she might have positioned herself within specific identity groups. Turning to the archaeology of Roman Britain, Mattingly then successfully identifies differences in the material culture used by region or by site-type. However, whilst this allows the identification of discrepant experiences of being Roman by three broad groupings, military, urban and rural (elaborated in greater detail in Mattingly 2006), the discussion of aspects of ethnicity other than status has vanished. Ultimately, his discrepant identities are based upon settlement type (not irrelevant in the study of identity), but with limited discussion of how these were involved in the creation of discrepant identity, and with the adult male again assumed as the norm. Mattingly's discrepancy raises a fundamental methodological problem: in (correctly) breaking apart the homogenising experience or identity of being Roman, and then further qualifying all other identities, how do we then write and archaeology of identity which is not focussed on the particular and the individual?

The final issue I want to raise here is that of power and hierarchies within society. In much of the work on identity within the Roman world, there has been a downplaying of the way in which different identities were valued in varying ways. Aspects of status were clearly bound up in the inequalities of Roman society, with the emperor and the magisterial elite accorded more power than the urban poor or slaves through their membership of these social classes. However, we need to remember that these power relationships could also exist within other elements of identity: women were considered unequal to men; similarly, children and the elderly less powerful than adults. The characteristics associated with each form of identity were valued in different ways, and returning to the example of the care of the body, the way in which a woman presented and cared for her appearance was valued as less serious or more frivolous than the way in which a man monitored his appearance, and this formed part of the way in which men were valued more highly than women within Roman society. The ideology through which gender identities were differentiated legitimized the inequality between men and women. It was accepted by both groups and internalised through their everyday activities, such as their grooming regimes. In spite of this, we need to accept that again, these power relationships were not set in stone, and as the multiples aspects of an individual's identity came together, there was the potential for a series of hierarchies to intersect to allow an elite women, for example, to appropriate elements of male identity, such as priesthoods. This instability creates levels of tensions and slippage within the social hierarchies of the Roman world. Power was inherently unstable, and constantly worked at (Foucault 1979). The discourses and performances which created the sense of identity were also used in the continual display and renegotiation of the social power of any single individual.

These various ideas and assumptions underpin the approach offered within this book. Any individual person is socialised into the group, and the ideologies of that society. They form allegiances, whether consciously or subconsciously, with particular sub-groups within that society, based on criteria of gender, or status, or religion, or profession. They internalise who they are through their identification with these groups, and learn ways of acting appropriate to who they are, and they use the material world around them within these routines. From this material record, whether archaeological or textual, we can begin to reconstruct something of these discourses through which identity was formed, and the differences between the different social groups. It is very rare that we can reconstruct the identity of named individuals, but we can understand the social structures through which they came to form their own sense of self. One criticism which has been made about an archaeology of identity is that we can never reconstruct the identity of individuals in the past: we can never get into their heads to establish who they thought they were. However, this is, in many ways, a misunderstanding of the power of this theoretical approach. In focussing on the discourses as well as the people, the approach advocated in this book, we can explore the way in which individuals made sense of their place in their communities – as distinct from the way in which any specific individual charted their own particular trajectory.

An archaeology of Roman identities

It is the aim of this book to provide such a theoretically-informed exploration of identity in the western provinces. This is not a straightforward undertaking. This has to be more than the identification of the previously invisible people of the past: it is more than an "add women and stir" approach, but with the addition of children, slaves and the non-elites (Brown 1997: 25). It constitutes a consideration of how such identities were formed within the past, and the way in which such formations were dependent upon material culture. Identity rests within practice and the routines of daily living, which incorporate the material culture of the archaeological record. Therefore our undertaking in writing an archaeology of Roman identity is the exploration of such practices. However, whilst there have been a number of studies of identity in the Roman world, some disquiet is emerging. In reality, much of the critique and new approaches have been applied to ethnic or cultural identity. The danger is that other aspects of identity are left unexplored. Perhaps more worrying is how few studies include explicit theoretical or methodological discussion of how to approach identity (Pitts 2007, Gardner 2013).

Identity is incredibly fluid, and the position of an individual within their local community will rest on a number of factors: their gender, age, occupation, wealth, rank, legal status, sexuality, as well as the potentially multiple aspects of their ethnicity. In exploring the question of personal identity in the Roman period, I am not looking for the individual, but rather the social structures which allow their actions to be meaningful and the discourse within which these identities are formed and differentiated. Thus the twin focuses of this work are the ideologies and social practices of identity: the ideas and behaviours attached to specific aspects of personal identity in the Roman world, and which the individual responded to in articulating their own identity. As Meskell has argued for gender, it is formed through "a complex assortment of networks of signifying practices, varying for individuals over time, as it intersects with other networks of signifying practices located in such concepts as class and race" (Meskell 2007: 29). Trying to understand these networks requires imposing an artificial division according to elements of identity, but also reducing the fluidity of the social practices to a more fixed discourse. Therefore, the book is divided into chapters, each of which investigates a particular form of identity, beginning with ethnicity, then status or class, gender and finally age. This is not an all-encompassing list: most obvious is the absence of a discussion of military identity, although other forms of professional identity are considered, and religious identities are also excluded. Similarly, this is not meant to be a complete account of the aspects of identity which are included: differences are negotiated through multiple forms of social practice, and it is not possible to cover them all in one book.

The material discussed is a reflection of approaches which have proved successful in Roman archaeology or archaeology more widely. A range of forms of material evidence are used, and different methodologies employed. Each type of archaeological material comes with its own set of potential and restrictions, as well as established methodologies, and consequently the approaches will differ. Furthermore, the way in which material culture was used in the formation of identity renders some identities more invisible than others. The power relations underpinning identity mean the archaeological record is to some extent the product of the processes designed to make specific groups less visible. There are three core approaches used in the following chapters. The first is the identification of the social practices through which identity is maintained and internalised. This has formed the basis for my previous work (Revell 2000, 2009) and has proved a fruitful means for understanding identity formation and relies upon a close reading of the material culture. The second is the exploration of the idea of boundaries, and the ways in which they were constituted and maintained. This is derived from the idea that part of the way in which group identities are formed is through the creation of differences with other groups, and that such boundaries are actively policed through, for examples, different social practices and material culture. However, the archaeological tradition of how we understand the relationship between the material record and groups of people is problematic. It is important not to fall into the culture-history approach of objects meaning ethnic groups, or even specific forms of personal decoration meaning particular genders and miniature items denoting children. Material culture is used in the creation of boundaries, as has been demonstrated from by the work of the Cambridge School of archaeologists in the 1980s (Moore 1986, Shanks and Tilley 1992). The multivocality of material culture means that the link must be explored and demonstrated rather than assumed. The third approach is to focus on the social structures and ideologies of identity: the conditions within which each person makes sense of their own world, and which go into the sense of self. This seemingly draws the attention away from the person, and seems contrary to argument for a peopled past. However, the reality is that for some, we are left with this as the most robust means of understanding how they were made different by being written out of the archaeological record.

The remainder of the book deals with the question of how we might go about an archaeology of Roman identity. It takes the form of three pairs of chapters. The first pair focus on the question of Roman ethnicity or cultural identities, looking firstly at being Roman as an ethnic identity, and then the question of regional identities, and how we reconcile these two levels of interaction. The second pair focus on status or class, looking firstly at how the elites placed themselves firmly and visibly within the material record, and secondly at the question of non-elite identity, and how we might explore the identities of those who have less power and fewer resources within the Roman social structures. The third pair deal with gender and age, and focus more on how categories are formed and boundaries maintained for both the dominant and the less visible identities. The geographical scope of this comprises the western provinces excluding Italy: Iberia, Gaul, the Germanies and Britain, and the temporal scope is the Principate, roughly from the time of Augustus to the mid-3rd century AD. Much of the material discussed draws upon a wealth of existing research, and reinforces the argument I have made elsewhere that in order to undertake a social archaeology of the Roman provinces, we do not need new data-sets, but to ask new questions of our existing data-sets (Revell 2010b). This book offers such a re-interrogation.

Chapter 2

Ideas of Roman ethnicity

Introduction

Since the 19th century, the transformation (or not) of the pre-conquest cultures to something more homogeneous and recognisably Roman has been the focus of research into the Roman provinces. There is a tendency for much of this work to be descriptive, or conceived within a framework which owes much to the ideas of culture-history: the study of the change from one bounded culture (indigenous, native or barbarian) to another (Roman). It is not my intention to go through the history of the academic study of Romanization (Freeman 1997, Hingley 2000, 2005), or the arguments for and against the usefulness of term 'Romanization' itself. As the term 'Romanization' has become increasingly contested the concept of identity has become seen as an acceptable means of replacing it (Pitts 2007). However, this raises the question of what constitutes a Roman ethnic identity. There is a danger of assuming that we know how this is defined and how this is demonstrated materially. In this chapter and the next, I want to think about how we can use the ideas about identity outlined in the previous chapter to explore some of the theoretical literature, and think about what constituted a Roman ethnic identity, how we might identify it within the archaeological record, and how it might interact with more localised, almost sub-ethnic identities.

Defining ethnicity

In the last 60 years, ethnicity has emerged as a central research question within humanities and the social sciences. Yet the terms ethnicity and ethnic group have been described as "among the most complicated, volatile and emotionally charged words and ideas in the lexicon of social science" (Nash 1989: 1). The term ethnic group, for example, is usually conceptually associated with that of an ethnic minority. The preconceived picture is one of the construction of a modern nation-state from a series of formerly autonomous, although possibly culturally-related, groups; because these diverse groups are incorporated into a single political boarder, they become described as ethnic minorities to distinguish them from the dominant group within the nation (Nash 1989: 1–2). Thus 'ethnic' is used to signify 'them' rather than 'us', or divergence from the norm (*ibid.*: 2). This uncertainty over the use of the term ethnicity is mirrored in a vagueness concerning its definition and characterisation. Before looking specifically at Roman ethnicity, I want to introduce some of these uncertainties, and question their implications for the study of ethnicity within the archaeological past.

The first element of this debate is the types of criteria used to define ethnic groups and to distinguish between them. Weber listed what he saw as the constituent elements of ethnicity (Weber 1968 [1956]: 385–98): a belief in a common descent; a common language and rituals; and shared conceptions of what is proper in terms of, amongst others, styles of clothes, housing, eating and drinking habits, and division of labour. However, he also sounded a note of caution: that under any rigorous analysis, any homogenising ideology of ethnicity begins to break down. Weber's definition produces an idea of ethnicity as something based on ideology or shared beliefs, but also on more mundane elements of shared practices and material culture. These elements have remained the core of subsequent definitions. Nash, for example, characterised ethnicity as: body (i.e. a biological component); a language; a shared history and origins; religion; and nationality (the right to a territory) (Nash 1989: 5–6). Smith proposed six principal features in defining an ethnic group (Smith 1986): a collective name; a common myth of origin or descent; a shared history; a distinctive shared culture (including language and religion); an association with a specific territory, even if the ethnic group no longer lives there; and a sense of shared identity and solidarity. For the early Medieval period, Bartlett defines ethnicity as being connected to customs, language and law (Bartlett 1994: 197–220).

In all of these definitions, we see an idea that ethnicity is a complex phenomenon which cannot be reduced to a single element. It incorporates elements of a belief in a shared past, but also a present common culture. There are aspects of behaviour or custom: ethnicity is connected to how the group live out their lives on a daily basis, and that this takes on a common material expression. Billig, for example, has argued for what he termed "banal nationalism" (Billig 1995): that a national identity is created through ongoing 'flagging' through shared practices, which have an ideological element connecting them to the idea of the nation. Looking at the national identity of America post-9/11, he argues that the nationalistic fervour is underpinned by banal acts such as the display of the *Stars and Stripes* in public locations such as town halls and classrooms, or the singing of the national anthem. We tend to overlook these in favour of the highly ceremonial acts of pomp and occasion, but it is important to give due recognition to the impact of these accepted and almost unthinking acts of group compliance. An objection could be made that Billig concentrates on the elements which relate more closely to patriotic nationalism rather than ethnicity, such as the national flag, or the national anthem. Nevertheless his point about banal flagging stands. Rather than seeing ethnic identity and patriotism as different phenomenon, explicit patriotism is the product of ethnicity under pressure. It is through the ongoing daily activities and symbols that a sense of common identity is maintained, and this serves as the preparation for events where that shared identity comes to the fore, for example during warfare. The flip-side of this, which may be relevant for the Roman world, is that there will be instances where ethnicity is taken as read, and is only apparent in its subconscious routine enactments.

A seminal paper on how to investigate ethnicity was that of Barth (1969) in which he argued for the importance of the study of boundaries between ethnic groups: not the physical divides, but the cultural symbols used to both denote but also to construct ethnic divisions. This entailed a move away from the study of the core, shared cultural symbols to studying how an ethnic group forms its identity within the context of other cultural groups, and maintains it as a response to the ongoing interactions with them. He proposed a reconceptualisation of ethnicity as something very dynamic, which had to be continually worked at rather than something primordial and unchanging. Furthermore, he set expressions of ethnicity within a context, not only socio-geographical, but also historical. The core element of Barth's work was the idea of boundary markers. These he defined as being either overt differences in material culture or values such as morality. Not all will be invested with significance: some will be downplayed or ignored. Consequently, there can be no universal defining criteria for the identification of ethnicity; the criteria need to be identified for each particular ethnic group.

These ideas of boundaries, instability and context have proved influential in later studies. The precise definition of these boundary markers has been developed, and so Nash, for example, describes them through the metaphors of blood (kinship), substance (commensality), and deity (or cult). As these are not always visible, they can then be expressed through surface pointers or secondary features, such as dress, language, house architecture, taboos, and possibly physical characteristics (Nash 1989: 10–14). However, this is not always straightforward, as there will be elements of common cultural symbols between adjoining ethnic groups. Eriksen uses the example of studies of the Lue, a contemporary Thai tribe who share language, religion and customs with the other groups in the area (Eriksen 1993: 10–12). In spite of this, they define themselves as a different group, which leads Eriksen to define ethnicity as "an aspect of social relationship between agents who consider themselves as culturally distinctive from members of other groups with whom they have a minimum of regular interaction" (*ibid.*:12).

This outline of the broader literature on ethnicity merely gives a flavour of the current debates on ethnicity; however, these authors do share a number of common assumptions which underpins the discussion of Roman ethnicity outlined in this chapter. The first is that ethnicity is not primordial, but rather is situational and contingent. Any particular manifestation will be dependent on the particular context, and should be located within it. A group's ethnic identity is formed in relation to other ethnic groups, and the characteristics of the ethnic identity serve to distinguish between 'us' and 'them'. The characteristics are variously defined, but include elements of a shared past, and a common set of cultural traits which may include language, religion, architecture, practices of eating and drinking, ways of dressing, and so on. Race itself is not a part (Mirza and Dungworth 1995), but a common set of physical characteristics may be: this may be skin colour, but might also be hair or eye colour.

One thing which is clear is that in many cases, these elements have ideological overtones. When listed, they may seem innocuous, but they become a way of judging one group over another, and in many cases, become a way to say that 'we' are better than 'you'. Thus customs of eating and the eating of certain forms of meat becomes subject to judgement: some animals are considered taboo to eat because they are judged either sacred or unclean. Other forms of meat are considered to be unsuitable for reasons long forgotten (for example, horse, dog and cat), but those that eat them are still considered to be different and less civilised. Within an imperial context, this can then be used as a justification for the rule of one ethnic group by another, that the conquering group is bringing civilisation to a less civilized people.

Archaeological approaches to ethnicity

The argument that an ethnic group will share certain customs provides ethnicity with a material dimension, as such customs incorporate the use of similar forms of material culture. It therefore provides the basis for an archaeological methodology for the study of ethnic groups in the past. The archaeological identification of peoples through their material culture goes back to the 16th and 17th centuries (Trigger 2006: 211–2). It has formed the basis for Anglo-Saxon archaeology in Britain, for example, where the textual sources describe the influx of a series of Germanic tribes into England in the centuries following the end of Roman rule. Artefact types, particularly brooch types, have then been mapped as a way to describe the territories of the ethnic communities and so specific brooches come to be regarded as indicating the presence of the Angles, the Saxons and the Jutes (Lucy 2000: 11–14, 155–73). Archaeological approaches became more rigorous in the twentieth century, influenced by the work of Kossinna in Germany, and then Childe in Britain (Jones 1997: 15–39, Lucy 2005: 87–91, Trigger 2006: 235–48). Childe described this methodology in the preface to *The Danube in Prehistory*:

> [w]e find certain types of remains – pots, implements, ornaments, burial rites, house forms – constantly recurring together. Such a complex of regularly associated traits we shall term a 'cultural group' or just a 'culture'. We assume that such a complex is the material expression of what would to-day be called a 'people'. (Childe 1929: v–vi)

In a footnote to this definition, he explicitly equates these culture groups or peoples with ethnicity.

Within these culture-historical studies of ethnicity, the material evidence was deemed to stand unproblematically for the identity of the ethnic group. By mapping the spread of specific artefact types (preferably more than one form of artefact), it was possible to map the extent of a specific ethnic group. The material culture was an inactive proxy for the people. More recent approaches have argued for a more active role for material culture in that it is used to define the group, and maintain its boundaries in relation to surrounding groups. Ian Hodder's ethnographic fieldwork studied tribal interactions in Kenya, and the role of material culture within such social interactions (Hodder 1982). He argued that tribal boundaries were maintained through specific forms of material culture, such as women's dress and ear-rings, pottery styles, and hearth positions. These strategies need to be seen in the context of various forms of interaction between the tribes, such as economic relations and intermarriage, making these tribal boundaries permeable. The material culture was used to signify tribal identities in the context of interaction between groups, not in a vacuum.

Perhaps the most influential archaeological study of ethnicity is that of Sian Jones (1997). Her book still remains the most comprehensive examination of the literature on ethnicity from the social sciences and from archaeology. Throughout, she stresses the difficulty in defining ethnicity as a concept in general, and its identification within the material record in particular, and this difficulty is exemplified in her application of *habitus* to the question of Romanization. She defines ethnic groups as "culturally ascribed identity groups, which are based on the expression of a real or assumed shared culture and common descent" (*ibid.*: 84). She further argues that ethnicity is a process involving the reproduction and transformation of the classificatory distinction between 'us' and 'them'. She argues for the adoption of *habitus* as a way to understand the relationship between ethnicity and culture: ethnic affinity is grounded in similar practices and experiences, through which systems of classification are both internalised and signified. Within this, material culture forms the expression and recognition of ethnic identity. However, in utilising this approach in the case of Romanization in Britain, the complexities of this become apparent (*ibid.*: 129–35). She advocates the adoption of a contextual approach which focuses on the negotiation of identity without applying the prior categorisation of Roman and native, and instead using all forms of evidence available from a particular context to look for the elements of transformation and difference. Ultimately she concludes that one of the problems of identifying ethnicity is the way in which it cross-cuts other aspects of social identity. Furthermore, the concentration on the local leaves unanswered the question of how we then understand the question of ethnicity at the larger scale of an empire: is there something which brings together the various peoples of the empire so that they form an imagined community of 'us' as distinct from a 'them' outside of the empire? How do we bring together such small-scale contextual studies to understand an empire-wide Roman ethnicity?

It is these complexities which have led some to doubt whether we can actually identify ethnic identity from the archaeological evidence alone. Such doubts were voiced by Childe, who questioned whether it was possible to attach ethnic labels derived from Classical textual sources to Bronze Age cultural groups (Childe 1930: 240–7). More recently, Hall has argued that it is impossible to study ethnic identity when the only available evidence is archaeological (Hall 1997: 111–42, esp. 42). Whilst he acknowledges that there is a material element to ethnic identity, his view is that we have to first determine the existence and name of the ethnic group from the textual evidence, and then identify which forms of material culture are used by the group (see Antonaccio 2010 for a detailed critique). Further doubts have been raised based on the question of self-ascription, that is how a group name themselves, and whether it is possible to identify ethnic identity in prehistory in particular (Shennan 1989: 14–17). Derks and Roymans have argued that some form of linguistic evidence is necessary to act as the evidence for how a group of people identified themselves (Derks and Roymans 2009: 3–4). The consequence of such arguments is that we would be unable to investigate ethnicity in pre-literate societies, or societies with only a partial literacy. It would render a purely archaeological investigation of ethnicity impossible.

Such doubts rest on a view that textual documents are more transparent than the archaeological evidence. They relegate archaeology to a secondary status to history: only capable of adding colour to the facts deduced from the textual sources. They also assume that the textual sources are a straightforward account, whereas in reality documentary evidence is more problematic. Geary's work on early Medieval France has demonstrated that contemporary texts were a means to manipulate the past: to create group identifications based upon past supposed ethnic differences, reinterpreting lines of ancestry to create identities which reinforced claims of power by early lordships (Geary 1983, 1994). Placing a reliance on such documentary sources in preference to the archaeological is not a solution to the problems of ethnic identification. These texts, whether literary documents or carved inscriptions, play the same role as other forms of material culture: they are used to create and maintain ethnic identities and the boundaries between them rather than being an objective reflection of them. Ultimately, the argument that ethnicity can only be adduced from textual sources is the result of a limited view of the definition of ethnicity, one which privileges self-ascription and naming over social practice and shared material markers. It further denies the ideological aspects of material culture: that ideas of descent and cult, core elements of many ethnic identities, can be expressed materially. Finally, it regards the object of study as the identification of the core elements, rather than the Barthian idea of boundaries.

A more fundamental question is whether it is appropriate to term group identity as ethnicity before the early modern period. Much of the work on ethnicity by anthropologists, for example, has been carried out on contemporary populations, in the context of complex nation-states. Crone, for example, argues that there was no shared, national material culture in the pre-modern period, as there were no cultural traits which were shared by all members of the group, and which were distinguished from those of its neighbours (Crone 1989: 88–92). Instead, there was a shared elite culture across independent political groups. Cultural integration was a requirement of and consequently connected with modernity (*ibid.*: 178–80). This echoes a lot of the research which equates ethnicity and nationalism, thereby seemingly negating its relevance to periods before the development of the nation-state. Other have argued that ethnic identities develop with the emergence of the city-states in the 3rd millennium BC, or with complex societies (Shennan 1989: 14–17 with references), suggesting that it is an applicable model for pre-modern societies. However, part of the problem comes down to how rigid the definition of ethnicity is in the mind of the writer. As seen above, there is no single, simple definition for ethnicity. The criteria for ethnicity in the context of the nation-state is not necessarily directly applicable to different forms of political organisation, but that does not negate the applicability of the actual concept of ethnicity. We need to be more explicit in our definitions of what ethnicity might be.

Rethinking Roman ethnicity

This raises the question of how we should define Roman ethnicity, an undertaking which is more difficult than would first appear. Dench has argued that "little work has been done on questions of specifically Roman ethnic and cultural self-definition" (Dench 2005: 26). The most influential was Gruen's work on the impact on Roman identity of encounters with Hellenism during the mid–late Republic (Gruen 1992, see also Farney 2007), and Laurence (1998) examines the complexity of ethnic ascription in Italy. The publication of Wallace-Hadrill's book arguing for the transformation of Roman cultural identity during the Augustan period has gone some way to remedy this (Wallace-Hadrill 2008), but there is still a noticeable lack of research on ethnic identity at Rome in contrast to the equivalent work on the Greek world. If this lack of research is the case for Rome itself, it is more acute within provincial archaeology. The traditional debate has relied upon monolithic groupings of 'native' and 'Roman', and in challenges to this, both the complexity of the pre-existing cultural groupings and the new resulting identities has been acknowledged and explored. Consequently, a rejection of Romano-centric approaches to ethnicity in the provinces has moved the debate on provincial identity forward, but without fully deconstructing what we mean when we describe something as 'Roman'. There is an unspoken, underlying assumption that we know what being Roman is, and its material correlates. In the discussion which follows, I want to think about how we might begin to define a Roman ethnic identity on a very broad scale, but focussing on the provinces. As a starting point for this discussion, I want to return to Smith's six criteria for ethnic identification (Smith 1986). This is not because I am convinced that it is immediately applicable to the context of the Roman empire. However, I think as a broad definition it provides a useful heuristic tool through which to think about how we might define a specifically Roman ethnicity.

Smith's first criteria of **a collective name** is one which is surprisingly difficult. We use the term 'Romans' in an ill-defined way: do we mean culturally Roman or a Roman citizen? Do we apply the term to someone born in the city of Rome, or within the Roman empire? I am not convinced there was any greater clarity in the ancient literary sources. Nevertheless, one thing is apparent: there are limited, if any, instances of anyone referring to themselves as *Romanus/a* within the epigraphic record of the western provinces. Where inscriptions do give some form of ethnic identification, it is in terms of more a localised identity, usually either the urban centre or the tribe they were affiliated to. Such descriptions tend to be situational: in the north-western provinces, they are generally used when a person is removed from the locale of their birth (Derks 2009b, Noy 2010). There is no compelling evidence for a collective name being part of the definition of Roman ethnicity: a distinction from both modern ethnic identity, and from Greek ethnic identity.

Smith further links ethnicity to the twin criteria of a **myth of descent** and a **shared history**. We are increasingly aware that these ideas of descent and history are a created phenomenon: a past is fabricated in order to hold a people together (Hobsbawm and Ranger 1983). Myths of descent have proved an important part of situating a community in relation to the wider world. Within the Greek world, associations with Heracles or with the heroes returning from the Trojan Wars served to provide a genealogy which tied a particular community into a wider Hellenic genealogy. This formed one part of a common Greek ethnic identity based in part on a shared kinship, articulated through the mythic origins of the community (Malkin 1994, 1998). We can potentially see a similar thing for the city of Rome, where the myth of Aeneas formed one means of linking Augustus and Rome with the wider Mediterranean through the myth of the Trojan Wars, although in this case, through a non-Greek hero. Underpinning these mythical origins is the idea of a shared blood, but the picture for Roman ethnicity is more complex than for Greek ethnicity. Dench has argued for the growing importance of a notion of Roman ethnicity based less on shared blood and more on the inclusion into the community of those who were not bound by ties of kinship (Dench 2005). The myths of Romulus' asylum and the rape of the Sabine women articulated a mythical past which allowed for the incorporation of manpower and wives from outside, and in particular, from the surrounding Italian communities. These myths are almost without parallel elsewhere in the Mediterranean world, and they have a particular temporal context within Rome itself. The story of the rape of the Sabine women becomes prominent from the 2nd century BC, once the Sabines were incorporated into the Roman state. The story of Romulus' asylum seems to appear in the textual sources from the time of Cicero onwards, with both becoming particularly prominent from the Augustan period onwards (*ibid.*: 15–25). Dench argues that they should be seen as evidencing a concern about immigration, mobility and cultural integration. It is no co-incidence that we see this concern in Rome at about the same time we begin to see the changes in the administration of the provinces, and the material culture of the provincial communities (see below).

The lack of explicit textual evidence within the provinces makes it difficult to discern whether we see these communities tying into this myth of common descent. Roymans has collected together the evidence for Trojan foundation myths in Gaul and Britain (Roymans 2004: 236–8). These hint at the possibility of provincial communities defining themselves through a shared descent, but the evidence is problematic. Roymans gives four examples, of which three are based on textual sources. However, none is without its problems, being either reported by Roman authors, or later sources. In the fourth case, the evidence is iconographic, and the epigraphic attestation of the Laurentes Lavinates, a college of priests associated with the Trojan foundation myth of Rome. However, if Dench is correct in her argument for the importance of myths emphasising the origin of Rome as a city of immigrants, we should perhaps question how far we should be looking for shared descent and claims of consanguinity.

More important seems to be the idea of a **shared history**. Carroll (2002) has argued that following the Augustan reorganisation of the Rhine area, new identities were constructed, including that of the Ubii. At the end of the 1st century BC, the tribe was transplanted from the eastern to the western bank of the Rhine, with the new urban settlement of the *Oppidum Ubiorum* founded by the Romans. This was promoted to a veteran colony by Claudius under the name of *Colonia Claudia Ara Agrippinenses*. Within these events, the family of Agrippa seems to have taken an active role: Agrippina appears to have petitioned for the granting of colonial status, as reflected in the colonial title, and it is possible that Agrippa was involved in the original migration of the tribe. The inhabitants of the town seem to have emphasised this link to their Roman past, terming themselves as *Agrippinenses* rather than *Ubii* as a reminder of this. This may represent part of a wider phenomenon suggested in the archaeological record whereby the succession of emperors became a shared history of the provincial communities, exemplified by the galleries of imperial statues in public spaces (Garriguet 2004, Revell 2009: 103–7)

Smith, as with most others, includes the criterion of **shared material, habits and ideologies** within his definition of ethnicity. This also seems to have been part of the definition of ethnicity in the ancient sources, where Roman authors used other groups of people as a way of exploring the boundaries of their own ethnic identity. This is not as simple as a polar barbarian 'other' (Woolf 2009), but the criteria selected for the discussion of other peoples points to the customs these Roman authors saw as defining the boundaries between different ethnic groups. From such descriptions we can begin to build up an idea of the characteristics prized by the Romans when considering other peoples in relation to themselves. They focussed on aspects such as: settlement organisation (most specifically planned towns); social organisation through laws and some form of ordered political system; and family organisation, with power resting in the hands of the elder males and recognition of legitimate lines of descent. Other indicators of a perceived level of civilisation were more technologically based, such as metal-working, complex weaponry and cereal crops. In the *Germania*, for example, Tacitus describes the Germans as not living in cities, but in disorganised settlements with inexpertly built houses (Tac. *Germ.* 16). On the other hand, their marriages are depicted as conforming to the Roman ideal of a chaste relationship between man and wife (*ibid.*: 18–19). He singles out those tribes whose marriages echo the *univira*, or woman who marries only a single man: he praises them for only allowing virgins to marry, and that these women do not desire other men, even when their husband has died. His descriptions of the Aestii, the Sitones and the Fenni stand as a direct opposition to Roman custom (*ibid.*: 45–6). They lack basic metal-working technology (iron or weapons), they have no houses or built settlements, they dress in skins and eat wild herbs (suggesting a lack of agriculture). Finally, relationships between the genders were skewed: amongst the Fenni, women and men took equal part in activities such as hunting, and the ultimate mark of the Sitones' lack of civilisation was that they were ruled by women.

One way to understand this is suggested by Woolf, who has argued that part of the Romans' sense of who they were was based upon a concept of *humanitas* (Woolf 1995, 1998: 54–76). Like many of the Latin abstract nouns, this is not easily reduced to a single English translation. It incorporated the aspect of a shared humanity in terms of treatment of other people, and proper respect towards the structures of society as a whole, but it also brought with it overtones of culture and civilisation (Veyne 1993). The description of the German tribes outlined above can be understood within these ideas of *humanitas*, in that these tribes, to varying degrees, have been described through their lack of the characteristic traits of Roman civilisation, that is, through a Roman lens. It was a concept which the Romans probably adopted from the Greeks, and came to symbolise their authority to rule over their empire (Pliny *NH* 3.39, discussed in Woolf 1998: 57).

One element which is seen by many as forming part of such shared customs is a common language, but this is something which is not apparent within Roman ethnicity. At a very basic level, Greek continued as the dominant language in the eastern half of the empire. In the western provinces where Latin dominates the written record, there are still examples of Greek inscriptions such as the dedication to Asclepius from Aulus Egnatius Pastor at Maryport (RIB 808), and the Palmyrene inscription at South Shields (RIB 1065). Nevertheless, the prominence of written Latin should be seen as part of the epigraphic habit, where inscriptions on stone were part of a symbolic relationship of inequalities, and writing a key part of the imperial administration. In Southern Gaul, there is evidence for a mosaic of written languages prior to conquest and in the Republican period, which come to be replaced almost entirely by Latin language written in Latin script (Woolf 1994). This prominence of Latin in writing masks the fact that bilingualism in speech was a feature of the Roman empire (Adams 2003, Mullen and James 2012). Adams has argued for a bilingual community at La Graufesenque, for example, based on the evidence of graffiti recording how much material each craftsman had in the kiln during a single firing (Adams 2003: 689–724). More than 160 such items are extant, and they show a community using both Latin and Gallic interchangeably, but without blending the two to form a hybrid, and whilst using grammatical forms appropriate to each. A similar situation is found at Pompeii, where we see the continuity of written Oscan until AD 79 (Cooley 2002). These and other such examples of bilingualism all act to remove any direct one-to-one relationship between the Latin language and Roman ethnicity.

Smith further defines ethnicity as **association with a territory**, which is surprisingly problematic for Roman ethnicity: the growth of the territory ruled by Rome would give the impression that this was matched by an equivalent growth in Roman ethnicity. However, the situation is in fact more complex. Roman expansion during the Republican period was a piecemeal conquest of land, alongside alliances and citizen colonies. From the late 3rd century BC onwards, there was a gradual development in the meaning of the terms associated with the empire revealing underlying changes in the conceptualisation of the empire and the people within it (Lintott 1993: 22–7, Richardson 2008). However, at this period, to see any connection between territory and ethnicity would be inaccurate. It is probably only from the Augustan period that we can confidently talk about the Roman state as such, and begin to assert that Roman ethnicity was at some level associated with a territory. Aelius Aristides in the 2nd century AD praised Rome for making the whole empire Roman, a suggestion that there had come to be some form of equation between the territory of the empire and Roman ethnicity, however imperfect that might be in reality (Aristides 63; Oliver 1953: 902).

This leads to Smith's final criterion of ethnicity as a **sense of solidarity**. Is this hinted at by the Aristides passage? There is an idea of an *orbis Romanus* amongst the writers at Rome, but it is more difficult to detect this within the provinces from the archaeological evidence alone. The incorporation of the provincial elites into the equestrian and senatorial orders at Rome certainly suggests this is the case amongst this particular group, but they are not necessarily representative of the whole of the provincial communities. More socially diverse were the military units, both legionary and auxiliary, and it is possible that here we can identify a more widespread sense of solidarity. By the 1st century AD, recruitment was increasingly from the provinces rather than Rome itself (Mann 1983), and work on the military in the last decades has emphasised the idea of a community of soldiers, in part bound together by rituals emphasising their loyalty to Rome and the emperor as well as to each other (Haynes 1999, James 1999). A second part of this sense of solidarity may be the spread of Roman citizenship, initially through the foundation of Republican colonies, but later through the grants of citizenship to individuals (Sherwin-White 1973). Rome's expansion of its citizen body outside of the boundaries of the city was unusual in Antiquity, and should be seen as a strategy of imperialism. Lintott argues that this created a bond with the emperor rather than Rome itself (Lintott 1993: 167), but this ignores the symbolic association between the emperor and the capital in the eyes of the provincial population: their loyalty to the emperor and their loyalty to Rome could well have been the same thing.

It is immediately apparent that a modern definition of ethnicity derived from the idea of the nation-state cannot be mapped unproblematically onto the Roman context. Modern ethnicity is strongly tied into the definition of the nation state, where it could provide a way to tie together a political institution which comprised groups of people who had formerly had multiple ethnic backgrounds. Whilst this could be seen as an analogy for the Roman empire (and other ancient empires), the criteria are not necessarily all applicable to the political and cultural structures of the Roman empire. As demonstrated, whilst helpful, Smith's criteria for ethnic identity do not all apply for a Roman identity, and this could similarly be argued for the definitions of other academics outlined above. Nevertheless, it is possible to begin to construct a definition for a Roman identity. We can envisage this as involving a distinctive shared culture, which set the group apart both from other peoples (at least in the literary imagination), but also from what went before. There are elements of a shared history, and myths of descent which tied into a common mythical past, although allowing the possibility of localised origin myths. The question of association with a geographical territory is something which we should perhaps see as looser and changing over time, and, similarly, a sense of solidarity as something which develops as more people are brought into the Roman imperial system through magistracies, military service or citizenship.

Towards an archaeology of Roman ethnicity

As argued in the previous section, a shared culture is an important element of Roman ethnicity, but how should we identify it within the archaeological record? Religion is often taken as a key part of shared Roman customs, but across the provinces, cultural change does not result in a uniform pattern in its material expression. In Roman Britain, we find two forms of material culture associated with Roman religion: temples and dedications on inscribed altars. However, temples concentrate in the southern, civilian areas, and usually take form of the so-called Romano-Celtic temple which consists of a central shrine, whether square, circular or polygonal, with or without an encircling portico. Inscribed altars are rare in the civilian regions, and instead cluster around military settlements (the frontiers and the legionary fortresses). Both forms of material culture are part of the post-conquest cultural change, both respond to an adoption of Roman cultural practices, but neither can be taken as a straightforward index of Roman ethnicity. This could be applied to all forms of material culture we describe as Roman: it is not possible to use the presence or absence of a single material type or artefact style to indicate Roman ethnicity.

Recent work has stressed the concept of Roman as a series of commonly-held cultural assumptions rather than a package of material culture, such as J. D. Hill's (1997) argument that the appearance of nail cleaners and razors on late Iron Age sites is evidence for new ideas about the body, cleanliness and appearance. Thus the appearance of new forms of material culture within the conquered territories represents more than the adoption of new goods, but is bound up in, and in some sense the product of, new practices and beliefs about how these lives should be lived. In a similar way, John Barrett, in a series of articles, has argued for a repositioning of the study of Roman imperialism and cultural change. He argues for a study of the common cultural values which penetrated the routines of the daily lives of the people of the provinces, and the ways in which these were expressed materially (Barrett 1989, 1997). A similar approach underpins Woolf's (1998) study of the Romanization of the Gallic provinces. He argues that Roman culture should be seen as encapsulating "the range of objects, beliefs and practices that were characteristic of people who considered themselves to be, and were widely acknowledged as, Roman" (*ibid.*: 11). Using this broad definition, he demonstrates how new forms of material culture were in fact part of a complex series of transformations in how people acted and how they conceptualised the world around him.

To return to Hill's example of bodily cleanliness, this is part of a series of beliefs and practices about the presentation of the body and the importance of grooming. The adoption of razors, nail cleaners, bath-houses, bottles for perfumed oils, hairpins and the like are the product of a view that a cultured outlook is reflected in the care devoted to the appearance and bodily hygiene. The adoption of these material items by the British reflects a similar outlook to that displayed on a more humorous level in Ovid's *Ars Amatoria*. In his advice to a lover on how to get his girl, he stresses the importance of grooming as the way to get a desirable lover: expertly groomed hair and beard, clean nails, and trimmed nasal hair. The correct care of the body was essential for the citizen at Rome: the grooming of the male body was part of the definition of civilisation, setting the citizen apart from the savages (Wyke 1994). The appearance of the material paraphernalia for such bodily grooming within the archaeological record can be seen as responding to the same discourse. In Britain, the local elites adopted toilet instruments (i.e. nail-cleaners, tweezers and ear scoops) in the century between the Caesarian and Claudian invasions; following the Claudian conquest, they became widespread within southern Britain, particularly in the countryside (Hill 1997, Eckardt and Crummy 2008). Likewise razors are attested in wealthy pre-conquest graves, and then seem to have become widespread. Combs are only adopted after the conquest period, the earliest dating to *c.* AD 50, with over 150 recorded (Pugsley 2003). In the case of Britain, we see the process of cultural change as being more than adopting new items of material culture, but as adopting new ideas and bodily practices.

This idea of Roman ethnicity as joining into a discourse presents certain problems, however. Work on ideologies has stressed that they are not static, with fixed boundaries and precepts, but rather changeable and subject to negotiation and contention (Foucault 1979, Shanks and Tilley 1982, Miller and Tilley 1984). Within the textual sources, whilst Ovid was advising his readers to shave their beards, Stoic philosophers such as Clement of Alexandria and Epictetus were concerned that the removal of the beard was an unnatural act which harmed a man's masculinity (Gleason 1995: 67–70). Ideas of the correct forms of behaviour change over time, and from Hadrian onwards, we start to see the emperors wearing a neatly trimmed beard on their statues and portraits. Furthermore, whilst the inhabitants of southern Britain were adopting toilet implements, those of Gaul seem to have given up their use after the Augustan period (Eckardt and Crummy 2008: 20). These apparently contradictory positions in reality point to the debates within such ideologies. The particular positions within the debate have changed, but the discourse of the correct way to care for the body remains as denoting the boundary between Romans and the Other. This bring us to Woolf's words of caution when dealing with the idea of ethnicity as a discourse: "there were so many kinds of Romans to become that being Roman did not mean assimilating to an ideal type, but rather acquiring a position in the complex of structured differences in which Roman power resided" (Woolf 1998: 245). In other words, we should not expect the people of the provinces to be slavishly acting in accordance with the literary accounts from Rome. A careful reading of these sources reveals debate and lack of agreement. Instead, the people of the provinces are joining in the debate: how should the body be cared for, and at what point a man's grooming routine failed to tread the fine line in the spectrum between savagery and effeminacy.

Consequently, an archaeology of Roman ethnicity no longer sees a single item of material culture as standing as a proxy for an ethnic identity, but rather as bound up in the practices and ideologies which set the Romans apart from the non-Romans. As seen in the discussion of Tacitus' *Germania*, an important element of this was urbanism: the ideal of a settlement system organised around a laid out urban centre which fulfilled a range of public functions, such as political organisation, religion and state administration. Thus, when we study urban settlements as evidence for Roman ethnicity, we are not merely looking at the form of the town (layout, public buildings, proportion of population living within the walls, etc.), but also the forms of practices it might allow, and whether these are part of shared practices and ideologies (Revell 2009). Any urban settlement encompassed a physicality, and so part of Roman identity should be seen as incorporating the physical remains of a specifically Roman form of town, with a broadly recognisable layout and range of building types. In accounts of the adoption of urbanism, this is the area where most work has concentrated: looking at the emergence of towns, with the fora, baths, temples and other public buildings which characterise Roman urbanism (Bedon *et al.* 1988, Bendala Galán 1993, Wacher 1995). However, we need to use these physical remains as the starting point for the beliefs and practices they enabled: how people lived within the spaces, moved through them, the knowledge this required, and the symbols and ideologies about correct modes of living which they were the product of and in turn engendered.

I want to pull some of these ideas together with respect to the town of Tarraco, the capital of the province of Hispania Tarraconensis, looking not only at the town itself (Macias Solé *et al.* 2007), but also at the surrounding hinterland (Carreté *et al.* 1995). The town developed out of a military camp adjoining the Iberian settlement of Kesse, with twin urban centres apparently co-existing during the Republic, and was later refounded as *Colonia (Iulia) Urbs Triumphalis Tarraco* (Ruiz de Arbulo 2006). By the 1st century AD the town possessed the facilities we would expect of an important provincial capital: a colonial forum, theatre and public baths in the lower town, and a temple to Divus Augustus in the upper town (Figure 2.1). During the second half of the 1st century, the upper town was turned into a more monumental complex, incorporating the temple, a provincial forum, and a circus, and an amphitheatre was

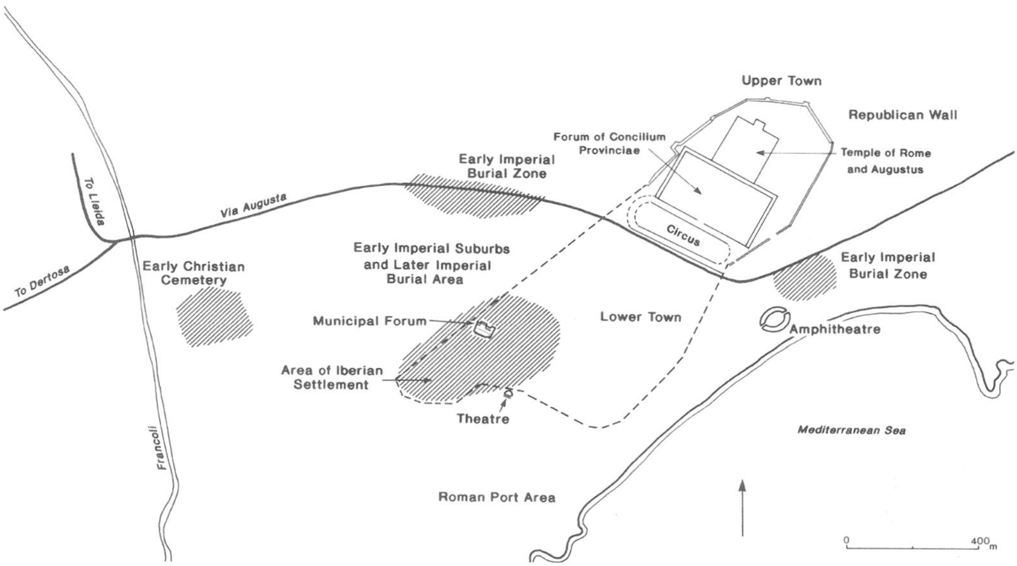

Figure 2.1 Plan showing principle known features from Tarraco (Carreté et al. 1995, fig. 3.1; reproduced by permission of S. Keay)

constructed outside the town walls in the early 2nd century AD. The development of the town is matched by changes in its territory (Carreté *et al.* 1995: 273–81). In the pre-Roman period, Kesse, el Vilar and a third un-named site all seem to have been local centres of some form. During the 2nd and 1st centuries BC, Kesse/Tarraco becomes dominant, with El Vilar being abandoned. Thus the people of the hinterland become completely dependent on Tarraco for urban facilities. A series of more elaborate villas concentrated on the plain to the north-west of the town and around the coastal strip, with a dense settlement of rural farmsteads throughout the hinterland. It has been estimated that only 13–20% of the total population of the territory actually lived in the town itself (*ibid.*: 278), the rest living in the town's hinterland or *territorium*.

From these very bald details, what can we say about the role of urbanism in the ethnic identity of the inhabitants of the region? Assuming they were granted a similar colonial charter to that of the *Colonia Genetivae Iuliae* (Crawford 1996: 393–454), then we can start to reconstruct some of the practices which centred the town within their daily lives. The citizens of the *colonia* were expected to take part in elections for the chief magistrates and priests, which presumably took place within the colonial forum. They might attend public religious events, whether sacrifices (possibly at the temple in the upper town), or games and dramatic spectacles at the theatre and amphitheatre. If they were prosecuted for debt, or involved in any other legal action, this was overseen by the colonial magistrate, with the trial presumably taking place in the basilica of the lower forum. The charter refers to market days, when presumably local people would have bought and sold their wares. They had an obligation to the colony to work for the community for up to five days per year, and could be obliged to take up arms as a local militia. From references to scribes for the keeping of records, presumably their tax obligations and any proof of property-ownership were also kept within the forum. The town council was responsible for the supply of water, with the ability to enforce the route of any water courses over an individual's land. There are other events which are not included in the *lex Coloniae Genetivae*, such as the payment of taxes, and the taking of the census. All of this is in accordance with the ideology of the community being organised through the urban centre.

It is tempting to say that such required behaviours only applied to the 13–20% of the population who lived within the town walls, but it must be remembered that these rules applied to all the citizens and the *incolae* who lived around the *colonia*. Presumably to fulfil their duties as a citizen of the *colonia*, the people of the surrounding territory were expected to come into the town, and take part in the same activities. Thus we have the situation where the people who do not actually live in the town itself come to share in an ideology of urbanism which disrupted their previous lives. Through such visits, even if only on an annual basis, they would become familiar with the public buildings of the town, how to act within them, and how to read the iconography decorating them. After paying their taxes, or voting for the following year's magistrates, they may have taken the opportunity to experience other aspects of the urban experience, such as a visit to the public baths, or purchasing specialist goods from workshops. They might pay a visit to the provincial forum to see whether any new statues had been erected or inscriptions put up. It is through such mundane activities that the ideology of urbanism was reproduced, and an affiliation to a Roman way of life reaffirmed amongst the wider population.

We can also argue that Roman ethnicity was in part the knowledge of a shared group of cultural symbols and myths. These have been encountered through different media, but formed part of the discourses of what it was to be Roman. This common cultural knowledge can be seen throughout the western provinces, usually within the pictorial language of decoration. There is a tendency to judge provincial art against a series of aesthetic standards based on Greek art, and to see it as of poor quality and worthless (Scott 2003). Nevertheless, its use demonstrates a familiarity with the images and, potentially, their meaning. One example of this shared culture language is myth, including those of the Olympian deities. There was a shared series of stories based around heroic figures (which included certain gods and goddesses) which were referenced in iconographic decoration. These were derived from the Mediterranean region, but not necessarily from Rome or Italy. Some of these were adopted from the Greeks by the Etruscans and the Romans. Other myths are more closely tied in with Rome, most famously the myth of Romulus and Remus, their suckling by the she-wolf and their subsequent founding of Rome. The iconography and deities of Egypt were also brought into this complex cultural mix as a form of Egyptomania (Versluys 2002). Such stories came to form a shared symbolic language for the western provinces as a whole. Whilst they may have been preferentially used by the elite (as I shall argue in chapter 4), their use as decoration on more mundane pieces of daily goods argues for a more widespread use through different levels of society.

Various kinds of material culture can be used to illustrate this idea of a shared cultural knowledge. One group is the intaglios or engraved gemstones from Roman Britain (Henig 2007). These show a sophisticated knowledge of iconography, even if the technical quality of their execution is of a variable standard. Within Henig's complete catalogue of intaglios from the province, the majority of the gems depict images associated with Roman myth, whether these are deities, personifications, heroes or some type of mythical animal. Approximately a third can be identified as deities (33.5%), of which the most frequently depicted are Cupid, Bonus Eventus and Mercury. A further 10% are unidentified male and female figures, of which some may be further examples of deities. In addition, some of the other categories may refer to divine attributes: the thunderbolt illustrated on three examples presumably relates to Jupiter, and similarly the 1st century AD example from Hod Hill in Dorset, which depicts a rudder and tiller, corn-ears and cornucopia, should probably be associated with Fortuna. Over 15% depict animals, some of which again may relate to deities, such as ants or cockerels. In some cases, the myths which are depicted take us to the myths of the foundation of Rome, such as the example from Corbridge which depicts Romulus, or the three examples depicting the *Lupus Romana* (this figure may be higher as there are a number showing wolves which might represent the she-wolf which suckled the twins). Other depictions represent people connected to the Trojan Wars, such as Achilles, Ajax and Ulysses. There are others which relate to elements of everyday life, but which refer to specifically Roman subjects, such as gladiators, actors and theatrical events, and chariot races.

These iconographical motifs are also visible on other categories of everyday material. Ceramic lamps are ubiquitous throughout the empire, and from the 1st century BC, decoration on the central discus was common (Bailey 1963). Unlike the gems, these were mass-produced items, with large production centres which then seem to have licensed smaller factories to produce the types for distribution within a certain region (Harris 1980, Eckardt 2002). In Roman Britain, these lamps show a similar repertoire of images to those depicted on the gem-stones. Eckardt lists a total of 105 out of a total of 325 picture lamps depicting deities, Bacchic scenes and myths (32.3%, Eckardt 2002: table 10). One example from Silchester depicts the goddess Fortuna holding a cornucopia, whilst those depicting Jupiter show him with an eagle and thunderbolt. As with the gems, there is the possibility of the attributes of deities being depicted without the deities themselves. Examples from Colchester depicting an eagle perched on a thunderbolt and others from London showing a peacock presumably represent Jupiter and Juno respectively. The depiction of these attributes called on the deeper knowledge of the owner or viewer: that their knowledge of Roman myth was sufficient to make the association between the attribute and the deity concerned.

Such motifs are common-place within museum collections of Roman material, and it perhaps this ubiquity which blinds the modern viewer to their significance. Cumulatively, they point to a common visual language shared by the peoples of the empire. Gems and lamps represent two very different scales of industries, but, in Britain, they use a common iconographic language. Such an analysis could be extended to other forms of mundane objects, particularly ceramic decoration. They are repeated throughout the empire, and so become a shared series of cultural reference points. Whilst mythological figures form one element of this, another is the importance of the image of the emperor, whether on coinage, or statues, or even his titles within an inscription (Noreña 2011). Again, this common cultural reference point forms one part of the shared knowledge of being Roman. The acts of both production and consumption tied the individual into a wider cultural *koine* and group identity.

The temporal context of Roman ethnicity

As many have argued, ethnicity is situational and should be seen as a work in progress. This is usually taken to be subject to the geographical context, but for Roman ethnicity, we also need to allow for the temporal context. The archaeological evidence is increasingly demonstrating that the process of ethnic change in the provinces does not follow a simple trajectory. From the second half of the 1st century BC, there is an increase in the material culture tied into the practices and ideologies of Roman ethnicity. One example of this is an increase in urbanism within the provinces, both in the number of chartered towns, and in the material from them, such as public architecture (Ward-Perkins 1970) and inscriptions (MacMullen 1982, Prag 2002). This is evident in the case of the Iberian provinces. Roman political control of this region began following the Second Punic War, and increased through a process of conquest which took the best part of two centuries. However, we see a delay in the adoption of Roman cultural traits; for example we only see evidence for the adoption of Roman architecture from the late 1st century BC onwards (Keay 1995). In the mid- to late Republic, Iberia was tied into a wider Mediterranean cultural *koine*, with a complex interplay of Iberian, Hellenistic and Carthaginian cultural forms evident (Keay 2013). The only town with evidence for Italic forms of architecture was the Latin colony of Carteia, founded in 171 BC by Roman citizens. In the second half of the 2nd century BC, there was evidence for an Italic-style temple, and the minting of coins with the name of the town in Latin. In contrast, at Emporiae, the site of a Greek city from the mid-6th century BC and under Roman occupation from the end of the Second Punic War, the Greek town (the Neapolis) show considerable rebuilding in the 2nd century BC, but using Hellensitic cultural forms, such as the agora with stoa, the temple of Asklepios, and the later temple to Isis (Aquilué *et al.* 2006). It is only in the Augustan period that the Italic-style forum is constructed. Similarly, Italica was settled with Roman soldiers wounded during the Second Punic War, but the appearance of Roman architecture occurs much later. The central area of the town seems to have been remodelled during the early 1st century AD, with a forum dating to the Augustan period, and a theatre to the Tiberian period (Keay 1997). At Saguntum there is evidence for a central settlement from the pre-Roman period, but the central area also underwent a new phase of rebuilding during the Augustan period (Figure 2.2), with the area around the Republican temple being transformed into a closed forum with porticoes, basilica and curia (Aranegui Gascó 1992, 2006). A theatre was constructed nearby, producing a central zone of monumental public architecture. Throughout the peninsula as a whole, there is little adoption of Roman or Italic cultural forms before 100 BC, and these only become widespread from the Augustan period onwards (Trillmich and Zanker 1990).

This fluidity of ethnicity within the provinces is related to a fluidity in ethnicity in Rome itself, where there was an ongoing renegotiation of what it was to be Roman. A core element of this has been the idea that Roman culture was formulated within the context of other Italian tribes during the early to mid-Republican period, and then in response to Rome's contact with Hellenistic culture, as most clearly argued

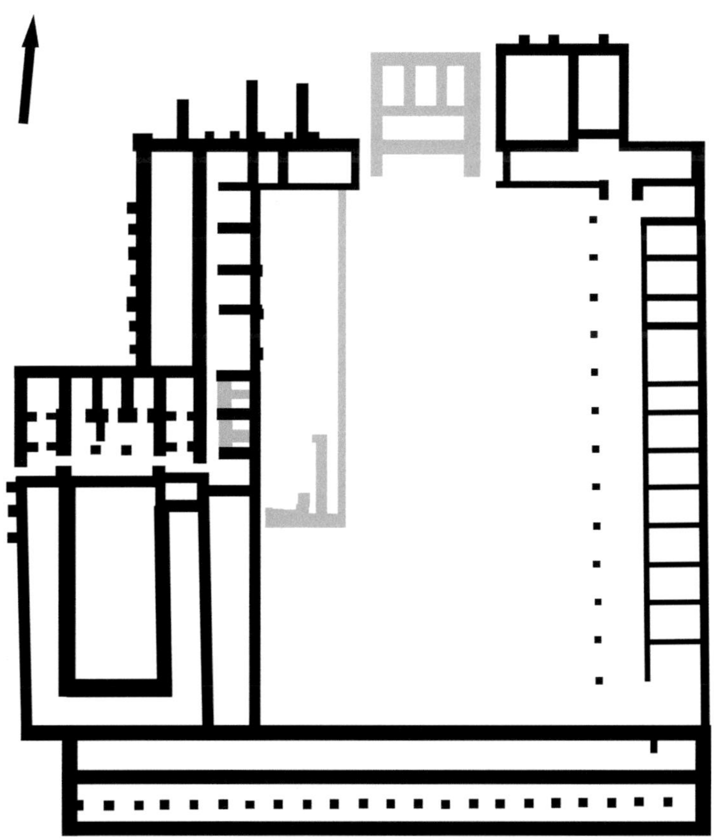

Figure 2.2 Plan showing hypothesised reconstruction of the forum, Saguntum; Republican structures are in light grey, Imperial period structures in black (adapted from Aranegui Gasco 1992 fig. 3)

by Andrew Wallace-Hadrill (2008). The reign of Augustus was a pivotal moment, with the creation of a new cultural and iconographic language to express the relationship between the emperor and his subjects in Rome (Zanker 1988, Haselberger 2007), and the emperor and his subjects outside of Rome (for example Zanker 1998 on Pompeii). At the same time, there were changes in the expression of the identity of the senatorial elite (Eck 1984), uses of honorific inscriptions (Wallace-Hadrill 1990), and so forth. Part of these changes during the late 1st century BC was a shift in the political relationship between Rome and the provinces. How far this can be completely attributed to Augustus himself, or how far Augustus was continuing a trajectory of change begun earlier is subject to debate, but regardless of this, it is clear that there was a very different relationship between Rome and its conquered territories in the early 1st century AD to that of the 2nd century BC (Lintott 1993). I do not want to go through the detail here, but a series of changes in how the provinces were administered drew the conquered peoples more closely into the system, with increasing rewards in the form of Roman citizenship. A central part of this was the extension of Roman urban status beyond the veteran colonies, and the foundation (forced or encouraged) of urban centres in areas with limited urban settlements. This changing imperialism is not only visible within the provinces, but also in the administrative structures at Rome for the governing of the empire, such as the mapping of Rome's territories, and the counting of resources through the census (Nicolet 1991). As argued in chapter 1, identity should be seen as fluid and in a state of constant renegotiation, and this is not only the case by region, but also by time.

Roman ethnicity and imperial power

This brings us to the question of how power was embedded within Roman ethnic identity. As argued earlier, identities are not neutral concepts, but are used in part to maintain and justify inequalities between different groups. Within the context of the Roman empire, ethnicity, albeit unintentionally, became bound up in Roman imperialism. Thus the adoption of Roman cultural traits was the acquisition of the dominant ethnic traits by the subjugated group. It became a means through which the power of the central authorities was maintained over the vast distances of the empire.

How far this was a conscious policy on the part of the imperial rulers has been a subject of debate. The most often quoted evidence for deliberate Romanization is the passage in Tacitus' biography of Agricola. Tacitus writes that whilst Agricola was governor of Britain "he gave encouragement privately and assistance publicly so that they built temples, fora and houses; and he praised the keen and chastised the tardy. In this way competition for honour took the place of compulsion" (Tac. *Agr.* 21.1; similarly Dio 56.18.2–3 for Germany). Using evidence such as this, Hanson, for example, has argued that "(it) was in the Roman interest to attempt to control the hearts and minds of the indigenous population – or at least of the élite, for 'civilised' (in other words Romanized) people were easier to control than 'barbarians'" (Hanson 1997: 76). He argues that this compulsion took place through urban development, local government, citizenship, the promotion of the imperial cult, and education. These structures were all mechanisms for the administration of the empire, and along with service in the army, formed a means of integrating the elites of the provinces into the Roman political system. Studies of the composition of the Senate and the army have demonstrated that increasingly men from the provinces replaced those from Rome and Italy (Hammond 1957, Mann 1983), showing the extent to which they could become part of the imperial framework. Whilst both the political magistracies and the military service acted as a stimulus for cultural change, it is unclear whether this should be seen as a deliberate policy on the part of the imperial authorities, or an unintended, albeit convenient, consequence.

Nevertheless, whether deliberate policy or not, there was an inequality within this process of cultural change in that it was largely a one-way flow, and that the growing acceptance of Roman cultural norms was an important factor in the stability of the empire. It aligned the customs and the outlook of the provincial communities with those of the imperial authorities, making their cultural norms seem correct and inevitable. It required in part a rejection of the local traditions and local systems of knowledge in the face of a new political reality. However, the outcome of these changes was not uniform, and there is a clear flexibility and fluidity in their interpretation of how to be Roman. The material correlates of claiming a Roman ethnicity were the product of a creative process, in part because ethnic identity was based upon shared practices and ideologies which could be expressed through stylistically different materials. The second factor disrupting any material homogeneity was the intersection of ethnicity with other aspects of identity: the discrepant experiences which Mattingly (2004) argues for. A further aspect of this was the idea of regionality; it is the significance of local and regional variability which I shall address in the next chapter.

Chapter 3

A Poly-ethnic Empire

Introduction

In the previous chapter, I argued for a Roman ethnic identity which was based upon links between abstract concepts, everyday practice and material culture. However, this expression of specific discourses of ethnicity did not result in an homogeneous package of material culture throughout the provinces; in fact, there is clear variability between and within provinces. This results in a fundamental paradox in the archaeological record of the provinces: the paradox of similarity and difference. We can identify certain reoccurring features, such as specific forms of building, coinage or pottery, but any apparent uniformity soon becomes a mirage. For example, we might argue that the forum was the definitive Roman public building, but there are marked differences between them at the provincial level, with the so-called tripartite forum of the western provinces, with forum, basilica and temple, in reality masking a degree of flexibility in arrangement between the elements (Gros 1996: 207–34). Adding to this variability are some from Britain and North Africa which lack the inclusion of a temple, and consist of forum and basilica (Goodchild 1946, Euzennat 1994). This raises the question of what precisely constituted Roman material culture, and how it related to an overall Roman ethnicity. It brings us back to the idea of identity as a discourse, a group of ideas about actions and behaviours worked through using certain kinds of material culture. The relationship between discourse-action-material allows for a degree of variability, such as that seen in the provincial fora, and that variability is reflected within the archaeological record. The aim of this chapter is to explore variability at a regional level: the form such variability might take, the explanations for it within the archaeological record, and how we might understand it within theories of ethnic identity.

Characterising variability

The elements of variability within the archaeology of the Roman provinces are wide-ranging, and cannot be reduced to a single element. Perhaps the most evident is within the typologies of specific artefacts, such as different styles of architecture. For example, J. T. Smith's work on rural villas demonstrates the variation within the style of villas (Smith 1997). In the Mediterranean region, these are centred on the peristyle, echoing Hellenistic styles of housing. Within temperate Europe they are initially row-type, later developing into the courtyard-style house. Finally in the Low Countries and Germany, they are a single structure divided between the household and the livestock. We similarly see variability within the ecofactual evidence, such as the remains of animal bones (King 2001). In Spain, although there are comparatively few assemblages, the evidence suggests a diet in which cattle is the dominant meat, but with a high proportion of pork. Southern Gaul shows a very different pattern, with the dominance of sheep and goat. Further north in Aquitania, Lugdunensis and Belgica, the diet was dominated by high cattle and pork percentages, and the Rhine provinces show a similar pattern, but with cattle outnumbering pork. In Britain, there was a change from predominantly sheep-goat consumption to incorporate large proportions of cattle and pig, but still retaining a considerable proportion of sheep. These forms of variability can be described as cultural variability, but there is also the impact of geography to consider. This is not to argue for geographical determinism, but that there were differences in availability of mineral resources, or the agricultural potential of the area. How these are then exploited will also introduce an element of variability into the archaeological record.

If we can identify this variability throughout the archaeological record, we then need to consider how this variability relates to the pre-conquest material record. At its most basic, we may be dealing with little or no post-conquest change. This tends to be most evident in areas on the margins of the empire. Cornwall, for example, demonstrates evidence of an imperial interest through the construction of small forts such as Nanstallon and Restormel, as well as evidence for the exploitation of the area for tin. The non-military, indigenous settlements consist of small farmsteads and villages (Quinnell 1986), which seem to be a continuity of the pre-conquest settlement types. There were no urban settlements, and there do not appear to have been small towns, and only a single villa-style structure. There is some evidence for imported materials, such as samian ware. However, these are of very limited quantities compared to elsewhere in Britain: at Trethurgy the excavated sherds suggested a minimum of 14 vessels for the whole settlement, and the majority come from a 4th-century AD midden, indicating the deliberate saving of the pots as exotic wares rather than seeing them as more mundane items, as was the case elsewhere in the province. Although subject to Roman rule, the archaeological evidence from this area demonstrates little impact on the daily routines of the area.

A second possibility is a post-conquest change, but which seems to retain elements of the pre-conquest forms. One example of that is the evidence for religion and the gods. Within the north-western provinces, one element of this is the apparent continuity of pre-conquest deities. Once assumed to be an unproblematic incidence of continuity, more recent work has demonstrated the complexity of how such deities were accommodated within a Roman cultural system (Webster 1995, Zoll 1995, Derks 1998). *Interpretatio romana* and double-naming all suggest that the idea of deity could be flexible, but the process of equating one deity with another was also a transformation process, potentially reinterpreting the pre-conquest deity in the light of the Roman deity. Even the process of depicting the deity in anthropomorphic form and creating a temple for them represents post-conquest changes in the conceptualisation of the divine. Such processes could be a creative way of creating a means of security in the new imperial context, as has been argued for the Gallic goddess Epona (Linduff 1979). This goddess is closely associated with horses: her name is linguistically derived from the word horse, she was seen as the protector of horses, and her iconography associates her with horses. Linduff has argued that her depiction represents a "visual schizophrenia" (*ibid.*: 824) between Celtic and Classical conceptions of art, a retention of existing art forms, but with new forms of figurative composition. Finally, the distribution of the evidence for her worship shows its concentration in central Gaul (particularly the area associated with the Aedui) and on the Rhine and Danube frontiers. This military material is connected with cavalry units, suggesting that these units used the deity as a way to understand their own position within the Roman military.

We also see stylistic variability in materials with no pre-conquest equivalent and so which are new adoptions. One example of this is in public architecture: within the Gallic, German and British provinces, we see forms of public architecture which do not accord with typologies from elsewhere in the empire, but which nevertheless represent a new form of building type. In the four Gallic provinces, theatres can be divided into two main types: the classical Roman-style theatre, which shares close affinities to those in northern and central Italy, and the so-called Gallo-Roman theatre (Sear 2006: 98–100). In the case of the latter, the *cavea* usually extended beyond the semicircle, and the stage was smaller than the width of the *cavea* and usually lacked the *scaenae frons* (Gros 1996: 294–8). These are more common in northern Gaul, Germany and Britain than the classical-style theatre. We also see differences in typologies of small finds between the south-east and the south-west of Britain as demonstrated by the work of Hella Eckardt and Nina Crummy on nail cleaners (Eckardt and Crummy 2008). The general distribution is concentrated in the southern half of the province, but the types break down into east and west distributions. The so-called "Baldock type" has a suspension loop at the top and a leaf-shaped blade; this is found in the eastern part of England, in particular around Verulamium, Colchester and in East Anglia (Figure 3.1). The bone disc type has a circular disc of bone at the top, and a copper alloy shaft, the upper part of which is decorated with a lattice design. This is found in the western part of England, and in particular, around the Severn Estuary (Figure 3.2).

Finally, we see the use of a Roman cultural language to create something distinctively new. Within the German provinces, Jupiter columns form a regionally distinctive manifestation of religious worship (Woolf 2001, 2003). As Woolf has argued, they undoubtedly take their inspiration from a Neronian monument at Mainz, but they did not become ubiquitous until over a century later, and their restricted distribution puts an emphasis on their local distinctiveness. The architectural and

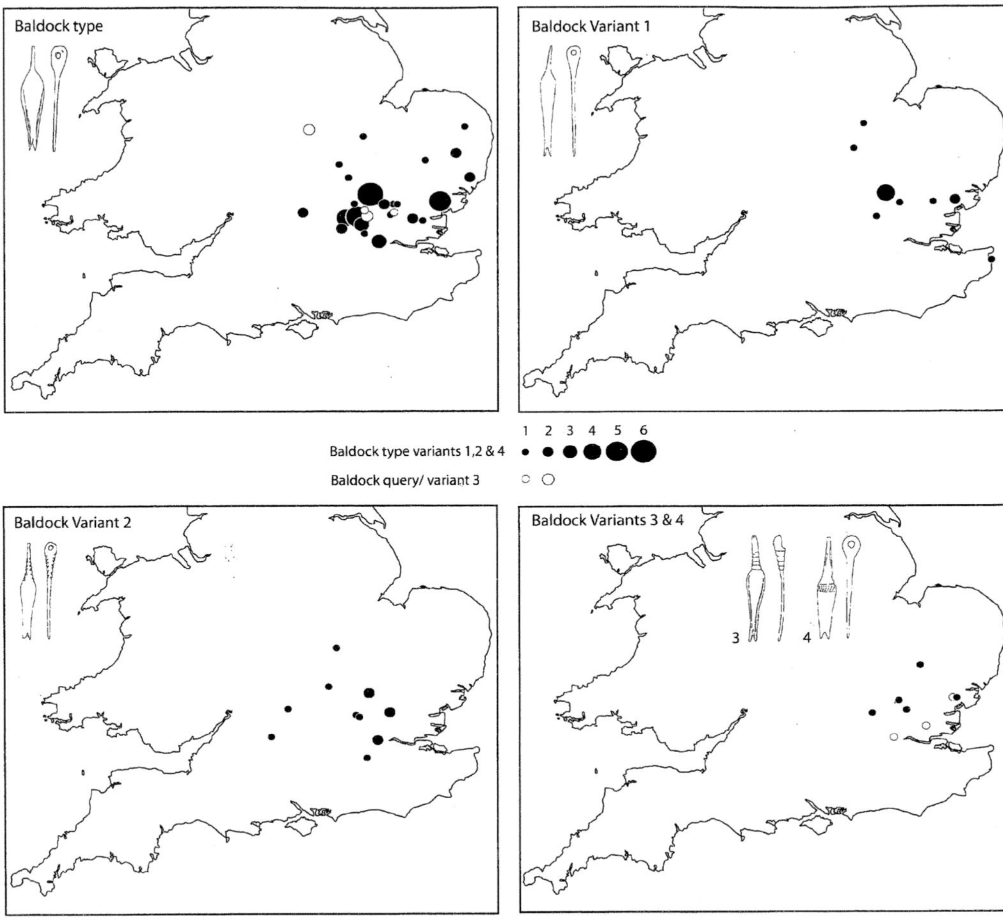

Figure 3.1 Baldock type nail cleaner distribution (Eckardt and Crummy 2008, fig. 29; reproduced by permission of authors)

iconographic language is particularly Roman: a two-part base, each of which might bear images of groups of deities, on which sat the column, often decorated with scales and with ornate capitals. On top of these stood statues of Jupiter. Inscriptions in Latin record their dedication, either on the base or on associated votive altars. The iconography and inscriptions point to the adoption of Roman styles of representation, but the way they were put together into a single monument was distinctly innovative. However, given this form of monument was developed decades after the conquest of the region, it cannot be accounted for as a continuity of pre-Roman cult traditions. Instead, we are seeing the development of a new form of practice within the region.

Such elements give some idea of the variability apparent within the archaeology of the provinces. This variability is not a single phenomenon, with predictable

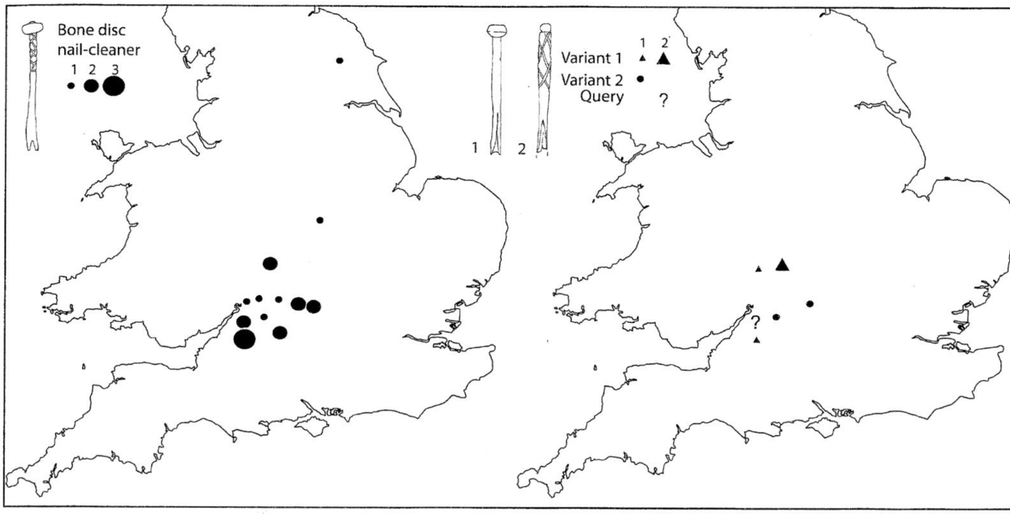

Figure 3.2 Bone disc type nail cleaner distribution (Eckardt and Crummy 2008, fig. 30; reproduced by permission of authors)

characteristics from a uniform interplay of pre-Roman and Roman cultural forms. It is more complex, and responds to different processes at play in the cultural changes provoked by Roman imperialism. However, if we take the approach that such forms of material culture are bound up in the formation of ethnic identity, then this implies that such variability is not meaningless. It requires archaeologists to account for this variability, and to consider the consequences for ideas of Roman ethnicity.

Explaining variability

How we account for this regionality has been a central concern of the work on cultural change within the provinces. A somewhat uncritical explanation sees these as somewhat imperfect levels of Romanization. The variability is caused by the differences in the pre-existing cultures, and these traits are not replaced by 'proper' Roman culture. This certainly underpins Haverfield's thinking on the Romanization of the provinces, and Britain in particular. Although he allows that the cultural change was not necessarily uniform, he argues that such differences were caused by the latent persistence of pre-conquest traits (Haverfield and MacDonald 1923: 9–22). He elaborates that the reasons for this persistence might be due to local and geographical conditions (*ibid.*: 12–14), or due to the racial inferiority of certain regions (*ibid.*: 173). An important part of rethinking Romanization has been a rejection of these simplistic assumptions, and to explore more sophisticated explanations for this variability.

One explanation for the persistence of indigenous traits has been cultural resistance to Roman rule. Whilst legally and administratively regions were incorporated into the Roman empire, the people retained their pre-conquest material culture as a way to articulate their resistance to Roman rule. Their use of material culture was an active statement of their refusal to be incorporated into Roman social norms. These arguments were originally made by Bénabou in relation to the Romanization of North Africa (Bénabou 1976). He used the evidence of religion and language amongst other elements to argue for the absence of Roman cultural traits. In the case of religion, he argues for the continuity of traditional African deities, and the Africanisation of classical ones through syncretism. Reaction to his thesis has been mixed (Mattingly 1996: 58–9), but he does raise the possibility that in some cases, the patterning in the evidence is the result of deliberate rejection of Roman ethnicity. Hingley, for example, has argued that the continued construction of round houses in Britain represents an act of non-compliance or resistance, although in this case, he questions who is being resisted, the imperial authorities or the Romanized local elites (Hingley 1997).

These explanations rely on a dichotomising approach to the material remains, based on a mutually exclusive polarization of cultural categories. A similar critique can be made of acculturation studies: although they allow for the multi-directional flow of cultural influence, it is still within the discourse of bounded, opposing cultural blocks (Slofstra 1983). Other explanations for the variability within the archaeological record have concentrated on the apparent hybrid nature of the provincial material forms. This was expressed by Collingwood in his account of Roman Britain: "it might be said that the civilization of Roman Britain is neither Roman nor British but Romano-British, a fusion of the two things into a single thing different from either" (Collingwood 1932: 92), and this fusion has been argued for most, if not all, of the Roman provinces since then. It allows for cultural change within the provinces to be represented as something more than a linear transformation to Roman cultural norms, providing a space for the non-Roman to remain in a positive perspective. This fusion has been the subject of a number of more theoretically informed explanations in recent years, which have been influenced by post-colonial studies. These have concentrated on the hybridity as the consequence of the process of negotiation by the conquered communities and have recast the provincial peoples as knowledgeable agents, employing deliberate strategies to deal with their changing world.

Such studies have argued against the focus on the material object as the carrier of the hybrid values. They have rejected the idea that a study of hybridity is the listing of the various elements from the contributing societies within the context of a classificatory grid (Jiménez 2011). Instead, such studies have focused on the people responsible for the material and the contexts within which it is produced. For example, Jiménez has demonstrated that certain forms of sculpture in Iberia during the last two centuries BC were the product of the intermingling of indigenous traditions with new Roman iconographic markers. She argues that they should be analysed using the idea of the speech act: such objects become a single utterance within a specific context, referring to specific understandings of similarity and difference. A related approach is that of Tronchetti and Van Dommelen, studying interaction between Sardinians and Phoenicians (Tronchetti and Van Dommelen 2005). They argue that hybridity should be seen as hybrid practices, as people meet and act in zones of colonial contact. Whilst these two studies take different approaches, they share the starting point of concentrating on the intentionality of the actors and the context of the act of production. The elements of hybridity are not seen as accidental, but deliberate, referring to the cultural meaning of different societies and using them in a knowledgeable way to situate a specific community within a contested cultural context.

Related to such post-colonial readings of hybridity has been the use of theories of creolization by Jane Webster in the study of art in Britain and Gaul (Webster 1997, 2001, 2003). Her work is based on models developed in African-American and African-Caribbean contexts. Although initially a linguistic theory, it was later applied to material culture within the same contexts, such as American plantation slaves who received artefacts from their European masters, but used them according to the underlying African-derived rules of slave culture (for example, Ferguson 1992). Webster argues that the post-conquest representations of the Gallic deities of Epona, Cernunnos and Sucellus might be seen as creolized representations (Webster 2001): they are represented in anthropomorphic form in classical art styles, but are usually connected with, or sometimes even replaced by, animal imagery. They are not syncretized with Roman deities, and they do not appear in divine marriages. Webster argues that in their post-conquest manifestations, they are neither Roman deities, nor purely Celtic, nor can they be seen as a syncretic incorporation into a Graeco-Roman pantheon; rather they stand outside the boundaries and instead represent, "an alternative creole pantheon in Roman Gaul" (Webster 2001: 223).

Such ideas of resistance, creolisation and hybridisation still tend to look to the culture of Rome as the main source of non-indigenous cultural forms within the process of cultural change. Other work has decentred Roman culture as the only response within an imperial context. Admittedly, this is not new, as it is over 40 years since Ward-Perkins (1970) argued that the models for public architecture in southern Gaul were derived from northern Italy rather than Rome itself. It has also been argued that Roman Britain looked to Gaul for new cultural trappings, continuing a cultural interaction evident in the Late Pre-Roman Iron Age (James 2001a: 190–2). The 1st century AD villa at Ditches in Gloucester, for example, does not echo Italian-style architectural forms, but rather the contemporary development of villas in northern France (Trow *et al.* 2009). Similar processes can be seen in the case of the *Totenmahl* (funerary banquet) reliefs from the northern provinces (Stewart 2009, 2010). They originated in Classical Greece and were popular during the Hellenistic period in the Greek world and Asia Minor. During the 1st century AD, they were adopted by soldiers on the Danube, and spread from there to the Rhine and Britain. However, although this seems a simple account of artistic diffusion, there are specific concentrations in distribution and variations in iconography which point to a local input into their articulation.

Underlying these recent approaches is a more nuanced approach to the development of new forms of material culture within the western provinces, and different readings of its significance. Whether we term this hybridism, creolisation, provincialism or bricolage (Terrenato 1998 for the final term), the underlying assumption is that the variability apparent within the archaeology of the western provinces is the product of human intentions and reactions, depending on their knowledge of what is appropriate within specific contexts. For this, they drew on both their own pasts and their new Roman presents, but also on other elements of the cultural mix of their local worlds. These choices were based upon messages they wished to communicate and customs they carried out as part of their daily lives. However, if this accounts for the heterogeneity of the archaeological record, how does this tie into ideas of ethnic identity?

Poly-ethnic contexts

Although there are various and contrasting explanations for the variability we see in the archaeological record, one thing they share is an assumption that ethnic identity is single-layered. Roman is set in juxtaposition to the pre-Roman group identity, and the ethnic identity of the community is assumed to be one or the other, or a new version created from the amalgamation of the two, or *ex novo*. However, this downplays the regional variability as being part of the process of creating a Roman identity. Whilst I do not disagree with the idea that there is no single, bounded interpretation of Roman identity, we do need to ask about the complexity at play, and whether this regionality might have a meaning in and of itself. There is an underlying question within this work which archaeologists have tended to shy away from, and that is how to reconcile the local with the global. To do this, we need to think about Roman ethnicity in a different way.

Amongst those studying ethnicity within modern contexts, there is an acknowledgement that the identity of a single person can encompass more than one element of ethnicity. For example, the transhumant Sami of northern Scandinavia maintain a distinct ethnic identity, which, in the 1960s, was seen as inferior by the dominant political groups. The coastal Sami of Norway presented themselves as Norwegian within public contexts, but within the home, spoke Sami and maintained their ethnic traditions (Eriksen 1991: 271–3, 2001: 266–7). This is the case in modern poly-ethnic societies, where the national identity derived from the nation-state can co-exist with the ethnic identity of descent. In the case of Mauritius, this island nation-state comprises groups descended from Africa, Europe and Asia: Hindus and Muslims from India, Europeans from France and England, those from China, and Creoles of Malagasy and African descent (Eriksen 1993: 23). When such communities possess multiple levels of ethnicity, that which is dominant is based upon the situation, the one which is appropriate for that particular circumstance. Specific aspects come to the fore as an individual person, or an individual community, interacts with others who are perceived as different. Therefore, if a Mauritian is interacting with a non-Mauritian, then their ethnic identity as a Mauritian is foregrounded. In contrast, when a Hindu Mauritian interacts with a Franco-Mauritian, then their Indian-Hindi ethnicity is foregrounded (Eriksen 1991: 269–70). The case-study of Mauritius provokes a fundamental question about ethnicity: is it possible for one person to hold more than one ethnic identity? This then leads to the question: if so, could this be applicable for the Roman period?

A closer analogy to this idea is the world of classical Greece, where this layering of ethnic identity is apparent. Here we see various forms of communal identity: polis, ethnos, federal, intra-Hellenic and pan-Hellenic (Malkin 2001). Thus a citizen of Syracuse could describe himself as a Syracusan citizen, a Corinthian colonist, a Siceliot (i.e. a Greek from Sicily), a Dorian or a Greek. The precise answer was situational and would depend on the context of who the Syracusan was interacting with. We can detect an interplay at Athens during the 5th century BC between their pan-Hellenic identity and their polis identity (Konstan 2001): when at war with Persia, Athenian ambassadors stressed their common Greek origin (Hdt. 8.144.2), whereas during the Peloponnesian War, Pericles stressed their Athenian ethnicity in contrast with the Spartans (Thuc. 2.35–46). One element used to construct these different layers of identity was sanctuaries. In the case of the Ionians of the western coast of Asia Minor, where there was an interplay between a pan-Ionian ethnicity and local identities, there were cult sites common to all Ionians, such as the interstate sanctuary to Apollo on Delos, whilst local sanctuaries formed an expression of local ethnic identities, such as the temples at Ephesus and Didyma (Crielaard 2009). The interpretation and reinterpretation of historical events can be used to negotiate these different elements of ethnicity, as Gehrke has demonstrated through the shifting interpretation of Marathon as a Greek victory or a specifically Athenian victory (Gehrke 2009). Neither Mauritius nor Classical Greece provide a direct analogy for the Roman empire, as in the Roman case, we are dealing with an imperial context and the relationship between an imperial power and its subject communities. Nevertheless, both the Mauritian and the Greek examples provide cautionary tales concerning the complex layering, or nesting, of ethnic identities, and possible analogies for the complexity we see within the Roman provinces.

One consequence of the dominance of the discourse of Romanization is that archaeologists of the western provinces tend to think of ethnicity within an 'either-or' framework. This is possibly a product of the hermeneutic relationship between the Roman empire and the nation-state. As the nation-states were formed, there was a political desire to quash the ethnic sentiment of the multiple ethnic groups incorporated into them. Alternative languages and ethnic symbols were suppressed, with perhaps only a reinvented traditional element retained (Hobsbawm and Ranger 1983). However, the nation-state is not necessarily an appropriate model for the Roman world. As we are increasingly acknowledging for the modern world, a person does not necessarily have a single ethnic identity. It is possible to have an adherence to different scales of groupings: village, region, language community, political country. These different scales of belonging can be tied into different forms of communal identity. Whether we term all of these ethnicity is contentious, and rests upon any individual researcher's definition of ethnicity: if ethnicity is associated with the largest scale of political institution (i.e. the nation-state, or in this case, the Roman empire), then these smaller, community-based identities are not ethnic identities. Conversely, the political origin of the nation-state may be seen as others as the non-ethnic element, whilst the sub-group represents the true ethnic identity (influenced by the idea of the ethnic minority). Perhaps we should acknowledge that both opinions are missing the point: that an individual can see themselves as part of more than one ethnic group, existing at different scales.

These analogies provide a different way to reconceptualise Roman ethnicity as layers of multiple ethnicities. The local ethnic identities, whether tribal or urban, are not antithetical to a Roman identity. A constituent part of Roman imperialism is that in specific circumstances, it allows pre-conquest ethnic identities to be transformed within a Roman system of cultural values. Consequently, certain aspects of the material variability may be flagging the local ethnicities rather than the sense of Roman ethnicity. For Italy, Farney (2007) has argued that Italic ethnic identities came to be subsumed within a Roman identity, becoming an 'intra-Roman' ethnic identity. These people maintained the markers of Italic ethnicities, such as their myths and shared histories, whilst tying them into part of the larger political and social construct of Rome. In the western provinces, we can see a similar process from the material culture. This complexity creates the possibility that for some in the empire, particularly those away from the frontiers, such local ethnicities are more important at a daily level than the more global, Roman identity.

Re-reading local identities

This raises the question of how we are to identify these local ethnicities from the archaeological evidence. The most explicit expression of their importance is, perhaps unsurprisingly, the statement of a local ethnicity on an inscription. In some cases, the origin of the person will be included within the text of the inscription. These are rarely the province of origin (Talbert 2004: 36, although see Birley 2008 for exceptions), but rather the more specific town or community. So, for example, at Cirencester there is a tombstone set up to Philus, which describes him as a *civis Sequanus*, from area of the upper Saône valley (RIB 110). The base of a column, also from Cirencester, carries an inscription recording the benefaction of the governor of Britannia Prima, who gives his origin as *civis Remus*, modern Reims (RIB 103). Both men self-identify as part of a more local community. In both of these instances, it is a blend of pre-existing community and Roman legal terminology: the Sequani and the Remi were both tribal names, with their urban centres Vesontio and Durocortorum respectively. However, the term 'civis' relates to the new Roman concept of citizenship of the community, within a new Roman legal framework (Woolf 1998: 78–80 for further examples).

The expression of these local identities is not always straightforward, and its use needs to be seen as situational. Derks' study of the statement of Batavian identity explores the contexts of the use of ethnic self-ascription (Derks 2009a). He compiled all known inscriptions giving a Batavian ethnic descriptor, giving a total of 63 direct attestations of Batavian ethnicity. This list is dominated by the formulae *natione Batavus*, *Batavus* and *(Ulpia) Noviomago Batavorum*, with a small number of alternative constructions. The most significant characteristic of the use of the ethnonyms is the context within which they were deployed. There are no inscriptions which mention a Batavian ethnicity within the Batavian territory. The inscriptions found within the Batavian territory which mention an ethnic origin are those which give a non-Batavian ethnic ascription. The inscriptions which do give a Batavian origin cluster on the frontier regions and at Rome, the latter being where they served as part of the imperial guard. This picture is reinforced by the fact that ethnicity is more likely to be mentioned by Batavians not serving within a Batavian auxiliary unit. The picture presented by this distribution is clear. Local ethnicities were most important in social situations where the person had been removed from their place of birth, or from the people who shared their ethnic identity, such as within the Batavian auxiliary units. When a person was setting up an inscription found within the Batavian territory, the assumption was that they were a local and so it was not necessary to stipulate the ethnic identity. Noy has argued that this was also the case for ethnic statements in Britain (Noy 2010), pointing to a wider practice within the frontier provinces.

However, this is not the universal picture, and a very different use of ethnic statements emerges in the Spanish province of Baetica. If we look at the epigraphy of the Conventus Astigitanus, it is clear that there is a markedly different pattern of use of local ethnonyms. The data were taken from the updated edition of CIL (Alföldy 1998); rather than a collection of the attestation of a single ethnic group, as in Derks' study, all local ethnic statements were recorded, as well as their context. The wider patterns of use will be discussed in the next section, but if we look at where an individual person is allocated an ethnic affiliation, this gives a total of 128 examples. Within this sample, there are multiple instances of individuals recording their ethnicity within their place of origin. At Ilurco, for example, there are four examples of ethnic statements, all found on epitaphs and all referring to an origin of Ilurci itself (CIL 2.5.682–4, 707). This phenomenon is not limited to funerary contexts: at Nescania there are five examples of ethnic statements, all referring to an origin of Nescania; three are on religious dedications (CIL 2.5.838, 840), and two on honorific dedications (CIL 2.5.847, 849). This does not exclude the ethnic affiliation of those who were incomers to the community being recorded. Of the eleven ethnic statement found on inscriptions at Aurgi, seven refer to an origin of Aurgi itself (CIL 2.5.29, 31, 32, 35, 40, 42). Of the remaining four, two people are recorded as having come from Cordoba (Patriciensis; CIL 2.5.25, 39), and one from Astigi (CIL 2.5.42). The fourth example is an epitaph recording that the deceased was originally from Tucci, and but was on his death an *incola* of Astigi (CIL 2.5.41).

This use of ethnonyms within the Conventus Astigitanus was markedly different to that on the north-western frontiers. In total, 57% of the personal ethnic statements recorded the same ethnicity as the place in which they were set up, with only 43% recording a different ethnicity. Why this is the case is less clear. The social importance of such ethnic identities is clearly very different to how it was perceived amongst the Batavians, for example. People recorded their ethnicity both when they were removed from their place of both, but also when they were in their place of birth. This suggests that there was not the same assumption that someone recorded without an ethnic statement was necessarily from the local area. An alternative interpretation would be that place of birth, and in particular, being born amongst the community where one was being commemorated (whether through funerary or honorific dedication) was of key significance within the community, and within the articulation of personal identity. These individuals, or the person responsible for the text of the inscriptions, were making quite explicit that they were part of that community. It demonstrates a high level of awareness of one's local ethnicity, even when one was living within the community one was born into.

If this idea of multiple ethnicities is apparent within the epigraphic record, can we also see it within the material record? This raises the question of whether the variability in the material was used by these peoples in the past to create and distinguish their regional identities. One moment when a regional identity may become more acute is during the movement from one context to another; in other words, when the regional identity is set in the context of those who are different, as in the case of the Batavian and British inscriptions. We have long been aware of the movement of people between areas within the empire, whether from the epigraphic evidence (Farland 1990) or, increasingly, from the isotopic analysis of the human remains (Eckardt 2010). One important driver to this movement was recruitment into military units. Studies of epigraphic evidence have demonstrated that both legionary and auxiliary manpower were drawn from outside of the province where the unit was garrisoned, particularly in newly conquered regions (Mann 1983). This brought soldiers from one region into another, and so the customs and material culture which were bound up in their regional identities were thrown into sharp relief.

One example of the identification of these regional identities from the material record has been published by Vivien Swan (Swan 1992, 2009). Although her primary aim was to understand recruitment practices, her methodology was based on establishing forms and stylistic traits within ceramic assemblages which did not match the local characteristics, but which were locally produced. One example of this was late Ebor ware, from the legionary fortress at York (Swan 1992). There was a tradition of ceramic manufacture in the region of the fortress from the AD 70s. The proximity of a series of kilns suggests that manufacture was either carried out by the legion, or by potters associated with the legion. During the late 2nd or the early

3rd century, there was a compete change in the forms manufactured in the local clays. These new forms included a number of distinctive forms of cooking vessels; one was a casserole-style vessel which had a rounded base and was generally wide and relatively shallow, with flanges for a lid. The second new form was a shallow dish, apparently for baking bread. These were very different to the local styles of cooking pot, which were smaller in diameter and proportionately deeper, tapering to the base. Within York and its environs, these new forms are generally found in contexts associated with the fortress and the *canabae*. Further examples have been identified at other military sites, such as the Antonine Wall, and possibly at Chester. The closest parallels to these types of vessels are found in the North African provinces of Proconsularis, Numidia, and Mauretania. Swan argues that the pottery was made by African potters for African soldiers, and that they represent the large-scale recruitment of African soldiers into Legio VI.

This particular case-study points to the potential of the archaeological evidence to identify different regional groups from variations in ceramic forms. Interestingly, in the case of this example, it is possible to go beyond the typologies themselves and identify different regional practices of food preparation. The wide, flat bottoms of the late Ebor ware casseroles point to food being cooked over braziers, usually comprising a pan-stand and a fire-basket in one piece. This contrasts with the cooking styles of the local British population, who used a closed oven. These different styles of cooking encompassed different routines, which would serve to highlight the boundary between the local groups and the incoming African soldiers. This may not be an isolated case, and Swan has extended this study to argue for the presence of Gallic soldiers in Britain from the distribution of tripod-vessels and vase tronconique (Swan 2009). In this particular instance, the differences are heightened by the military recruitment of those from different regions of the empire, probably creating a situation of enhanced awareness of these cultural differences and so the differing identities of individual peoples. Moreover, it is possible that in this scenario, regional ethnicities become dominant. If the aspect of identity which is dominant is situational and influenced by the dynamics of the specific social context, then we need to accept that within the context of York, it may not be the overall Roman/non-Roman identities which are paramount, but the regional ethnicities as different groups of Romans interact.

This is a rather extreme case-study, due to the movement of people from one area to another, and the cultural differences between them being brought into sharp relief. More contentious is using ethnicity as the explanation for typological distinctions in material culture in a less confrontational situation. For example, there are clear differences in the typologies of various forms of material culture between the eastern and western halves of southern England. Reece (1995) proposed this division based on the difference in coin loss patterns between the eastern and western halves of the province in towns, small settlements and villas. This is repeated in other forms of material, and the rigorous analysis of material usually relegated as 'small finds' has strengthened Reece's argument. We have already seen that there is a regional difference in the distribution of nail-cleaners, and metal hair pins also follow this broad east-west pattern (Cool 1990). Hair pins seem to have been a post-conquest innovation, and Cool identifies three localized distribution patterns for the 1st and 2nd centuries AD: one which covers East Anglia and spreads down to the west country, but which is dominated by finds in the Thames and East Anglian areas; a second which focuses on London and north Kent; and a third which focuses on the western half of England, particularly the Severn estuary.

Can we interpret these distribution patterns as relating to local ethnicities? The distributions cannot be tied to a single civitas group, and instead cover multiple groups. Nevertheless, these could be seen as regional identities, which comprise a number of civitates. The temptation is to see this as a continuity of the political groupings represented by the regional distribution of Iron Age coinage (Kimes *et al.* 1982), and this could well be the case. However, it raises a fundamental methodological problem, which brings us back to the issues raised in chapter 2 about the identification of ethnic identities from archaeology alone. There is no textual evidence, neither epigraphic nor literary, to point to such regional groupings. However, the paucity of inscriptions from the civilian zone of Britain compared to other provinces perhaps makes it unsurprising that we have no references to supra-local identities. Nevertheless, an explanation may be provided by the context of these identities, and the interaction between different ethnic layers. Within the Roman imperial system, the local identity, revolving around the urban centre, took precedence. As ethnicity is situational, and was being played out within the context of Roman imperial structures, it can be argued that the local identity, based on the urban centre, took primacy. Nevertheless, this does not eradicate the other levels of identity, and in this case, the regional identities still had some significance in structuring the distribution patterns of artefact types. Thus, we can imagine that a person from Colchester would primarily see themselves as a citizen of Colchester, but would also identify broadly with the eastern half of southern Britain, and that a similar situation would apply for someone from Cirencester, with their western identity being subsumed under their urban identity, but still being a factor in their overall sense of self.

This case-study of regional identities in southern Britain demonstrates the possibility of identifying regional identities from the artefactual evidence alone. It relies upon a rigorous study of the corpus of material in order to identify these patterns, and it is this lack of contextual and typological study which has perhaps rendered previous approaches unsatisfactory. The interesting feature of many of these forms of evidence (Latin inscriptions, nail cleaners and metal hair pins) is that they are the product of the post-conquest cultural changes. All could be used as evidence for an adoption of a Roman ethnic identity, demonstrating the multivocality of material culture: that it can be used to signal both a Roman and a regional/local ethnic identity, depending on the scale of interaction. It mirrors the multiple elements of individual identity, that each individual has multiple aspects of their identity and the one which is foregrounded is dependent upon context. Consequently, these local ethnic identities do not necessarily stand in opposition to a wider Roman ethnic identity. Instead, we are seeing ethnicity as multi-layered within the complex scales of interaction within the complexity of the Roman empire.

Local ethnicities and Roman imperialism

This idea of multi-layered ethnic identities raises the question of the relationship between these different levels. In particular, as this is an imperial context with an unequal power relationship, how these local ethnic identities were impacted on by the process of incorporation into the Roman empire. Eriksen has argued that in equivalent modern contexts, there are three ways of dealing with poly-ethnic societies by the dominant authority (Eriksen 2001: 284–6):

1. segregation: physical segregation accompanied by an ideology of inferiority
2. assimilation: the disappearance of the minority
3. integration: participation in shared institutions, but the maintenance of the group identity and some degree of cultural distinctiveness

I would argue that in most cases, we are dealing with processes of integration. The local groups share in important institutions of Roman imperialism, such as political organisation, urbanism, and economic exploitation. This draws the group into the wider Roman ethnic identity through such shared institutions, shared practices and shared ideologies. However, this also entails the maintenance of the local identity which involves the continuity of local traits, as each local ethnic group interacts with other groups in the vicinity.

However, this does not mean that the process of integration left the local identities unchanged; instead, they are subject to significant transformations. This is clear if we return to the case study of the *Conventus Astigitanus*. Each particular ethnonym is presumably derived from the pre-conquest local identities, but it is expressed in a way which shows a change to Roman concepts of settlement and social organisation. As we saw in the previous chapter, urbanism was a central part of a Roman ethnic identity, and was one of the important mechanisms through which the imperial authorities ruled the empire. The appearance or transformation of towns was a key part of the cultural transformations, with political activity at their heart. When we look at how the people of the *Conventus Astigitanus* expressed their local ethnicities, it is clear that they are doing so through the language of the urban constitution. The communities describe themselves through Roman legal terms, predominantly *res publica*, *municipium* and *colonia*. For example, at Tucci (*Colonia Augusta Gemella Tucci*), six imperial dedications are all set up in the name of the *Res Publica Tuccitanorum* (CIL 2.5.74–80), and three honorific dedications in the title of the *Colonia Augusta Gemella* (CIL 2.5.88, 96, 157). Similarly, two dedications at Cisimbrium are set up by the *Municipium Flavium Cisimbriensis* (CIL 2.5.291–2). The overall community is now described within the political ideologies of Roman urbanism, representing the transformation of a local identity within a Roman framework. In certain cases, we see the idealisation of this through the dedications to the Genius of the community, such as the dedications to the *Genius Municipi Nescaniensis* (CIL 2.5.838–9) and the *Genius Municipii Florentinorum* (CIL 2.5.619).

In a similar way, we can see some of the people describing their local identity through the medium of their place within the community. This is clearest when we see the community describing themselves using terms such as *cives* or *incolae*, referring to their legal position as a citizen, or resident non-citizen within the Roman town. At Ipsca, for example, an honorific dedication was set up by the *plebs* of Ipsca (CIL 2.5.387), and at Oducia, in a fragmentary inscription, an honorific dedication was set up by the *municipes* (CIL 2.5.1330). A more complicated phenomenon is that of individuals who describe themselves as members of the local community, but through their precise position within that community. So, for example, we see magistrates who describe themselves as magistrate or priest of a specific *municipium* or *colonia.* A complex process of self-description is occurring in these instances, as the statement of individual identity primarily records their political rank (see next chapter), but also includes their local ethnicity. At Astigi, a priestess and two priests stipulate that their priesthoods are those of the *colonia* itself, qualifying their title with variants on *Colonia Astigitana* or *Colonia Augusta Firma* (CIL 2.5.1162, 1171, 1179). This means of description was not restricted to the elite, as witnessed by the epitaph of Graecinus, which states that he was *colon(iae) Aug(ustae) Firm(ae) servus*, a slave of the town of Augusta Firma (CIL 2.5.1176).

These examples demonstrate the impact of Roman imperialism on local ethnic identities, and it is important to remember the imbalance in power relations at play here. This was not a neutral transformation, but a strategy of control by the imperial authorities. It was potentially a process of removing local forms of identity, and although the group may have remained, the relationships within them and potentially between them were recast within a Roman ideology. How many of these towns were formed from identifiable ethnic groups is difficult to say for certain and has been subject to considerable debate. Nevertheless, even if they were all individual tribal groups, arguing that such local ethnonyms represent continuity from the pre-conquest period is not credible. The choice of language evident within these inscriptions, coupled with the architectural evidence for the development of Roman-style urban centres, demonstrates how these previous local identities were transformed into something which adhered with Roman ideologies. The means of forming and distinguishing between these groups has changed in response to the political authority of Rome. In some cases, this process leads to the complete assimilation through the act of forgetting. In the previous chapter, we saw how the Ubii emphasised their links with a history of empire; however, this involved the downplaying and gradual forgetting of their previous history. During the 1st century AD, inscriptions referred to them as Ubii, but by the 2nd century AD, they described themselves as *Agrippensis*, apparently forgetting their previous ties and identity (Carroll 2002).

It is becoming increasingly evident that this process of assimilation is somewhat variable, and should be seen as incorporating elements from the pre-conquest societies. Whilst this can clearly be seen on a macro-level, and is perhaps unsurprising, smaller-scale studies also show that this process can differ between regions. This has been argued by Roymans for northern Gaul and the adjacent Rhineland area (Roymans 1996). The two regions integrated into Roman social systems quite differently, dependent upon the demands made upon them by the imperial authorities and the reaction to this by each group. Initially, both groups were subject to military exactions, but from the late 1st century AD onwards, two zones develop, one an outer zone of frontier civitates where troops were raised and stationed, and an inner, demilitarised zone which produced few troops. Whilst the tribes of both regions had been dominated by a military ideology prior to this period, only those within the frontier zone retain it into the 1st century AD. Here we see the maintenance of the martial ideology, with continued weapons deposition in native cult sites, rivers and native burial contexts, and the persistence of the warrior elite. This contrasts with the south-western area of Gallia Belgica, where there is a clear break in weapons deposition and no mention in the textual sources of military leaders.

These different trajectories are also evident in other elements of daily practice. In the late Iron Age, both areas practised mixed agricultural economies, but in the north cattle-raising was dominant, and in the south, arable. After conquest, these differences in agricultural economy increased. In the frontier zone, there was a major intensification in cattle and horse breeding. The primary product was cattle, and the archaeological evidence shows an increase in size of the cattle, indicating an emphasis on meat and hide production. Within the inner zone, there was intensification in grain production, with a specialisation in spelt wheat and bread wheat as commercial crops, and a decline in the proportion of emmer, barley and millet. Roymans argues that this is due to the variable system of taxation, with taxation in kind leading to the intensification of the dominant agricultural economy in each region. This had some profound unintended consequences, as the southern arable zone witnessed the development of a villa landscape, with elite competition manifesting not only through their construction of new villas, but also through elaborate funerary monuments depicting the arable farming which underpinned their status. In contrast, there was a marked absence of villas in the northern, pastoral region. Instead, there is a continuation of the local style of housing (the Wöhnstallhaüser), although elements of Roman-style architecture, such as the portico, are added to them, pointing to some developments in form (Figure 3.3). It is argued that these differences in martial and agricultural ideologies are echoed in the selection of Roman deities for cult worship: the northern regions adopting the martial and pastoral Hercules, whilst the southern region worshipping Mars, a martial deity, but with powers over agrarian prosperity within Italy (see also Derks 1998).

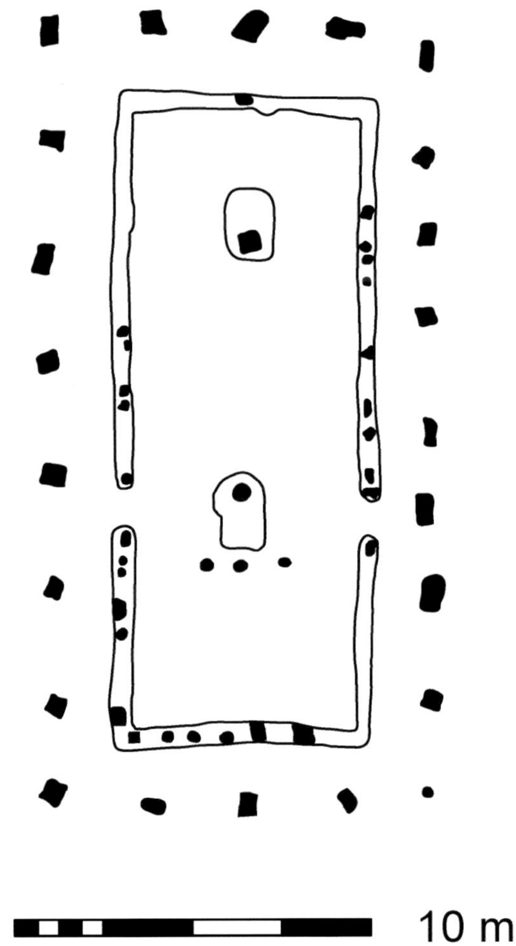

Figure 3.3 Plan of house 12, Druten (S. Hakenbeck; adapted from Roymans 1995, fig. 4)

One form of interaction between majority and minority ethnic groups which is not considered by Eriksen is that of ethnogenesis: the creation of new ethnic identities, and it has been argued that this is the case for the Batavians, on the lower Rhine (Roymans 2004). The tribal organisation of the lower Rhine area seems to have gone through fundamental changes in the mid-1st century BC, possibly part of a restructuring of the frontier by Julius Caesar. Certain tribes seem to drop out of the record, most markedly the Eburones; whether they were wiped out or forcibly assimilated into other tribes is unclear. The Batavi appear at this time, apparently a sub-group of the Chatti from the eastern bank of the Rhine who were presumably forcibly moved to the western bank and amalgamated with the existing population of the region to form this new tribal group. Roymans argues that a social group was organised around a military leader from the Chatti and his entourage (*comitatus*), and that he then amalgamated the immigrant and indigenous groups (Roymans 2004: 55–65). This leader was granted citizenship by Julius Caesar or his representative, and may have been formerly tied to Caesar as a personal client.

The development of cult centres at Empel, Elst and possibly Kessel acted as focal places and, over time, Nijemegen emerged as an urban centre. The epigraphic evidence demonstrates that they continued to use the ethnonym of Batavian to describe themselves through to the 2nd and 3rd centuries AD, with a limited number using the urban centre of Noviomagus for self-ascription (Derks 2009a). It is possible that the early alliance with Caesar was emphasised through public monuments as a way to tie their past into that of Rome (Roymans 2004: 211–20). These included a marble head of Julius Caesar dated stylistically to the Augustan period, and a column-shaped monument dedicated to Tiberius, both found in Nijmegen. The Batavians occupied a privileged place in the military structures, as they formed a prominent part of the emperor's personal bodyguard, as well as providing large number of auxiliary troops. Their importance as a source of military forces is demonstrated by the estimation that every family would have provided at least one son as a soldier (Willems 1984). Furthermore, studies of military equipment and horse-gear have demonstrated that whereas these items cease to be found in the interior of Gaul following Caesar's conquests, in the frontier region they continue to be found in non-military contexts, both ritual sites and rural domestic contexts, suggesting their symbolic value (Nicolay 2002). It was only at the end of the 1st century AD that these items decline in the frontier region. Whilst 'common-sense' would dictate that this martial ideology was responsible for the way in which the Batavians were incorporated into the empire through their military service, van Driel-Murray has argued that this was in fact the product of the way in which they were incorporated into the empire:

> [f]ar from making use of 'traditional ethnic bonds' or 'primordial martial qualities', military service itself can be seen as an active factor in shaping these attachments and creating new ethnicities which answer the stereotypes demanded by state security. (van Driel-Murray 2002: 202)

It is tempting to see local identities and the retention of apparently pre-conquest ethnonyms as the rejection of Roman imperialism, when in reality the opposite is true. Roman imperialism relied on the incorporation of pre-existing political groups into the social and political structures of empire in a way which changed them. These new local identities were transformed into a Roman concept of local ethnic identity, in the main through urban affiliation, but in other instances, through the creation of the *civitates*. In neither case was this anything other than a disjuncture: in the case of urban identities, a new language of membership through citizenship was created, whereas the relationship between the pre-conquest Iron Age tribes and the post-conquest *civitates* in the north-western provinces was not an innocent process. In the most extreme cases, such as in the case of the Batavians, we see the forcible movement of peoples by the imperial authorities and the creation of new ethnic identities. The Roman empire was maintained through these local ethnicities, recreating them within a new imperial language.

Ethnicity and Roman imperialism

This chapter and the previous one have focused on the idea of ethnic identities within the western provinces and their role within an imperial context. Whilst the two chapters have focused on different scales, the global and the local, there is a danger that these become conceptually separated from each other, or that in some way they are seen as in opposition: competing academic definitions of ethnicity within Roman scholarship. Instead, within complex, large-scale socio-political entities such as the Roman empire, ethnicity has the potential to be multiple and multi-layered. It is not a case of being Roman or being Batavian, for example; instead the two exist but at different scales. Nevertheless, both aspects of ethnic identity are played out within localised moments of interaction: even the more global Roman identity is maintained through the agency of the individual actor on a local stage (Revell 2009).

Unlike the modern identities of the nation-state, which actively supressed regional identities, the Roman system incorporated them, in effect creating and recreating local identities. This raises the interesting proposition that two or three generations after the process of adoption of Roman ethnicity, for the people of the provinces their Roman ethnicity was no longer the one which took primacy: instead this assumed a background significance and was unconsciously recreated through their daily practices. Instead their local identity may have been more significant, as they interacted with and distinguished themselves from the peoples of the neighbouring communities. This would have been more true for the people of the inner provinces, such as the Iberian provinces, than for the peoples on the frontiers, who would potentially have been in regular contact with those from outside of the frontiers of the empire who were considered not Roman (either by themselves or others). Alternatively, even these local ethnic identities may not have been uppermost in the minds of the peoples of the provinces, and it may have been their social rank which was under stress and so foregrounded in their social practices. Therefore, it is to the question of social rank which I shall turn in the next two chapters.

Chapter 4

A New Provincial Elite

Introduction

In the previous two chapters, I have looked at the complexity of ethnic identity within the Roman empire, and to a certain extent, this is a reflection of the existing research on the topic of identity as a whole within Roman archaeology. However, Roman imperialism impacted on more than the ethnic or cultural identity of the provincial populations. It also had the potential to disrupt more localised social structures and other aspects of social identity: the process of incorporation could lead to fundamental changes to the underlying social organisation, and also to the routines and materials through which identity was maintained. In some ways, this is implicit within the current paradigm of Roman imperialism, as proposed by Millett (1990a, 1990b). Within this model, Roman imperialism impacted on structures of social rank and the way in which this was articulated. For the western provinces in particular, a core part of this argument is that elite status was no longer articulated through the ideology of the warrior leader, and instead became expressed through the urban magistracies. This did not necessarily rely on a change in the actual personnel occupying the top rungs of the social ladder, but rather a change in the ideologies, practices and material culture they used to express that status.

The aim of this chapter and the next is to move beyond ethnic identities and consider social rank or status, and to explore the ways in which certain social practices and forms of material culture became bound up in the maintenance of such identities. Through this, the changing ideologies of rank and gradated rank will be explored. These chapters form a complementary pair: chapter 4 explores the question of elite identity, whilst chapter 5 focuses on the non-elite. The analysis of elite identity may seem to already be centre-stage within Roman archaeology, but in reality there is a certain methodological problem within this. Just as we saw in previous chapters how the definition and maintenance of a Roman ethnic identity is assumed to be self-evident, so elite status is assumed, and taken to be unproblematic. It is seen as less of a problem, but rather an inevitability. This is true for most archaeological periods, but it is particularly the case for the Roman period due to the nature of elite status and materiality. One aim of an ideology of elite status is to render that privileged position as part of the unquestioned order of the world. Such an ideology serves to mask the arbitrary nature of social hierarchies and to make the fluid seem fixed and natural. Its expression through praxis and material culture places the elite at the centre of the system, representing their particular view as the dominant one, and the correct one. One potential consequence of this is that the elite differentiate themselves from the rest of society merely through their greater visibility, whether within the textual sources or the material ones, and their view is represented as the ideal. For example, the study of Roman domestic housing has tended to concentrate on elite residences, in particular, the country villas, as these are constructed of materials which are more likely to survive archaeologically than the houses of the rural poor (stone as opposed to timber). These are studied as the normal style of Roman housing and Roman practices of living. Even for those wishing to study non-elite ways of living, the rural villa is taken as unproblematic rather than as a form of material culture which is very deliberately designed and used in such a way as to continually affirm the status of its elite owner. It is only recently that work on such buildings has looked explicitly at their role in the creation and maintenance of an elite ideology, and the presentation of the fluid as permanent (for example, Purcell 1995, Scott 2000).

If we are to understand the nature of elite identity within the western provinces, we need to question this assumed inevitability, and look at the way in which this dominant ideology was constituted, and how it was maintained through social practice. However, alongside this, we need to acknowledge that elite identity did not exist in isolation. Instead, it was one part of a complex continuum of social rank. It was not enough for one person to say "I am a member of the social elite", but relied upon others to acknowledge this, both other members of the social elite, and also members of the non-elite. There is a temptation to see the changes to the ideologies of elite status promoted by Roman imperialism as only impacting on the elite themselves, but for their status to be secure, the rest of the society needed to understand these new social systems of elite self-definition and to agree "Yes, you are a member of the social elite".

Defining class in the Roman world

One of the most fundamental changes to provincial society brought about by Roman conquest was the change to the system of social rank. We have already seen the importance of urbanism as part of the post-conquest changes, and this brought with it the system of urban magistrates. These magistrates were the positions of authority at a local level, and so, as Millett has argued (1990b), the local elites in order to retain their positions of power within the local community, adopted not only the title of magistrate, but the behaviours and material associated with it. This is witnessed through the epigraphic record, where we see the adoption of urban magistracies as a means of self-definition by the elites. One example of this is the four generations of the family of Epotsorovidos (CIL 13.1036; Wuilleumier 1963, King 1990: 66, Maurin *et al.* 1994: 79–95, no. 7). His son, Gaius Iulius Agedomopas, was given citizenship, presumably by Julius Caesar, and by the time of Tiberius, his great-grandson Caius Iulius Rufus was a provincial magistrate, constructing Roman style monuments at his home town of Saintes and the federal centre of the Tres Galliae at Lyon. This family epitomises the impact of wider processes of change: a new means of elite definition based upon that of the city of Rome.

The adoption of these magistracies as a new system of elite self-definition is a largely uncontroversial consequence of imperialism, however they were only one element of a complex system of rank within the Roman world. Within the constitution of the city of Rome, social rank was based on a series of legal and economic criteria: citizenship, freedom and wealth (Beard and Crawford 1999: 40–7). These were a series of scales rather than polar oppositions, and produced a complex hierarchy of multiple levels which problematises apparently simple classifications. The amount of wealth a person owned was used to place them into a specific rank, but they were also distinguished between free and unfree, and then between freeborn and the manumitted (Gaius *Inst.* 1.9.11). So, for example, an ex-slave could hold more wealth than a free-born person, but their servile birth made them legally inferior, placing them in an ambiguous position within an apparent scale. The move from republic to principate placed the imperial family in a unique position at the top of this social hierarchy, but the system overall and the criteria underpinning remained largely the same (Alföldy 1985: 94–5).

These criteria for social rank were then imposed on the provinces. Although there were some changes in the system, and some elements were adapted to the local context (such as the property qualification needed for decurion rank), the principles underlying it remained largely the same during the first two centuries AD. The Roman people were divided into a series of orders or ranks, officially at least enshrined in law through property qualifications and the census based upon wealth, citizenship and free/unfree status (Alföldy 1985: 106–33). These can be divided into the upper orders and the lower orders. At the top of this was the senatorial order, and next the equestrian order. Within the towns of Italy and the provinces, power was wielded by a third upper order: the decurions. Outside of Italy, there is limited evidence for the top tiers holding local magistracies. For example, in the Iberian provinces, in the larger towns such as Tarraco some local magistrates were of equestrian rank, but this was rare in the small Iberian towns. Below this stood the lower orders, classified according to whether they held citizenship or not, how much wealth they held, and whether they were slave or ex-slave. This allocation of ranks was, in theory, applied to the whole population of the town and its territory, thereby extending this system of social status beyond the elites.

In thinking about elite identity within the provincial context, the most important element of the upper orders is the decurions and local magistrates. These were the elite of an individual town rather than an empire-wide group as was the case for the senatorial and equestrian orders (Alföldy 1985: 126–31). There is a tendency in many accounts of the provincial structures to suggest we know how it operated, and that there was an homogeneity in detail; however, in reality, the available evidence shows variability in the detail. Membership of the *ordo decurionum* was based upon wealth, gender, age and the holding of a public magistracy. The actual wealth qualification was variable: the often-quoted figure of 100,000 sesterces is attested in some cities, but it was not the criterion for all. In North Africa, for example, 100,000 sesterces was required to be a decurion at Carthage, but in other smaller towns, it was a little as 20,000 sesterces. Allied to this was political participation, and for the wealthy, election to magisterial position. There was a system of elective magistracies: colleagues of leading magistrates (variously *duovir*, *quattuorvir* or less frequently *octovir* depending on specific town charter) and a junior rank of aedile, all of whom held office for a single year, although re-election is attested. In this way, the local elites were encouraged (or forced) to adopt the role of urban magistrate in order to maintain their social standing within the shifting political context (Drinkwater 1979). Together, they formed the town council, responsible for the wider running of the town, and again this is adjusted to suit the local conditions as the frequently cited figure of a council of 100 in reality masks a variability in size. Frustratingly, the criteria from membership of the council is unknown: whether it was only ex-magistrates, or a wider selection of those with decurion rank.

In addition to the formal qualification of wealth and election as magistrate, elite rank also rested on the more nebulous qualifications of family standing and moral worth, which can in part be treated together. There is an underlying idea that each person was judged according to their moral standing, which was revealed to others through their everyday actions. Trying to define this moral standing is complex: it is summed up within the Latin terms *virtus* or *mos*, neither of which are easily translated into English. Both are connected with ideas of morally appropriate behaviour, *virtus* originally with martial valour, but later taking on the elements of ethical qualities (McDonnell 2006), whilst *mos* can be seen as moral behaviour or morality, *mos maiorum* in the positive sense of ancestral moral qualities. Edwards has argued they were bound up in the power structures of Rome and a form of "symbolic capital" (Edwards 1993: 1–33). The idea of morality was used by the elite to monitor and discipline the activities of its own members, as when Cicero, writing to his brother Quintus, praises him for the way in which he conducted himself when he was governor of Asia. Cicero lists the factors which contributed to Quintus' prestige (*dignitas*): his integrity, self-restraint, sense of propriety, household governance, and his ability to form friendships wisely (Cic. *ad fratrem Quint.* 1.1.18). Morality and good standing were further associated with family and ancestors: to be a member of a distinguished family was an indication of a young man's potential. Who you were and who you were descended from was an indicator of aptitude for office and eligibility as though the deeds of the ancestors were revisited in their descendants. The multiple nature of the criteria for elite status leads to an element of flexibility within the system, as exemplified by the way women and freedmen could be incorporated.

Public performance

If we are exploring how the position of the magistrate became central to the definition of elite status within provincial communities, we need to look beyond the immediate evidence for the presence of these magistrates and think about how specific forms of material culture were drawn into this. Furthermore, we need to go beyond the position of the magistrate himself, and think about how this was something which was acknowledged by the wider society. In doing so, we are able to move beyond the specific members of the elite, and think about how the changing social structures were something which impacted on the whole society. If the elite magistrate stood at the top of the social hierarchy, his power relied upon the active acquiescence of the rest of society, not necessarily in their conscious agreement to this inequality, but through their participation in the social practices through which this elite status was now reinforced. This moves us substantially beyond the idea that the new political structures only impacted on the elite themselves, and that the non-elite carried on as before. The membership of the social classes may have been constant, but the changing nature of that relationship was more than a superficial veneer to the social structures of society.

At Rome, politics was based upon large public spectacles which brought the whole citizen body together within the town (Nicolet 1980, Bell 1997, Patterson 2000). Activities such as voting or trials were communal events, and consequently the public spaces of the town were drawn into the display of political power. Through the use of and movement through these places, a man of magisterial rank marked out his elite state in various encounters with those of his political class and the rest of the population. This model of political spectacle was inherent within the urban charters in which politics was expected to be organised through this principle of popular participation, but with the privileging of elite activity. These twin elements are exemplified in the procedure for the election of magistrates in the charter granted to the *municipia* of the Iberian provinces during the Flavian period (González 1986, Fear 1996). It was envisaged as a communal event, with the citizens of the town coming together to vote within the forum. The election itself was supervised by the elder of the two serving *duumviri*, who summoned each voting group to cast their votes within their own enclosure (González 1986: 188–9, chaps 51–9). As each magistrate was elected, he immediately swore an oath in front of the gathered assembly to carry out his duties as prescribed within the charter. It was through such public performances that we can identify how the new forms of social status went deeper into society, creating elites and non-elites alike.

The focus of this magisterial authority was the forum, and the architectural layout of such buildings was drawn into such performances. In order to demonstrate how the space might have been drawn into such political performances, I shall use the fora-basilicas of Roman Britain as an example. It is tempting to think of these as the poor relation of those in the Mediterranean provinces, but we need to take a more situated perspective: how the forum was invested in by the community, and the way in which certain areas were highlighted through a more elaborate decoration, or through the ways they were accessed (or not) both physically and visually. The areas associated with the performance of magisterial power were the tribunal and the council chamber (the *curia*). The separation of those with political power from those without it was negotiated through who had access to these areas, and the hierarchy was signalled by whether these areas were marked out as privileged through their position, how the movement of people through the spaces was controlled, and any differentiation through their decoration. The tribunal formed a platform for use by magistrates. It was not a necessary part of the forum, and the position was variable (Gros 1996: 235–60). However, in the fora of Roman Britain, it was invariably placed within the basilica at one or both ends of the central nave. The basilica at London seems to have had a single tribunal at the eastern end: this was a raised platform set within a circular apse with an antechamber separating it from the main part of the nave (Brigham 1992). It was highlighted through different wall-painting designs to those in the nave, with the antechamber painted in a scheme of red panels decorated with spiralling green stalks and coloured flowers, and a robed figure of some kind, and the apse itself may have been lined with marble veneer. Similarly, within the Silchester basilica, the northern apse was decorated in reds and yellows, with some decorative elements, in contrast to the plain white with red bands in the nave (Bird 2000). The tribunal in the basilica at Caerwent was emphasised using architectural elements: engaged columns and possibly a balustrade (Frere 1991: 225).

The second area associated with the elite and the decurions was the council chamber. Here the *ordo* was both physically and visually removed from the more public areas. The only certain example is that at Caerwent (Figure 4.1). One of the rooms in the rear range contained a small platform, with benches along two sides (Ashby 1906, Brewer 1993). The walls were decorated with wall-painting, and the floor with a mosaic. It could only be entered via an antechamber, distancing the council members further from the rest of the population. The council chambers in other British towns have proved more difficult to identify. At Verulamium it was likely that it was one of the three free-standing buildings at the southern end of the forum, opposite the basilica (Cotton and Wheeler 1953). Others were presumably rooms within the rear ranges of the basilica, or around the forum piazza.

The rhetoric of the space of the forum-basilica, created through the activities of those using the building and the decoration of the various areas, privileged the figure of the magistrate through his visible access to the tribunal, and his non-visible use of the *curia*. The ways in which people negotiated such spaces created a hierarchy based around political power, setting the elite apart from the non-elite. The prominence given to the magistrate through the architecture was enhanced through his costume and accessories. In contrast to the plain white *toga virilis* of the ordinary Roman citizen, the magistrate could wear the *toga praetexta* with it broad purple band. He was attended by slaves owned communally by the town, and was entitled to *fasces*. The colonial

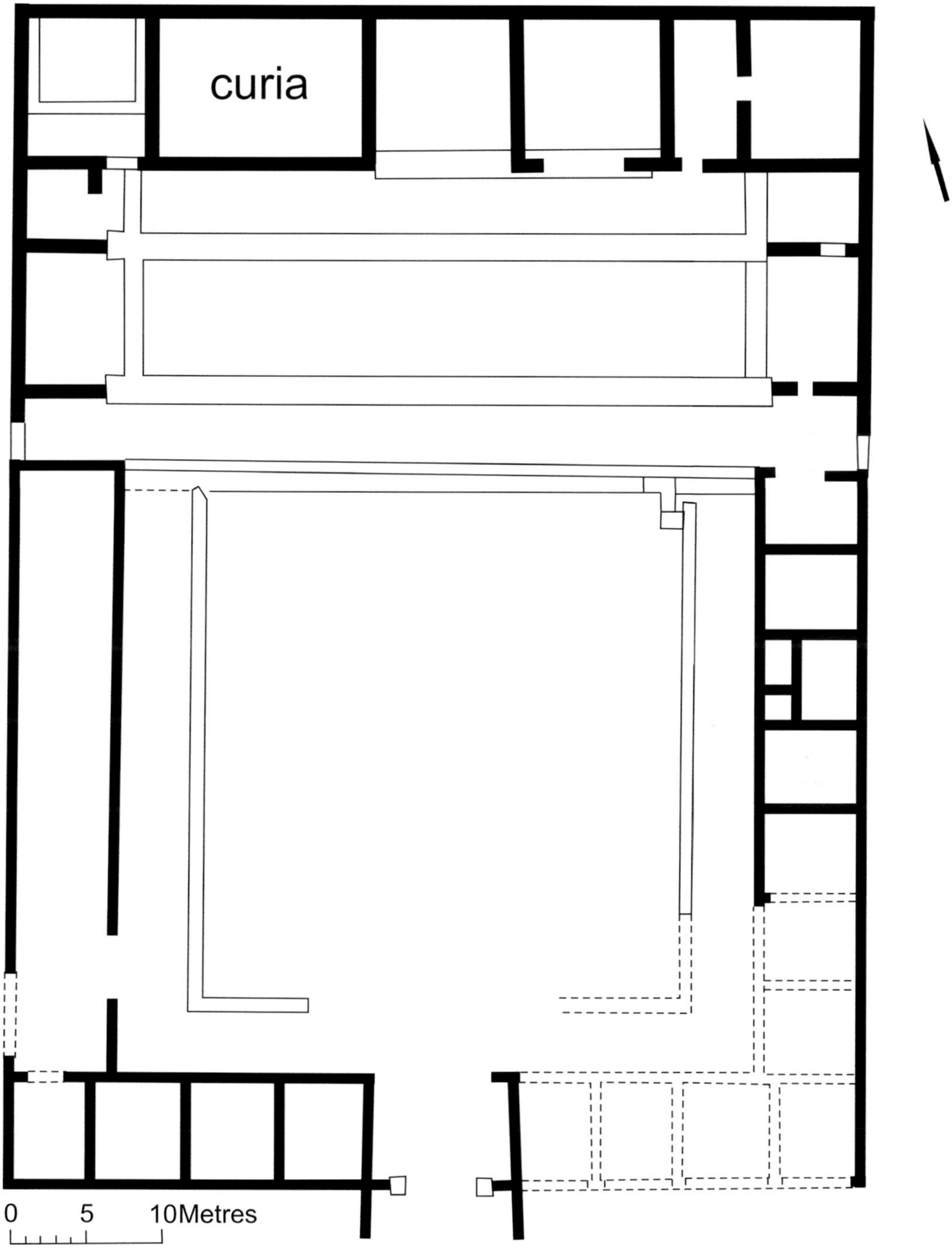

Figure 4.1 Plan of Caerwent forum, with location of probable curia marked (adapted from Brewer 2006, 39)

charter from Urso indicated that for his year of service, each *duovir* was accompanied by two lictors, a servant, two scribes, two messengers, a clerk, a herald, a haruspex and a flute-player. The aedile, as the junior magistrate, had a similar entourage, but fewer in number (Crawford 1996: 393–454, chap. 62). These symbols of political status were a visible manifestation of the power and prestige of the magistrate, marking him out in a crowd and proclaiming the magisterial office on which his social position was based. As he moved through the town or attended public spectacles, his rank was visible to all through his costume and his entourage of attendants.

This magisterial authority was also visible in other public spaces within the town, recalling and reinforcing the ideologies at play within the forum-basilica. In this way, the public buildings of the town were implicated in the maintenance of magisterial authority: the magistrate who took centre-stage within the forum-basilica also took a prominent role within other social occasions. The public nature of Roman urban life ensured that he was continually on display to an audience of the rest of the community. He was required to finance a number of theatrical and gladiatorial shows each year: provision of religious spectacles was part of the duties of the *duoviri* and the aediles in the *lex Ursonensis* (Crawford 1996: 393–454, chaps 70–1). He and his colleagues would preside over such events, with specific areas in theatres and amphitheatres reserved for his use (Revell 2009: 167–8). Spatially, he was separated out from the general population, the privacy and comfort of these areas marking his elevated political rank. However, these private boxes or seats were also highly visible, and so the rest of the audience would not only be watching the entertainment on offer, but also the magistrate who was responsible for that year's shows: was he acting appropriately; did he deserve their respect.

A magistrate's political position also included religious leadership, and so communal religious rituals, such as festivals or sacrifices, became a further means for the demonstration of elite rank. Public religion was characterised by large-scale, community-wide festivals, with a set calendar. Some were connected with the imperial cult, some may have been adopted from the religious calendar at Rome, and others would probably have been local festivals. Urban charters mention religious observances, games and banquets for the community (González 1986: 194, chap. 77). Political and religious authority were linked: the *lex coloniae Genetivae* mentions that the elected magistrates were responsible for deciding upon the religious calendar at the founding of the town, which festivals were to be held and when (Crawford 1996: 393–454, chaps 64–72, 125–8, Rüpke 2006). These magistrates had the authority to preside over these festivals and sacrifices (Gordon 1990), giving them a visible position. During the sacrifices, for example, the priest or magistrate would symbolically transfer the victim from the human to the divine realm (Revell 2000). Such events involved the wider community of the urban citizen-body, again making the authority of the magistrate contingent and subject to challenge.

The public architecture of the town formed a means to differentiate between the various ranks of the urban population. There were a series of roles to enact: urban magistrate, local citizen and the disenfranchaised (women, children and slaves). Ability to access, to participate or to view within the forum, the temple or the amphitheatre all provided a location for the magistrate to demonstrate his authority. The way in which the people negotiated these spaces created a hierarchy based around political power. The rhetoric of the space, produced through the layout and differential decoration of particular areas, privileged the person of the magistrate through his visibility and his access to specific areas. The public nature of these activities, involving the rest of the community, produced moments of uncertainty: it was where he might affirm his power, or be judged as lacking in ability. Political power was dependent on the continued demonstration of fitness for power.

Writing political power

The forms of elite activity outlined above are largely ephemeral, with no lasting trace except in the memory of the participants (although this aspect should not be underplayed). One way to make such activities more permanent was to record them on stone through an inscription. Within the provinces, public architecture and the political performance of magisterial authority increases from the time of Augustus onwards. Broadly simultaneous with this is the widespread adoption of inscriptions on stone within these towns. The temporality of the epigraphic habit is a known phenomenon: initially charted by MacMullen (1982), the majority of inscriptions in the western provinces date to the first three centuries AD. At the same time, the mosaic of local languages is replaced with inscriptions written almost inclusively in Latin (Woolf 1994). Explanations for these have been tied into changes in the way in which social position was expressed at Rome, with the adoption of honorific inscriptions from Greece (Wallace-Hadrill 1990). This form of public display was then adopted by the provincial elites to emphasise their fitness to hold their political rank (Mackie 1990, Meyer 1990, Woolf 1996). The epigraphic corpus is dominated by epitaphs, estimated at three quarters of all inscriptions in Latin (Saller and Shaw 1984: 124). The remainder are overwhelmingly concerned with the maintenance of elite status within the community, whether through political or religious activity.

Such inscriptions recorded the acts of benefaction from the elite to the community and honorific dedications given in response. These acts of providing buildings, games or gifts of money or food were memorialised in stone, the name and magisterial titles of the donor continuing past the moment of giving. To take three examples from Perigueux in Aquitania, inscriptions record the donation of a temple and baths by M. Pompeius Libon, an amphitheatre by Aulus Pompeius, and a sequence of fountains (Bost and Fabre 2001: 87–91, 110–2 and 113–7 respectively). Libon was part of a prestigious local family: he states that he was priest of the imperial cult at the federal cult centre at Lyon (*sacerdos arensis*), and that his father had held the same post. The same family is known from Lyon, where an inscription records four generations of the family (CIL 13.1704). Aulus Pompeius paid for the construction of the amphitheatre and its decoration, the inscription stating that it was from his own money (*de sua pecunia*), and the works were completed by a second member of the same family, presumably Pompeius' son. He too lists his achievements: commander of a legion and *praefectus fabrum*. The third example records the donation of a fountains by L. Marullius Aeturnus. He records that he was a local magistrate, a *duovir*, and that he paid for the fountains and the infrastructure to maintain them from his own money. Three inscriptions record his actions; although they are fragmentary, they seem to contain identical texts. It is possible that they refer to a series of fountains throughout the town, each text associated with a separate fountain, and the duplication of the texts spreading their message through the physical space of the town.

A second form of political inscription is the honorific dedication. These were set up to honour a particular individual, often in acknowledgement of their acts of munificence to the urban community. These inscriptions acknowledge the obligation from the townspeople to the individual, making clear the respect owed to him due to his rank. Again from Perigueux is an example of a dedication to Titus Ligurius Masculus, a *curator civium Romanorum*, set up by his son. As the magistracies were of fixed tenure, inscriptions became a way of recording that an individual had held these positions, and in these cases from Perigueux, here and above, we have seen how both imperial and local magistracies were included within the text. This reiteration of the *cursus honorum* served to both articulate the magisterial identity of the individual, but also to reinforce the system through which that identity was formed, making the authority of the magistrate independent of the office-holder as an ongoing part of the discourse through which elite status was understood. In some cases, such inscriptions acted as the base for a statue of the magistrate, portrayed in his toga. Inscription and statue together formed part of a symbolic system and for those unable to read the inscription, the statue provided a reminder of the power of the elite (Stewart 2003: 83–9).

There was a reflexive relationship between these inscriptions and the sites they occupied, with statues and dedications adorning the public spaces of the town, reinforcing the connection between political status and the physical setting of the town (Revell 2013). At Munigua, in Baetica, the forum has the highest concentration of inscriptions outside of the cemeteries. Set within the porticoes encircling the forum was a series of niches, and in these was a pair of status bases, one each to Rufinus and son Rufus, both of whom had twice been elected *duovir*, and both of which were set up with the permission of the town council (Figure 4.2). Elsewhere within the forum were two further plaques recording its construction by Lucius Valerius Firmus, and a statue base to Bonus Eventus, also within a portico, from a *libertus* to celebrate becoming *sevir* (CILA 2.1054, 1074–7). Similarly, excavations at the town of Baelo Claudia demonstrate that of the inscriptions which can be given an approximate location, just over half came from the forum and its associated buildings (Bonneville, Dardaine *et al.* 1988, Sillières 1995). At Singilia Barba, fragments of nineteen inscriptions were found within the forum area, including an honorific statue set up to a *duovir* by the *cives* and *incolae* (CIL 2.5.789). This states explicitly that the bronze statue was to be set up publicly in the forum, reinforcing the relationship between political space and political activity.

Figure 4.2 Dedication to Lucus Quitius Rufus. Museo de Arqueologia, Seville (author; reproduced by permission)

This pattern is repeated throughout the western empire, where honorific inscriptions and statue bases were a frequent part of the decoration of the forum (Lefebvre 2004, Revell 2007). Religious dedications tended to be placed within the temple precinct, although again these were used an opportunity to reaffirm political office, such as the dedication by Marcus Sentius Marianus to Apollo Augustus, set up within the Traianeum at Italica and recording that he had served variously as *aedile*, *duovir* and augur (CILA 2.342). He used this inscription to record his dedication of a statue weighing 100 pounds in silver. The inclusion of the weight of the statue makes the link with the money expended on this dedication, and Roman magistrates were not shy about mentioning how much they spent on such acts. This had the dual effect of reiterating the wealth upon which his social position rested, but also of emphasising his *pietas* towards the gods and so his moral worth.

Political inscriptions record the good deeds paid for by the elite, and the honours granted to them by the community in recognition of these. The inscriptions were markers both that these individuals were considered worthy of public note, but also the acts which entitled them to this status. Such inscriptions need to be read as a statement of the criteria for rank within these provincial communities. Wealth was implied through the expenses incurred through the donation of buildings, games and so forth (Duncan-Jones 1982), whilst political office was stated within the text of the inscription. However, the two further elements tied into elite status are more nebulous: family and *virtus*. We have already seen the importance of mentioning genealogies in the inscriptions of Caius Iulius Rufus, the great-grandson of Epotsorovidos, and M. Pompeius Libon, both of whom gave three generations of ancestors. This importance of family connections is also seen in Baetica (Revell 2013). In Singilia Barba, a pair of dedicatory statues were set up to two members of the Hirii family, probably father and son (CIL 2.5.786, 799). Similarly in Munigua, L. Quintius Rufinus and his son M. Quintius Rufus were honoured in a series of inscriptions within the public spaces of the town (CILA 2.1060, 1074–5). The Quintii both served twice as *duoviri*, making it clear that political ability and elite rank passed from one generation to the next. The inscription could also stand as a statement of the *virtus* of the dedicator: his *pietas* to the gods, or alternatively his generosity to the community. In this way, the inscription became part of the demonstration of the moral worth of the magistrate.

As with the political routines within the forum, it is possible to go beyond the upper rank of the elite. It is common to concentrate on those responsible for their production, or being honoured in the text, but their location within the public spaces of the town indicate that they were intended for a wider audience. The question of how many people could interpret these has been hampered by questions of levels of literacy within the Roman world, with Harris' estimate of more than 90% illiteracy casting a long shadow over the debate (Harris 1989). However, writing can be used in different ways through form, context and intention of writing. Inscriptions called upon different literacy and interpretation skills to reading literary texts. The patterning in these inscriptions can be seen in the limited messages conveyed, as well as the limited vocabulary and frequent abbreviations. This is reinforced by the repetition in the materiality of the inscription: its position and public display, and in some cases, its role as the base for a statue of the political magistrate. We can question how far reading such political inscriptions actually relied upon reading the text, as opposed to recognising the kind of things it might be referring to, based upon a number of visual clues. For the non-elite, it also brought with it a recognition of the new ideologies of rank, and the role of politics within it. For the elite, these forms of material culture marked their position at the top of the social hierarchy; for the non-elite, it marked their exclusion. Nevertheless, as Nicola Mackie has argued, it marked a relationship of honour and esteem: the act of generosity from the donor, but also the act of recognition and the granting of *honor* by the community (Mackie 1990).

The discourses of domestic architecture

The performance of elite identity was not confined to activities within the public spaces of the town. The houses of the elite similarly formed a way to structure social relations and to maintain the elite position of power. Within the modern world, there is a tendency to view public and private as separate spheres: once someone has retreated behind the walls of their home, they are safe from the stresses of the outside world. Such a binary view would be alien to a Roman magistrate, whose house was an extension of his public life, blurring the distinction between public and private (Wiseman 1994). The house was an important place for political activities, although of a more informal nature than those which took place in the forum. The result of this was that there was a level of anxiety that the house should correctly express the rank of the magistrate. This provides us with the social context of the elite house: it was a place where the elite man was on display to both his peers and those of more lowly status.

Research into the social significance of the house and its decoration has flourished in the last 25 years (Gazda 1991, Wallace-Hadrill 1994, Zanker 1998). Much of this relates to Pompeii, as here, uniquely, the archaeological evidence allows a detailed analysis of domestic space on a large number of buildings with their decoration and furnishings reasonably intact. Similarly, for many, the textual sources from Rome can be applied to Pompeii, allowing the symbolic significance of the various elements of the house to be reconstructed (although for a counter view, Allison 2001). Work on domestic space within the western provinces is patchier, and less ambitious as here we are left with the typical state of low walls (or even foundations), fragmentary decoration and uncontextualised household goods. In the excavation of towns, there has been a preferential excavation of public buildings, possibly as these are thought to tie into narratives of urban development and Roman imperialism, whereas domestic architecture produces evidence for social relations and more private concerns. Furthermore, there is limited synthetic work on urban domestic architecture (AA.VV 1991, Perring 2002 are exceptions to this). There has been more work on villas, and for these, work has focussed on the relationship between spatial layout and decoration, and social relations (for example, Smith 1978, Ellis 1991, Scott 2000).

When looking at the provincial town-house, it is immediately clear that there is a wide variability in their layout. The atrium house has been seen as the traditional Roman house, based largely on the writings of Vitruvius, who sees this as the epitome of Roman domestic architecture, and seemingly confirmed by excavations at Pompeii. This equation is disrupted by the Greek-influenced peristyle house, and the appropriation of Greek architecture by the Roman elite (Wallace-Hadrill 2008). This complexity is then increased when we add the provinces to this. In North Africa, Spain and Southern Gaul the axial peristyle house is the dominant type (Meyer 1999), which consists of an axial suite of rooms comprising entrance, peristyle and *triclinium*. In the north-western provinces, we see less Hellenising influence, at least during the first two centuries AD. This is in part a product of the cultural variability which we saw in chapter 3, and feeds into the idea of regionality within the western provinces.

Given typology of layout does not provide a satisfactory answer to what makes a typical Roman house, the alternative is to think about what the social role was of the Roman house, and how it was used by its inhabitants. This removes the actual type from the equation: it was possible to fulfil the social role of the house using different layouts and room-types. To understand the attitudes towards houses at Rome itself, we can turn to the attitudes expressed within the textual sources. As well as the architectural handbook of Vitruvius, there are numerous references within other writers which give a hint of the social significance of the elite house and its decoration (Nevett 1997). Cicero, for example, clearly appreciated the ideology of the house as symbolic of a man's political standing: he argued that a man of rank needed a house to enhance his prestige through its appearance and decoration (Cic. *de Off.* 1.138-40). As a *novus vir* from outside of Rome, his house represented the public face of his political achievements (Wiseman 1994: 98, Hales 2000). In 62 BC he moved into a house on the Palatine, overlooking the forum and, metaphorically, the Roman people. When he was exiled from Rome, his house was pulled down as a symbol of his disgrace, and a shrine to Liberty erected in its place. On his return, he campaigned for the site to be returned to him as a symbol that his political authority had been restored. For Cicero, his house was part of his political persona and his political status. This idea is reinforced in the architectural treatise of Vitruvius. He explicitly links house form with the rank and occupation of its inhabitants: for example, those reliant on small-scale agriculture would need spaces for the storage of goods and beasts, whilst those with a political career would need spacious and elegant reception rooms (Vitruvius 6.5.2). Whilst this can be given a functional explanation, the underlying assumption is that a visitor would be able to read the rank and occupation of the owner from his house.

It is possible to distil from the textual sources something of the principles underpinning that discourse of what made an elite house (Gazda 1991, Thébert 1993). As the elite house was involved in large-scale political activity, in essence an intersection between public and private space, large easily accessible areas were needed for receiving guests and enacting political business. In addition, there should be other spaces, similarly public, but more discreet and less accessible for the reception of more privileged political guests, such as fellow magistrates. The house should be an expression of the wealth and prestige of the owner, as expressed through the architectural detail, such as columns and gardens, and the decoration (e.g. marble, wall-paintings, mosaics). These elements should also be a display of the learning of the owner – his knowledge of myth, etc. and the ability to place them in appropriate places. Finally, as the house was in some sense a public space, it should adopt the vocabulary of public architecture, through provision of colonnades, baths and in some cases, honorific inscriptions to the owner. However, the Roman ideal of *moderatio* meant that these elements had to be carefully judged – it was possible to go over the top, and this laid the owner open to just as much ridicule as was heaped on Trimalchio in Petronius' *Satyricon*, the caricature of nouveau riche bad taste (Hales 2009).

The materiality of the house

As argued, the Roman elite house cannot be reduced to a typological requirement, and the variability of elite housing within the archaeological record shows that the elite of the provinces were not concerned with acquiring atrium houses as such. Instead, the key concern was how the house differentiated between those of differing social rank through both the spatial layout and the decoration. The underlying idea of the house was the open-ness to guests from outside of the immediate family, but at the same time, restricting physical and visual access to others. Some of these guests would be of lower social rank to the owner, possibly tied by ranks of patronage and obligation. In Rome, this is associated with the *salutatio*, the formal reception of the clients by the patron (Wallace-Hadrill 1994: 12, Laurence 2006: 165–6); however, we should be careful about how we apply the evidence for very specific activities from Rome to the provinces (Allison 2001). Instead we need took look for more general characteristics, such as a focus on the entrance to the house, large rooms, which might be easily accessible to visitors, and whose decoration intimated the wealth and learning of the owner, but also the ability to restrict access to others. If we look at the elite town-houses of the Iberian peninsula and southern Gaul, we can see certain characteristics being repeated.

In Italica, a group of elite houses survive within the Hadrianic extension of the Nova Urbs (Rodríguez Hidalgo and Keay 1995). The smallest of these, and the least complex in layout, is Casa de los Parajos (Rodríguez Hidalgo 1991). The peristyle was a colonnaded area covering 25% of the floor-space of the house and held a water feature at the centre (Figure 4.3). A series of rooms led off it on two sides, with a large central reception room and two further suites of rooms comprising the third side. This reception room on the central axis is the largest room in the house and has traces of marble on the walls. It is traditionally identified as the *triclinium*, and if this is not correct, it was certainly the most important reception room. This room

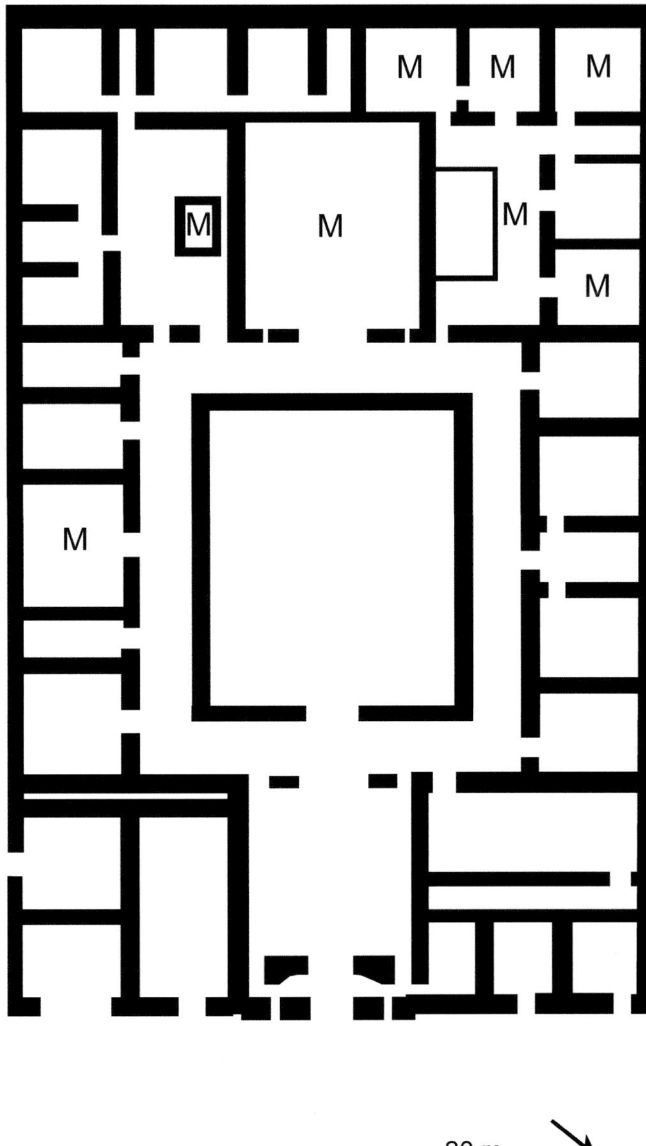

Figure 4.3. Plan of Casa de los Pajaros, Italica. Location of mosaics shown (m) (S. Hakenbeck; adapted from Mañas Romero 2010, fig. 15)

seems to have overlooked an open area to each side, each with a central water feature surrounded by further suites of rooms. The north court is set around a pool and comprises a series of apparently richer rooms, decorated with elaborate mosaics, including depictions of Tellus and Medusa (Mañas Romero 2010). The south court was a colonnaded area, with a central marble water feature and fountain. The house takes its (modern) name from the other key reception room opening onto the peristyle, this one in the centre of the south side. This was paved with a mosaic of panels, each depicting a different form of bird.

We see similar characteristics in the other houses in Italica. Although the known plan is incomplete, Casa de Hylas clearly incorporates the same open spaces of the peristyles and large reception rooms (García y Bellido 1960, Rueda Roigé 2002–3). The layout is more complex, and it lacks the simple axiality evident at Casa de los Pajaros, but there is the potential for zoning and social differentiation. Elaborate mosaics decorate key reception rooms; other elements which show an adherence to the demonstration of wealth and the language of public architecture include marble column bases, Corinthian capitals and water features. The largest known house in Italica is Casa de la Exedra (Rodríguez Hidalgo 1991). Again, it has large public rooms arranged according to principles of symmetry and axiality. There is a clear demonstration of wealth in the space: the gardens, the use of water, and the elaborate decoration such as mosaics and marble. Facilities echo those of public architecture, particularly the private baths suite and the long, thin palaestra, as do decorative features such as the use of marble and the Corinthian capitals in the north court. This conspicuous incorporation of decorative elements derived from public architecture as well as the duplication of their functions has led to the argument that this was some form of semi-public building rather than a private house (Rodríguez Hidalgo 1991), however, there are parallels for such elaborate facilities in a domestic context.

These characteristics are also fundamental to the elite houses in the town of Vaison-la-Romaine in Narbonensis (Goudineau and Kisch 1999). Here, a series of large town houses has been excavated. They adhere broadly to the axial peristyle type, but their overall layouts are more complex: primarily, the axiality is less clear, with no evidence of the vistas through the house from the entrance. However, once inside the house, we do see the idea of axes and vistas becoming important. In the Maison au Dauphin, the focus of the house is on the large peristyle garden (Goudineau 1979). Here we see the juncture of two axes at right angles to each other: the axis through from the entrance into the peristyle, and the axis formed by the rooms of the peristyle area. There is a pool at the centre of the peristyle, with a pair of reception rooms facing each other across it, their entrances aligned with the intercolumnation of the peristyle. One contained an exedra, and the other overlooked the northern portico of a second garden and its pool. This emphasis on peristyles, gardens and water features is repeated in all of the excavated elite houses at Vaison, such as Maison à la Tonelle which had an external room set in the garden which may have functioned as a dining room (Goudineau and Kisch 1999). The Maison de Buste en Argent was entered from the Rue des Boutiques through a large vestibule area. The house contained two open peristyles, and two large peristyled gardens, both with water features. To the rear of the house was a bath suite. Again, there is no single axial layout: the entranceway led to the first peristyle, but behind that is a perpendicular axis from a large open room through to the smaller of the two gardens. The Maison á l'Apollon Lauré has only been partially excavated, and so the overall layout cannot be reconstructed, but it too has a large garden with a pool at the centre, suites of rooms arranged around axes, and at least one suite of baths. These houses were decorated with floors of marble and mosaics, and walls of painted wall-plaster.

In both Italica and Vaison-la-Romaine, it is possible to identify the adoption of a similar discourse of domestic architecture, in spite of any differences in the precise layout of the houses themselves. They demonstrate an understanding of the role of domestic housing in signalling elite status which is similar to that in Rome and Italy. They display an ordered layout based around ideas of axes through the building, and roughly symmetrical arrangements of rooms. All show a hierarchy of space in decoration, and areas of relative public-private access, allowing the possibility of distinguishing between visitors of different social rank. The emphasis on the open spaces of the peristyle, gardens and water features creates the potential for specific vistas, and an adherence to the ideals of leisurely living. There is a demonstration of wealth through facilities and decoration, particularly in the use of marble, elements of which echo the characteristics of public architecture.

There is a second element of display within the elite house, but in this case, the display is more symbolic. Bound up in the idea of elite rank was the privileged access to specific forms of cultural knowledge. This *paideia* was preferential knowledge of Roman and Hellenistic culture, both the literary works, but also grammar, oratory, medicine, astrology and other arcane forms of knowledge (Elsner 1998: 106–13). *Paideia* forms part of elite self-representation, allying the local elites with provincial officials (for example, Brown 1992: 35–41). This learning found its physical manifestation in the personal items used by the elite. Depictions of mythological images on dining vessels, jewellery, caskets and the decoration of their houses all pointed to the familiarity with these cultural symbols by their owners. Such items were not hidden away, but were placed on display as a form of conspicuous consumption of cultural knowledge. Sarah Scott (2000: 126–7) has argued this for 4th century AD mosaics in elite villas: mythological scenes within reception rooms represented the knowledge of the owner to visitors, both his peers and his estate workers. This is also the case for the earlier imperial period, and can be seen within the decoration of provincial houses.

Returning to the elite houses of Italica, we can see these ideas at play within their decoration. Little of the wall painting survives, but the mosaics give a clear indication of the kinds of images chosen. There are two complete catalogues of the mosaics (Blanco Freijeiro 1978, Mañas Romero 2010), many of which were figurative. Returning to the Casa de los Pajaros, it takes its name from the mosaic in the main reception room which consists of a series of 33 panels, each containing the image of a single bird, each one different. The rooms surrounding the eastern patio were heavily decorated with mosaics, including ones depicting Medusa and Tellus. Just as this was one of the smallest of the elite houses in the town, so its mosaics were not the most decorative. The mosaic perhaps most imbued with the *paideia* of the owner was the so-called Lovers of Zeus mosaic from the Casa del Mosaico de las Metamorfosis (Blanco Freijeiro 1978: 25–6, Mañas Romero 2010: 215–6). This large mosaic (6.85 × 6.88m) consists of a series of panels in a geometrical arrangement. At the centre is a disputed male figure holding pan pipes, and at the four corners, the four Seasons. Interspersed between these are depictions of Zeus and his various amorous encounters: Leda and the swan, Io transformed into a cow, the rape of Ganymede, Danae and the golden shower, Europa and the bull, and Arcas and Callisto. To be able to read the mosaic, the viewer needed to identify the myths depicted in the various panels, linking them with figure of Zeus and ideas of transformation. This was a knowledge which not all viewers would possess, creating a privileged viewer. Other houses contain mosaics with Bacchic motifs, demonstrating the owners' knowledge of Hellenistic motifs and culture. The Casa del Planetario was decorated with a mosaic depicting Bacchus and Ariadne at the centre, surrounded by panels depicting Bacchic revellers, satyrs, centaurs and panthers (Figure 4.4).

The mosaics of Italica are typical of those within elite houses throughout the western provinces. We see an elite demonstrating and maintaining their status through their claims to a form of knowledge not necessarily shared by the rest of the society. In chapter 2, I argued for a common cultural language of images which would seem to negate this argument (and see also chapter 5), but it is the element of learning which underpinned the use of these images. To return to the Lovers of Zeus mosaic, the connection between the various myths is not obvious. To make these connections required that the viewer have a detailed knowledge of the specifics of these myths: to make the connections that all of these characters had been raped by

Figure 4.4 Bacchus mosaic, Casa del Planetario, Italica (author)

Zeus, in many cases involving a process of metamorphosis. Guests to the room of a similar or superior rank would be expected to be able to understand these allusions; guests of a lower rank to not understand them.

Rejection of the model?

So far, I have presented a rather straightforward picture of new criteria for elite rank and new materials for its maintenance. However, was this applicable to all parts of the western provinces? In Roman Britain, at least, the evidence for the acceptance of political activity is more problematic. This comes from the analysis of the epigraphic and iconographic evidence: when we begin to look for concrete evidence of named local magistrates within Britain, there are very few examples. This absence is further accentuated by the lack of statues or reliefs depicting the British elites wearing togas or in the act of delivering a speech. This is reinforced by Tom Blagg's analysis of the incidence of munificence in Britain and the social status of benefactors (Blagg 1990). In other provinces we can see the magistrate taking an active lead, but in Britain, munificence was more likely to be funded by collective bodies, such as the group as a whole (e.g. *Civitas Cornoviourm*, RIB 288) or a *collegium* (*collegium fabrorum* at Chichester, RIB91). Blagg's calculations give 17.8% of benefactors as corporate bodies, as opposed to 6.3% by civic magistrates or priests (Blagg 1990, table 4), whereas in both Gallia Lugdunensis and Germania Inferior the numbers of corporate benefactors are lower (3.4% and 2.9% respectively) and at Lugdunensis, the proportion of civic magistates and priests is much higher (22.3%), although in Germania Inferior, it is not substantially different to Britain (8.7%).

There are two possible (although not mutually exclusive) explanations for this: that there was a lack of competition for elite office, and so consequently less need for the inscriptions and iconography to preserve the deeds of a magistrate; or that there was a more deep-seated rejection of the idea of the magistrate within the differentiation of social status. Returning to the attested magistracies on the inscriptions from the province, it is noticeable that the majority of the individual magistracies mentioned are religious: *seviri* (for example, RIB 678 from York) or *Augustales* (RIB 154 from Bath), both usually connected with the imperial cult. The only political magistracy mentioned is the *aedile* Marcus Ulpius Januarius, who paid for a new stage for the theatre at Brough-on-Humber (RIB 707). However, there are more attested members of the town-councils, the decurions: from York (RIB 674) and from Gloucester (RIB 161) for example. The tombstone of Volusia Faustina names her as a citizen of Lincoln, and gives her husband's title of *decurio*, and there is a possible second example of a decurion, although the text is fragmentary (RIB 3174). Furthermore, inscriptions from York and Caerwent refer to political decisions or actions on the part of the *ordo* (RIB 3195, 311 respectively). All this suggests the adoption of political activity as a means of mediating status, but not the element of competition for the more prestigious annual magistracies.

Therefore we are left with a somewhat nuanced picture of political activity in the province. The forum was clearly a significant part of the mental landscape and daily routines of the people using the towns of Roman Britain. The continued investment through to the end of the 3rd century AD demonstrates that they were not an imperial imposition ignored by the local populations. In certain cases, this investment was on a substantial scale, such as at London, Silchester and Caistor-by-Norwich (Frere 1971, Brigham 1992, Fulford and Timby 2000), but in others it is minor alterations, such as the blocking or unblocking of doorways, the amalgamation or division of rooms, and the insertion of new decoration or hypocausts (Revell 2007). This suggests that they were an important symbol for the community. References to political bodies suggest the presence of political constitutions, but the relative invisibility of urban magistrates suggests that this was operating in a different way.

Another feature which seems to contradict the epigraphic evidence is the domestic architecture in and around the towns. In this instance, we see the increased investment of wealth in terms of construction in stone and decoration with mosaics and wall paintings (Perring 2002: 36–41). Some of these features can be seen in building 28.3 in Verulamium, for example. Here, a timber-framed town house was constructed in the middle of the 2nd century (Frere 1983: 236–41). Although the excavations have not revealed the entire plan, the house seems to have been arranged around a central courtyard. A hierarchy in room function is apparent from their decoration and the relative investment of wealth in them. The most elaborately decorated room is room 9, with a mosaic of nine panels, the central one containing depictions of an urn and two dolphins and the surrounding ones, geometric designs (Neal and Cosh 2009: 349–51, no. 348.47). The walls of the room were decorated with painted veneers with an architectural design, of which the surviving section shows a main zone of red panels with what appears to be an elaborate candelabrum in between (Davey and Ling 1982: 188–91). The corridor outside of this room was painted, and in this case, the architectural design was of panels divided with columns, designed to look three-dimensional (*ibid.*: 184–7). The panels were painted to imitate marble. This house was roughly contemporary with the examples at Italica, and it is very easy to be rather derogatory about it in comparison. Nevertheless, it demonstrates that the member of the Romano-British elite who owned it was fully aware of the rhetoric of domestic architecture: to conspicuously display wealth through the decoration, to create a hierarchy of rooms, and to imitate the features of public architecture. In this, s/he was not alone: there were elaborately decorated villas within 15km of the town, such as Gorehambury and Park Street (Niblett 2001: 96–100), and there are suggestions of a 2nd century mosaic workshop producing mosaics of a similar style for the local elite.

This complicates the picture of elite rank within Britain. We see the adoption of political architecture through the forum, and domestic architecture through town houses and semi-urban villas. We also see some evidence for the *ordo decurionum* and urban institutions such as the *collegia*. However, we do not find the inscriptions recording individual acts of munificence, or setting up honours to magistrates, nor do we find the togate statues common elsewhere. The system of social rank in Britain had changed to be broadly similar to that throughout the western provinces, of a rank based upon political activity and conspicuous display in and around the towns. However, the idea of competition for individual honour through political activity and munificence was absent. The Romano-British elite shared certain elements of their lifestyle and outlook with the urban elites from Iberia and Gaul, but not all. It is unlikely that this was exceptional. There may have been other areas where this was also the case, such as areas with heavy elite recruitment and sparse urbanization, and there is a similar lack of inscriptions recording magisterial munificence in Belgica and Germania Inferior (Blagg 1990: table 4). This warns against making sweeping assumptions about the adoption of magisterial authority as the basis for elite identity. In reality, we are looking at a more dynamic situation, which retained the potential for different responses to the magisterial model.

Chapter 5

Looking for the Non-elite

Writing in the gaps

In the previous chapter, I have explored the ways in which the elite in the western provinces learnt new ways to define and maintain their privileged position within these communities through their magisterial status and their use of architecture, sculpture and inscriptions. Fundamental to this has been the idea that the ongoing use of these materials, the repeated routines of daily life, formed the way in which this sense of self was internalised. However, this forms only one part of the story, and it raises the question of how the other ranks of Roman society also understood their position within the social hierarchies. As Barbara Bender (1992) has argued, it is not enough to just reconstruct the lives of the elites: we have a responsibility to think about the ways in which the non-elites also understood their place within the wider communities.

In trying to do this, we are confronted by two problems from the outset. The first is that at one level, both the archaeological and the historical evidence is biased towards privileging the power of the political elite. The concern of those of elite rank was to maintain their status and to demonstrate it to the rest of their community through moments when they interacted with others. These interactions revolved around the privileged consumption and display of specific forms of material culture, and the ability to obtain different forms of material, or use them in different ways from other sections of the population. Many of our literary texts were written either by or for the elite and formed part of the justification for their privileged social position. Fundamentally, they are more visible within our evidence because they made themselves so in order to maintain their social position. The second problem arises in part from this, and that is that research into the Roman period has tended to concentrate on the elite. This can in part be traced to the history of both archaeology and ancient history, where scholars tended to identify themselves with the Roman elite. Their sense of social position was in part derived from the consumption of specific forms of classical materials (languages, particular texts and art works) and so there was a preferential study of these.

This positioned research into the material culture of the elite at the heart of classical archaeology, and by extension, the archaeology of the provinces. There has been less excavation and collection of the material left by the non-elite. We have a mental template of 'Roman' which is not always explicitly acknowledged, equating Roman-ness with towns, villas, inscriptions, sculpture, dining customs and the like. This has resulted in the preferential excavation of villas as opposed to non-villas, the study of inscriptions on stone as opposed to the graffiti on *instrumentum domesticum*, and the collection of statues and mosaics as opposed to more mundane and portable items of art. These biases in the recovery and recording of evidence have had an impact on the kinds of analytical and synthetic work which can then be carried out: the picture presented by the elite material has been taken as the norm. There are some exceptions to this, in particular the work on slaves and gladiators, but these are particularist in approach, and do not always add to our understanding of identity as such. What follows is not intended to be an exhaustive account of the possibilities of non-elite lives, as the term non-elite covers such a large proportion of the population. In this chapter, my approach is to focus on some of the methodological issues at stake, and to consider ways in which we might begin to understand the lives of the non-elite within the Roman provinces.

Finding the non-elite

Within current accounts of the archaeology of the Roman provinces, we have tended to overlook the impacts of imperialism on the non-elites. This does not mean that we have ignored them completely, but that until recently, we concentrated on the wider changes, such as urbanism or intensification of agriculture, in an abstract sense, depersonalised from the impact on the daily experience of the lives of the conquered peoples. It is difficult to argue that Roman imperialism did not have the potential to impact on the social relations of the provincial societies, but we have not necessarily thought of this in depth, and this is what I want to examine here. One exception to this is Millett's model of Romanization, in which the non-elite adopted new forms of material culture as an act of emulation of the elite (Millett 1990b). This has been a problematic element of Millett's argument, as ideas of emulation have proved controversial. The non-elite adoption of elite material culture is not an inevitable part of human nature, but needs to be contextualised within its social, political and economic setting. This is not to discount the idea of emulation within the Roman provinces, but it does need to be more explicitly explained with reference to the particularities of elite/non-elite interactions.

An important element of the introduction of post-colonial theories to Roman archaeology was the idea of the subaltern experience: the experience of the non-elite within the imperial context. This raises the question of how we might then begin to understand the constitution of non-elite identities. As argued in the previous chapter, there was a fundamental restructuring of the power relations within provincial societies, and this was more than a cosmetic change at the top rank of communities. It necessitated a changing relationship between elites and non-elites. Just as the elite were learning to be urban magistrates, so the free members of the community were learning to be urban citizens. I have already argued in chapter 2 that the post-conquest cultural changes and the development of urbanism involved new routines for the whole community which located the towns within their lives. Aspects such as voting for magistrates created and confirmed social authority through political office for the non-elite, as it acted as a reminder of their lack of authority. In this way, their active participation as a citizen symbolised the changing structures of rank, and their place within that hierarchy. At the same time, we see a transformation in the economic basis of the society: an increase in the scale of economic activity, the development (in some areas) of a market economy, and the development of specialist industries (Hopkins 1980, Woolf 1992, Bowman and Wilson 2009). This transformation of the economy in the western provinces created different kinds of daily practice and social relations within the communities. These all relate to aspects of the creation and maintenance of social identity, particularly of the non-elite. Whilst they do not adhere to our stereotype of 'Roman', they do show the potential impact of economic expansion on the social relations within the provinces. These had the potential to create new forms of social relationships based upon economic transactions, manufacturing skill, and ownership of the means and outcomes of production.

The political and economic transformations which accompanied incorporation into the Roman empire had the effect of transforming the basis of social rank not only for the elite, but also for the non-elite. These new roles, relationships and social practices all point to wider changes in non-elite identity. Some of these aspects will have been enshrined in law, but others were more informal, and tied up in changing local relationships. Whichever is the case, we are confronted with the methodological problem of how we identify the non-elite archaeologically. As discussed in the introduction, we tend to interpret the changes through the lens of the elite, whether they are the political changes or the economic changes. This has rendered the non-elite invisible; therefore, how might we make them visible archaeologically?

One approach has been to attempt to identify the particular material culture of the non-elite. This has included the examination of wider settlement patterns through field survey or the investigation of non-elite forms of artefacts. Nevertheless, there are problems with this approach. The first is that there is a difficulty isolating the precise category of artefact which denotes the non-elite. Morris (2001) has tried to identify slaves in the silver mines outside Athens from their material culture. Historical accounts attest their existence in large numbers, and give some evidence for their origins. Nevertheless, there does not seem to be a single form of material culture which identifies them, and Morris concludes that they used the material culture of their Athenian masters. For the Roman world, Millett's model of Romanization postulates that Roman material was initially adopted by the elite, and then 'trickled down' to the rest of society (Millett 1990b); this similarly raises the question of how we would distinguish a specific non-elite material culture.

Fundamental to the search for specific non-elite artefacts is the idea that each form of identity is bound up with an essential form of material culture: that we can label certain forms of artefact or building type as elite or non-elite. Furthermore, this approach sees rank as being dichotomous (elite and non-elite) or comprising a series of rigidly separated groups. Both assumptions are problematic. Some critics of models of Romanization caricature it as an elite-only phenomenon, with the non-elite retaining items of their pre-conquest material. However, work on the archaeology of colonial period America suggests that this is not the case, as in certain circumstances the non-elite were able to acquire (or were given) the same forms of material as the elite (Silliman 2010: 32–4). Looking at Roman material, we cannot label Latin inscriptions as being the exclusive product of elite activity given that the epitaphs, which make up the majority of the corpus, were also set up by and for other, non-elite, sections of society (Hope 2001). Similarly, in Britain, we have examples of timber-built houses with stone-built bath-houses, such as the aisled building at Barnwell in Eastern England (Upex 2008: 130, fig. 43). The main part of the building was an aisled building, apparently divided into two zones, one used for agricultural purposes, and at the other, living quarters. Built onto this side was a bath suite consisting of a cold room, a hot room, and a possible changing area. The multiple entrances suggest there may have been internal walls, although no remains of these survive. Such domestic buildings point to the gradations of status: the people using these forms of material culture are not immediately recognisable as the elite of the community, but they do have sufficient resources to acquire expensive goods, suggesting they are not the poorest within the community. More importantly, they demonstrate the problems with looking for 'non-elite' materials.

A further problem is that this approach does an injustice to the complexity of the material evidence. The recent theoretical approaches of object biographies demonstrate that a single artefact can be passed from one person to another, acquiring different meanings in the process. Thus, as Peers (1999) has demonstrated, an artefact used to symbolise family relationships and the intimate and domestic within communities of fur traders could become a curio of the exotic and the anonymous with its sale. In the course of its life, a single object could be used in the creation of very different identities. Furthermore, different groups engaged in common economic, cultural and political relationships which revolved around shared social practices and material culture (Thomas 1991). This can make it difficult to separate elite and non-elite materials: as material culture is tied up in these practices, it cannot necessarily be attributed to one group or another. However, a more critical approach to human-material interactions can allow us to understand non-elite identities within the Roman provinces. I propose to concentrate on three core ideas. The first of these is the idea of entanglement, although in this case, I shall deal with entangled spaces. This is the idea that spaces were inhabited by more than one group within society, and that difference was structured by either the patterns of use, the areas accessed, or the times when they were accessed (Silliman 2010). Laurence (2006) has demonstrated this for the townscape of Pompeii, where the public spaces of the city were used by different groups within the society, but that their experience of the town was temporally dictated. Similarly, Wallace-Hadrill (1994) has argued for the houses being occupied by different social groups with access to different spaces.

The second of these approaches is that of an archaeology of labour, which has been used as a means of understanding prehistoric and historical archaeology, but which has, as yet, seen limited application to Roman archaeology. Silliman (2001) has explored its potential for colonial contexts. He defines labour as: "the social and material relations surrounding any activities that are designed to produce, distribute, or manipulate items for personal use or for anyone else or any activities whether material or not that are *required or appropriated* for use by someone else" (*ibid.*: 380, original emphasis), and which could be voluntary, or could involve coercion or force. He argues that labour should be seen as a routinised series of activities, which involve the use and production of certain forms of material, and through which a local web of meaning was created. This element of routinisation is important: as we have already seen, it is repeated social actions which lead to the sense of the self, the practical consciousness which we draw on and which allows us to understand how we fit into a specific identity. Dependent upon the roles taken within labour, distinctions are drawn between the participants involved: ceramic tablewares are usually tied into consumption and feasting, but the same social situations involve the alternative practices of serving and cleaning (Silliman 2010). The increased demand and consumption of goods in the Roman empire created new industries and scales of production, and it is the idea of the production of goods which I shall address explicitly.

The third of these is the idea of institutional ideologies and constraints. The idea of structuration theory is one where social agent and social structures exist in a duality: the agent maintains social structures through social practice, but at the same time, their practices are formed through social structures. Thus, people act within a social context, and that context will include rules about what is and what is not permissible for that particular individual. Some of these may have been enshrined within law, and others will have been part of social custom. Although somewhat imperfect and partial, it is through these constraints that we can begin to understand the wider ideologies and prejudices, and the wider attitudes towards a person of a certain identity. The non-elites would not necessarily have welcomed these prejudices towards them, and we will see examples where the dominant ideology was contested. Nevertheless, they were not immune to the impact of these social structures, even if their reaction was to reject or subvert them.

Entangled spaces

I want to deal with the idea of entangled spaces first, and here I want to return to urban public architecture. We saw in chapter four how the identity of the elite magistrate was maintained through a privileged experience of the public architecture of the town, in particular the forum and basilica. Many of these activities were carried out in circumstances in which a large portion of the rest of the community was present. The elite magistrate had a particular role to play during these encounters, and, in part, it was through their differential experience of these encounters that their more powerful identity was maintained. Nevertheless, these public spaces were used by more than one group, and as such, they can be seen as entangled spaces. To demonstrate this, I want to look more closely at the architecture of public entertainments.

We have already seen that the theatre and amphitheatre were places where the urban magistrates could occupy a prominent position through their role in sponsoring the games, but this was in the presence of the rest of the community, making these places where different experiences were possible. An important part of the creation of different experiences is where each social group was allowed to sit. Any analysis of this begins with the *lex Iulia theatralis*, the Augustan law on seating restrictions in the theatre reconstructed by Rawson (Rawson 1987). Using both the accounts of the law and other circumstantial evidence, she reconstructs an idea of seating in the theatre and the amphitheatre reflecting the complex hierarchies of society in Rome. This included seats for the senators and the 14 rows allocated to the *equites*, but also sections for soldiers, the *plebs romana*, married men, and freeborn boys, with slaves consigned to the rear of the seating. In this way, all those present internalised their own position within society, not in terms of a binary polarity between elite and non-elite, but as part of a graded system of status. However, it is debatable how far we can apply this to the theatres and amphitheatres of the western provinces. There are conflicting pictures from the urban charters. The *lex coloniae Genetivae* stipulated that seating should be divided according to similar guidelines (Crawford 1996: 393–454): places were to be reserved for the local magistrates and those with *imperium* in all shows (§125), and in theatres, the *orchestra* was to be reserved for local and Roman magistrates, senators (including former senators) and the sons of senators (§127). However, the *lex Irnitana* allowed local custom to continue, subject to ratification by the local magistrates (González 1986: §81). Nevertheless, the charter is clearly underpinned by the assumption that there would be some form of hierarchical ordering to the seating, ordered by formal rank rather than by ability to pay.

Whilst these laws clearly privileged the experience of the urban elite, it is possible to gain a different picture from the viewpoint of the non-elite. They were at risk of substantial penalties if they did not follow these laws: if they had the temerity to sit in a seat reserved for these magistrates, they could be fined 5000 sesterces (Crawford 1996: 393–454, §125). However, as at Rome, we should not see the theatres and amphitheatre as only divided into spaces for the elite and the non-elite. The epigraphic evidence for reserved seating, collected by Kolendo (1981), reinforces a more complex picture of social rank. At the amphitheatre at Nîmes, 25 places were reserved for the boatmen of the rivers Ardeche and Ouvèze, and 40 places for the boatmen of the Rhône and Saône (CIL 12.3316). It is possible that further places were also allocated for the ship-owners of Arles, the *navicularii Arelatenses*, although the reading of the inscription is unclear (CIL 12.3317). At the federal amphitheatre at Lyon, places were reserved for the butchers, and at Saintes, for the harness makers or armourers depending on the reconstruction of the text (CIL 13.1052).

These divisions were accentuated through the architecture. The complex system of dividing the seating within amphitheatres provided a sophisticated system for creating spatial hierarchies (Golvin 1988: 346–54). The amphitheatre was divided into three vertical zones, the *ima*, *media* and *summa cavea*. Each of these was divided into horizontal sections, the *cunei*, each *cuneus* into a series of row, and each row into seats. Thus, the *cavea* was divided into a series of zones which could be allocated to different social groups. The divisions between the levels of the *cavea* could be marked with low walls (or *maeniaria*), and access to them was often segregated. Similar methods were used within the theatres, but with the addition of the *orchestra* as a further zone of differentiation. In contrast to the Greek theatre, in the Roman theatre this was used to seat the most important members of the audience. Throughout the building, construction materials and decoration could be used to further emphasise the social hierarchy: for example marble was preferentially used in the *orchestra* and lower rows, dying out the further up the seating.

We can see the architectural delineation of rank at play in the theatre at Italica (Rodríguez Gutiérrez 2004). Here, the tiers of seating were divided by solid barriers. The *orchestra* and bottom rows were lined with marble, unlike the rows behind. Reconstruction of the widths of seats, although tentative, further suggests that those in the front were provided with larger and therefore more comfortable seats than the rest of the audience in the rows behind them. In the town's amphitheatre, the audience was similarly divided into segregated groups. Multiple entrances led to a complicated series of passages, ensuring that those of different rank were kept apart from the moment they entered the building. Those at the front had reached their seats via two gates to the side of the main entrance, whilst those further up had different entrances and access routes, thus segregating the audience completely (Roldán Gómez 1994: 218–23). The galleries used to access the upper tiers of seating were narrower than those for the lowest banks of seating, with proportionately fewer stairways, but more people to accommodate.

Through the architectural layout of these buildings, we can see that rank was not just a case of the elite distancing themselves from the rest of the population. This was a factor at play, but the non-elites also used these spaces as a way of internalising their own place within the local community. Through their different roles within such occasions as the theatrical *ludi* and gladiatorial games, they confirmed the varying levels of rank, and the ways in which they were regarded as a hierarchy. The ordinary citizens in the middle tiers may well have had their subordinate position to the decurions reaffirmed during these occasions, but at the same time, it was an opportunity to proclaim their rank as free male citizen, as opposed to a slave, freedman, or visitor. These blocks of people of similar social standing and shared occupation were not only a display of the differences between the various groups, but also a means of fostering a sense of belonging to a social group, promoting an internalisation of each person's place within the local hierarchy. In particular, the evidence for the seating by *collegium* demonstrates how the blanket term of non-elite could be broken down into smaller identity groups.

These ideas can be applied to the other public buildings of the town. Different people took different roles within them: some took roles of authority, others participated, others acted in service roles. On some occasions, the paraphernalia used within activities could also aid in distinguishing one group from another. Multiple textual sources describe visits to the baths as involving use of towels, oil, and the drinking of wine. The rank of the person was marked out by the quality of these materials: did you bring high quality towels and the best vintage of wine? were you anointed with fragranced oils? did you bring your own slave to guard your clothes? Or alternatively, did you have scratchy towels, vinegary wine, cheap oil, and were forced to have the general-purpose baths slave attend your goods? Were you visiting the baths, or working there? All of these apparently trivial aspects of the bathing experience served to make the baths entangled spaces, experienced as a continuum of experiences from the slaves stoking the furnaces to the richest patron.

Roman labour and the production of identity

The social practices of production and manufacture provide a second means of understanding the social identity of the non-elite. The daily routines of work are involved in the creation and maintenance of the sense of self: these routines form part of a person's knowledge of how to move around their own world and also form the basis for relationships (both equal and unequal) which form a sense of a person's place within the wider society. Certain forms of labour will involve specialisation, leading to the formation of ties between these specialists, but also a knowledge and responsibility which will not be accessible to all, creating a sense of pride and self-definition. During the Roman period, the majority of the population were probably involved in agricultural production, but the post-conquest period also sees the development of specific industries, and new forms of goods, and it these I shall concentrate on within this section, looking in particular at different scales of production between specific industries.

One form of material culture which increases in quantity in the western provinces is personal jewellery. We get some idea of the production process of such objects from the Snettisham jeweller's hoard from eastern Britain, who seems to have specialised in the production of silver jewellery (Johns 1997). This is a relatively small 2nd century AD hoard which contains scrap metal, unset gemstones, finished products and manufacturing tools and equipment (Figure 5.1). The presence of both tools and scrap metal suggests that this was a person (or more likely, a small group of people) who were engaged in both production and selling, rather than just selling the completed goods. This could have been a peripatetic workshop: the tools for

Figure 5.1 Snettisham jeweller's hoard (© Trustees of the British Museum)

producing both metal and gems were relatively lightweight, and there is no indication of buildings associated with jewellery manufacture in the immediate vicinity of the hoard, although admittedly excavation in the area has been limited. The jewellery was both cast and wrought, with the jewellers deliberately using different qualities of silver alloy for each production method. They drew on parallels from both gold and base-metal jewellery for the forms they made. One of their most common products was snake jewellery, with both rings and bracelets being made in this style. The workshop also seems to have manufactured some gold jewellery: there are no examples of finished items, but scrap gold and a burnishing tool with traces of gold on it points to someone working with gold. The level of specialist metal knowledge possessed by the members of the workshop is demonstrated through the deliberate collection of good quality silver coin for recycling. The coins are dominated by a specific Domitianic issue with a consistently high concentration of silver, in preference to a similar period issue which had less silver (Burnett 1997).

The hoard also contained a total of 127 gems, all carnelians, of which 17 were already set in rings. A detailed analysis of the cuts in the stones demonstrates that the gems can be ascribed to three different engravers, suggesting that they were the product of a gem workshop rather than a single producer. One seems to have been more experienced than the other two, and produced higher quality gems; presumably he was the head of the workshop. A second seems to have been his apprentice, but it is unclear whether the third overlapped with him, as their styles are somewhat distinctive. Stylistic comparison of the gems has pointed to the work of these three engravers being found further afield in Wroxeter, Leicester, Verulamium, and the Hadrian's Wall area (Kleibrink 1997). Either the engravers were mobile, or their customers were; probably it was a combination of the two. The assemblage is dominated by depictions of deities, in particular Bonus Eventus and Ceres. Ceres is depicted in two separate forms: in one she is depicted with a dish, ears of corn and an ant; in the second, with the dish and ears of corn, but no ant. The fourteen gems which show female personifications also suggest a knowledge of classicizing iconography. Four depict Fortuna with a rudder and a cornucopia, whilst a further ten show a female personification holding a cornucopia and a patera.

Here we see a small group of people whose work patterns were dominated by their production of portable pieces of jewellery. It seems likely that they did not work from a fixed workshop, but travelled with tools and raw materials, producing and selling goods within the region and possibly the whole province. The workshop either comprised one or more specialist metalworkers, or it contained both metalworkers and gemworkers together, or these were not specialist skills, and the jewellers were proficient in both. The metalworkers had specialist knowledge of the properties of different metals and metal alloys, and the methods for their working. Those producing the gems had knowledge of the characteristics of the various raw gemstones, as well as a sophisticated knowledge of classical myth and iconography. It is likely that the group represented by this workshop was tied into a wider network of people from whom they bought the scrap metal or the unworked gemstones. The knowledge and skill suggests an apprenticeship system, and specialists working together. Thus, for this group of workers, their sense of identity was based around the daily routines of manufacture, and their links both within the workshop itself and with other suppliers and customers.

The detail we can reconstruct for labour patterns using the Snettisham jeweller's hoard is in stark contrast to that for the larger scale-industries. In these cases, it is more difficult to identify individual contributions as securely. Therefore we need to think about a different scale of analysis, and different levels of interpretation. In such cases, we can reconstruct a more general picture of work patterns and relationships. Within the Iberian peninsula we see a substantial increase in the scale of mining of metals: gold, silver, copper and tin. Production was already established prior to conquest, but post-conquest, there was not only an increase in levels of production, but also a change in the ways in which mining was embedded within wider social relations. It would be inaccurate to see this as a uniform transformation, and there were substantial differences in the expansion of mining throughout the province of Tarraconensis, for example between the region around Cartago Nova and the north-western region (Orejas and Sánchez-Palencia 2002). The following analysis will focus on the north-western region of Tarraconensis and Las Médulas in particular.

The north-western region of Iberia was an important source of gold, and the archaeological traces of its production still form a visible scar on the landscape. During the late Iron Age, gold mining was small scale, and seems to have been embedded in the dominant form of social and political organisation: the *castro* (Sánchez-Palencia and Fernández-Posse 2000). These were autonomous enclosed hilltop settlements occupied by relatively small population groups and apparently controlling the surrounding agricultural area. This changed substantially post-conquest, with intensive exploitation by the imperial authorities. New forms of Roman and Hellenistic technology were introduced, which required an expansion of the workforce, but also greater control of hydraulic resources. Different forms of extraction were used, depending on the depth of the gold deposits below the surface of the ground (*ibid.*: 168–88). For deposits just below the ground, streams of water were diverted to create shallow trenches; once a vein was found, it was followed, in certain cases using series of parallel channels. Where the seam was further down, the technique described by Pliny as *ruina montium* was deployed. In this case, underground galleries were created through which the water was run, thus causing their collapse and the exposure of the metal. A second stage was needed to wash the gold from the debris. Following this, the waste material needed to be removed.

The intensity of this scale of production led to the development of specialist skills amongst the workers. It relied upon a substantial management of the local water resources, including aqueducts and storage reservoirs to guarantee the supply, as well as the management of the flow of the water during the process of extraction and washing. Others might be responsible for the creation of the subterranean channels, or the removal of waste material. A large ancillary workforce would also have been needed, producing tools or working the land to produce the food for the mining specialists. This is reinforced in the *lex Vipasca* from the copper and silver mining district of northern Portugal (Domergue 1983), which lists some of the concessions (possibly monopolies) granted to other trades, and lists amongst them barbers, shoemakers and fullers. The importance of these ancillary workers should not be downplayed, as it has been estimated that in South American mines in the 16th century, approximately two-thirds of the total workforce were actually providing such support services (Edmondson 1987: 60).

In the case of Las Médulas, we see an entire community employed in or dependent upon mining gold. Whether they were actively involved in the process of extraction or in the supplementary industries, the practices of mining will have permeated the routines of their daily lives as their livelihoods were dependent upon the success or failures of the mines. There are some details we do not know, such as the timetable for daily work or whether there was a shift system, but these will have structured the working day of the community as a whole. Given the danger involved, there may have been superstitious beliefs or practices designed to give a sense of control over the danger and ward-off the likelihood of some form of accident. These may have been instituted in religious festivals, whether it was holding dedicated festivals connected with mining, or incorporating specific rituals into more established festivals. There may have been particular illnesses and injuries which were the product of the mining process which would also have created a group mentality. Evidence from Jordan points to industrial pollution from exposure to copper and lead which would have impacted on the overall health of the community such as gastric illnesses, cancers and osteoporosis (Gratton *et al.* 2002). Both suffering and caring for the regular occurrence of a restricted range of illnesses had the potential to create shared experiences and bonds of suffering within the community which they would not have shared with those who were not exposed to the same dangers.

Although there will have been an overall sense of belonging to the mining community as a whole, there may also have been sub-groups within it. An individual's sense of personal identity will have been drawn from their role within the overall industry. For some, it will have been the specialist hydraulics knowledge, for others, the agricultural labour required to supply the community. Each of these trades will have had their own particular routines within the overall mining process, and different forms of knowledge. This knowledge and the work activities will have differed from those of the other jobs. In this way, an individual was situated within the sub-groups of the overall community. In addition to this, Domergue has argued that whilst there is no evidence for *damnatio ad metella* in Iberia, it was likely that mines were worked by a combination of salaried workers and slaves (Domergue 1990), adding a further axis of differentiation into the society. The effect of the different specialisms may have been reinforced by changes in settlement organisation. Prior to the expansion of the mining activity, the *castros* were multi-functional and autonomous. After the conquest, there was an increase in the number of settlements associated with Las Médulas, and they start to take on different roles within an overall network (Sánchez-Palencia and Fernández-Posse 2000: 368–72). Some settlements seem to have housed workers involved in agriculture, others with the aqueduct system, others with the actual working of the mines. A final group seem to have taken on specialist support functions: the village of Orellán for example seems to have concentrated on the production of metal tools, both for the various stages in the mining process, but also for the farming community. This level of specialisation means that, unlike the *castros*, none of these were independent, but each formed part of a complex network. In this way, an individual was part of a village which reinforced their working identity, but which also reinforced their identity as part of the overall mining community.

The complexity of reconstructing such activities and relationships of labour is reinforced when we look at the production of ceramics. This is one of the most extensively researched industries within Roman archaeology due to the durability of the material within the archaeological record, and the consequent ability to use it for dating and to answer other questions such as the extent of trading. Less attention has been paid to the human processes of its production, but here the work of Peacock (1982) stands out. It is easy to talk about the Roman ceramics industry as though it was a single phenomenon, represented in most people's minds by the large-scale production of finewares such as terra sigillata. However, Peacock has argued for varying scales of production, from household to quasi-factory. Activities such as extraction of raw materials, forming and finishing, firing and distribution would differ in levels of specialism between the different scales of production, thus creating different daily routines and levels of knowledge and therefore sense of identity.

Within Peacock's scale of production, the smallest scale would have been household production, that is making ceramics purely for the use of the immediate family.

Ceramic work will have been on a very ad hoc basis, producing goods on an infrequent basis, as and when required. The next stage is that of household industry, which produced a small surplus of vessels which would then be sold providing additional income for the family. This would have been a seasonal activity, with labour restricted to the members of the household, with the possibility of a single person undertaking all the stages of the production, and involving limited technological expertise. One example of this scale of manufacture is Malvern ware, from western England (Peacock 1982: 81–5). The production was restricted to the immediate area of the Malvern Hills, as demonstrated by the petrological signature of the tempers, but there was not a single point of production, suggesting that it was carried out in a series of households. The pots were hand-made, and dominated by cooking wares. Distribution was limited to within a 50km radius, and was on a small scale, with Malvern ware rarely making up more than 10% of the assemblage from a single site. This all points to a household industry, either sold directly to consumers through local market towns, or sold on to itinerant peddlers, who then sold it throughout the surrounding area. This formed one part of the overall economic activity of these farms and so pottery production was unlikely to have played a major part in the self-identification of the members of the family, forming instead part of their general farming activities.

The scale of production represented by Malvern ware is very different to the skills and routines of the massive sigillata industries of southern Gaul. In reality, this comprised a series of production centres, of which La Graufesenque (Condatomagos) is the best known. The evidence from here points to the small settlement being dominated by this single, exceptionally large-scale industry (Peacock 1982: 122–8). There was a large overall work-force, organised into separate workshops of varying sizes. These workshops had an estimated life-span of between 25 and 30 years each, with a large workshop potentially producing over 400,000 vessels during its lifetime (Allen 2013). The majority of the potters seem to have been free men, with limited evidence for slaves amongst their number. Instead, slaves seem to have been used for the more menial jobs, such as the collection of wood, the collection and the puddling of the clay, and the polishing of the moulded wares (Marichal 1988: 226–8, no. 169). Workers specialised in various stages of the process and stamps on the finished vessels demonstrate the expert roles: mould-maker, bowl finisher, potter and proprietor. A further group of workers specialised in the firing process: tally lists on pot sherds listed how many pots each potter or workshop had within a specific kiln load. There seems to have been an internal hierarchy within some of the workshops, with foremen, and particular potters overseeing the production of specific forms (Hartley 2002). There may also have been a centralised system of distribution, pointing to a final specialist stage in the process.

La Graufesenque seems to represent an exceptional level of specialised production, even for the sigillata industries. Nevertheless, it demonstrates the ways in which this level of manufacture would have led to the creation of particular forms of identity based on labour routines. As witnessed at Las Médulas, there may have existed two levels of group identification, one as a part of the pottery industry as a whole, but the second as a specialist within that, with the possibility of a hierarchy based on perceived levels of skill associated with each of the individual roles. This is very different to the scale of production for the Malvern wares, leading to more specialised professional identities. Hingley has argued that these potters have access to Roman cultural forms, such as the use of mythological symbols and the use of Latin on firing dockets (Hingley 2005: 99–101), suggesting some form of familiarity with Roman cultural forms, as with the Snettisham jewellers.

The significance of these specialist professions was accentuated by the *collegia*, or professional associations. The study of the *Collegia Centonariorum*, the traders of woollen goods and garments, shows that social activities were used to bind the group together, such as banquets, religious activities and shared tombs (Liu 2009). These groups seem to have differed in size from 93 to several hundred, and included members of freeborn and freed status. There are examples of them being accorded particular benefits, such as exemption from *munera* or legal guardianship. A number of inscriptions record the *Collegia Centonariorum* setting up honorific inscriptions, including some to their patrons, showing how membership of the *Collegium* could tie individuals into the wider social relationships of the community. Such activities would have helped maintained the cohesion of the group identity, but within the local context, would also have visibly marked out the group to the rest of the community. The *collegia* are a formal manifestation of a much wider formulation of identity within the Roman west, and that is the way in which work or labour, its routines, specialist skills and the relationships it created became a way to create a sense of shared identity with specific people, and a line of differentiation with other groups.

Discourses of slavery

The third approach we might use to investigate the identities of the non-elites is to focus on the social structures through which they formed their sense of self: the social structures which enabled or constrained their actions. This may form one means of understanding the identity of the slaves within the Roman provinces. Slaves formed a substantial proportion of the Roman population: Scheidel, for example, estimates that they comprised between 7% and 13% of the total population (Scheidel 2011: 292). Historical research into slavery has a long tradition, however, it has focussed more on the legal and economic role of slaves than on their place within Roman social structures and their social conditions. This has begun to change, in tandem with work on the Roman household, and with some overlaps (for example, Joshel and Murnaghan 1998). Most of this work is derived from textual sources, whether literary accounts, jurists, papyri or epigraphy, and consequently most relates to Rome, Italy or Egypt. Even discussions which claim to study slavery in the Roman world generally focus on Rome, Ostia and Pompeii (for example, Joshel 2010).

So far, the archaeology of slavery has proved problematic, and Walter Scheidel has gone so far as to argue, "it is unreasonable to expect archaeology to make a significant contribution to modern reconstructions of the Greek or Roman slave-systems" (Scheidel 2003: 581). The difficulties have been ascribed to the fact that slavery was a legal status (Morris 2011): a slave was someone who was defined as the property of another person, and consequently deprived of a number of legal rights. The argument follows that as archaeology cannot detect legal status, it cannot unambiguously identify slaves and so cannot produce an archaeology of slavery which is not dependent upon textual evidence. At first sight, it could seem that there is a certain amount of truth to this claim. The only detailed archaeological argument for the identifiable presence of slaves was in Carandini's publication of the excavations at Settefenestre (Carandini and Filippi 1985). The more typical picture is represented Thompson's survey of the archaeological evidence for Greek and Roman slavery which produced a depressingly small quantity of conclusive evidence (Thompson 2003). Criteria he considers diagnostic include small, cell-like rooms attached to rural villas and means of restraint, such as shackles. However, perhaps the issue is less with the evidence as with the questions being asked.

One approach which has proved profitable for historians of ancient slavery has been comparative approaches, using the better-documented slave systems of the new world to understand those of the ancient world (Lago and Katsari 2008). It is only recently that archaeologists are beginning to adopt a similar strategy and look to New World archaeologists for alternative methodologies. For example, Joshel (2013) argues that material traces of slavery are written into everything within a slaveholding society, such as domestic architecture. Using the ideas of 'a geography of containment' and a rival (slave) reading of space, she demonstrates how both the urban and the rural house in Italy might have constrained slave mobility through continuous work and surveillance, but may also show how slaves evaded such constraints, such as using small rooms adjacent to open service areas to escape surveillance. This approach echoes the ideas of entangled spaces discussed earlier, and exploring how material culture was used to maintain the boundaries between the free and unfree within such shared spaces is one way to understand the practices through which identity was formed, and similarly, alternative readings.

Similarly, in a series of papers, Jane Webster has turned to the question of slavery in Roman Britain and the use of comparative approaches in archaeology (Webster 2005, 2008). She focuses on the use of creolisation theory by New World Archaeologists, that the slave experience can be understood better by looking for the way in which materials were used rather than identifying a diagnostic material culture of slavery. She uses the graffiti from an underground room at the villa of Chalk, Kent, to argue that this was a slave *ergastulum* or prison (Webster 2005: 166–8). This approach is based on the proposition that frequent claims of ownership of goods, for example through marking them with graffiti, is common amongst slave societies. This makes her identification of this particular basement as for the accommodation of slaves persuasive, but we currently do not know enough about slave quarters in Britain to distinguish between their living quarters and specific *ergastula*. She also looks for evidence of enslaved Britons in Roman Britain. However, here her argument is less convinving. Through the analogy with North American slaves who built their own quarters using traditional African building forms, she argues that the round-houses found in otherwise Roman settlements were the quarters of enslaved Britons. However, without other forms of supporting evidence, there is no evidence that these were built by unfree as opposed to free Britons retaining the building methods for other reasons, such as the differentiation between the elite and the non-elite, or the preservation of a memory of the past.

Whilst such approaches may allow us to recognise the presence of slaves in a particular context, can we move beyond identifying presence to understanding identity? The essential characteristic of slavery was that the slave was a means of providing labour, and, consequently this labour would have formed an important element in their identity. Thus many of the arguments made in the previous section about work practices and specialisms would also have applied to the slave, and in fact both mining and ceramic production are industries where slave labour is attested. This opens up an alternative approach to slave identities. If in some ways their daily routines were similar to those of the freeborn poor, what was it that set them apart? How was the boundary maintained between these two groups, who may well have been working side-by-side on some occasions? Rather than looking for a unique material culture of slavery, perhaps we should be focusing on these differences. It is possible to identify the boundaries between slave and free identities by focusing on the wider social structures which created slavery and slaves, that is the other side of Giddens' duality of structure (see chapter 1). In this, as Roman archaeologists, we have access to a long history of textual scholarship on the topic. However, this is not to advocate a 'handmaiden of history' approach which takes the textual descriptions of the slave experience at face value and tries to map them onto particular items of material evidence. A more nuanced reading of the literary and legal accounts provides an idea of the key unspoken elements of the Roman slavery system which created these differences.

Here, I shall focus on a bill of sale for a slave from Roman London (Tomlin 2003, Gardner 2011: 418–9). This records the purchase of the slave girl Fortunata by Vegetus, a slave of Montanus, himself an imperial slave. The tablet points to one of the key elements of ideology surrounding slavery: that they were bought and sold for a price, in this case, for 600 denarii. In this respect, however important they were, all three were merely commodities, subject to the whims of their masters. Where Fortunata was sold is unclear: the tablet was found in London, so was this where she was put on sale? The archaeological evidence for slave markets is contested, and, in most cases, they were probably temporary and make-shift (Trümper 2009), and it is likely that in London at least, she would have been sold in a multi-functional space, such as the forum-basilica. Iconographic evidence of slave sales suggests the slave was displayed to the prospective buyers for examination, possibly standing on a box to make her more visible. In this, her difference in rank from the free population was made explicit. Within the letter, there is a hierarchy amongst the three slaves mentioned. Fortunata was bought by Vegetus, and he describes himself as the assistant of Montanus. However, all three were imperial slaves, and so ultimately owned by the emperor. Vegetus bought her with his *peculium*, a sum of money available to him to conduct the emperor's business. Both Montanus and Vegetus would have been sent to Britain to carry out some administrative role on the emperor's behalf (Weaver 1972), these positions of authority and the license it gave them potentially blurring the boundaries between free and unfree.

The tablet also provides what is almost a guarantee of the quality of the slave just purchased, stating that she is in good health and does not wander or run away. This was part of the information about the slave the vendor was required to provide by law (Gardner 2011). In this we see the criteria through which the quality of the slave was judged by prospective purchasers. That she neither ran away nor wandered off ties into Joshel's idea of the constrained slave, in that part of her value lay in the fact that she accepted these constraints. For those who did not, as Roth has recently argued, their punishment could be chaining which then lowered their value when resold (Roth 2011). Fortunata is described in the tablet as 'girl' (*puella*), typical of the infantilising terminology used to denote slaves. There is no indication as to her actual age, and she may well have been an adult woman, but in this legal document, her standing is diminished through the use of the term. Similarly her name, Fortunata, literally the lucky girl, is a reminder of the misnomers frequently given to slaves as their names. It also includes her tribal origin, the Diablintes, following the requirement to give her place of origin (Scheidel 2011: 303). However, this does not indicate whether she was born free or as a slave. If the latter, the recording of the place of birth as a slave undermines some assumptions about the geographical sources of slaves.

Whilst this tablet tells part of the picture, there is one key element missing, the violence which characterised the relationship: violence towards slaves, and a fear of violence from them. A master had the power of life and death over his slaves, and Suetonius describes how Julius Caesar, when he found out that his secretary Philemon had promised Caesar's enemies that he would poison him, had Philemon executed (Suet. *Jul.* 74). Suetonius groups this amongst Caesar's acts of leniency, and comments that no further punishment was carried out, referring to the expected punishment of crucifixion. Later, in his life of Augustus, Suetonius describes how Augustus treated his slaves (Suet. *Aug.* 67): he broke the legs of his secretary for betraying the contents of a letter, and had the attendants of his adopted son drowned for not attending to him with sufficient care. In both, habituated violence towards slaves is the underlying norm, and this is reflected in the *Senatus consultum Silianum* passed in AD 100 which stated that if a master was killed, all his slaves were to be questioned under torture, and any who could have prevented the death were to be put to death (Gardner 2011: 430–3). This law not only evidences the violence towards slaves, but also the other side of this discourse: the perception that slaves might be a danger to the safety of the *familia* and the household. It is difficult to imagine the archaeological evidence for this violence, but from these and similar texts we can say something about how violence had the potential to define the relationship between owner and slave.

The archaeology of slavery has traditionally been ignored in spite of the acceptance of Roman slavery within popular culture. Part of this is undoubtedly due to the difficulties of securely identifying slaves from the material evidence. Nevertheless, they formed an important part of the population of the western provinces, although we cannot be sure of the overall proportion. There are two issues at stake here: how we identify slaves from the freeborn poor and, furthermore, whether we can even talk about a 'slave' identity given the diversity in occupation, skill, place of servitude. Their invisibility in the past means that this will always be a difficult area of research, but the work of Joshel and Webster has begun to show alternative methodologies for their identification.

Multiple interpretations: the gladiator

With slaves and similar subordinate groups, it is tempting to present aspects of identity as static and monolithic, particularly when we have limited evidence, but in reality, there could be an element of ambiguity, and the discourses of identity could at times be conflicting. An identity group which was deemed weaker or secondary by the dominant group could reject such judgements themselves, or even a third social group could have a different view altogether. This introduces the question of how far the discourses of identity were internalised, and the idea that they could be challenged and alternative readings adopted. One example of this is the gladiator, which was a somewhat contested figure: on the one hand, they were marginalised, but on the other, a frequent figure in iconography and literature. This blurring has caused problems to those who try to fit them within pre-defined categories. It reinforces the idea that any discourse through which identity is formed contains elements of flexibility, polysemy and contradiction.

One element of this discourse of gladiatorial identity is that of the shame ascribed to the gladiator: that they were marginalised from the rest of society due to their supposed lack of honour and reputation (Gardner 1993: 135–40, Edwards 1997). Edwards has argued that this is because they were perceived as selling their own flesh, providing entertainment for the masses which was seen as the antithesis of the traditional Roman virtue of *gravitas*. Within the legal codes of the 2nd and 3rd centuries AD, they formed part of the legal group of *infames*, but they were separated out from the 'honourable citizen' from the time of Julius Caesar onwards. The (probably) Caesarian *Tabula Heracleensis* excludes gladiators and the trainers of gladiators from election as urban magistrate (Crawford 1996: 355–91, ll.108–25), and at Sarsina in Umbria, Balbus donated a burial place to the residents of the city, but explicitly excluded those who had hired themselves out as gladiators (CIL 12.2123).

The figure of the gladiator, along with the actor and the prostitute, can in some ways be seen as the 'other' to the male, Roman citizen, as "[p]aradigms of the antithesis of honor, they occupied a crucial place in the symbolic order" (Edwards 1997: 67). This marginalisation of the gladiators in law was coupled with their segregation within the arena. In many amphitheatres, the service areas, used for the preparation of the events and for gladiators awaiting their turn in the arena, were separated off with their own entrances and corridors. Where the amphitheatre did not have the architectural complexity to allow for this, the division may have been made by the times when the different groups could access these spaces. This may have been the case in the amphitheatres in Roman Britain, for example, where there do not seem to have been separate service areas (Wilmott 2007).

In spite of the apparently scandalous position of the gladiators, they were closely associated with the elite magistrates (Wiedemann 1992). As part of their duties, magistrates were required to provide religious festivals for the community. The *lex coloniae Genitivae* states that *aediles* were required to provide three days of festivities in honour of Jupiter, Juno and Minerva (Crawford 1996: 393–54, chapter 71), which was to include one day of either games in the circus, or gladiatorial games in the forum. Inscriptions, such as that from Cordoba detailing the provision of gladiatorial games to celebrate the dedicator's election as *flamen* (CIL 2.7.221), record such *munera*. This link is reinforced through the appropriation of the image of the gladiator and gladiatorial games in the houses of the elite. From Reims, in Gallia Belgica, comes a mosaic consisting of a series of small panels containing individual gladiators interspersed with beasts from the *venatio* (Stern *et al.* 1957: 33–5, no. 38). Another mosaic from the territory of the Aedui in Lugdunensis, of which only the central panel remains, depicts a *myrmillo* with his weapons and armour (*ibid.*: 114–15, no. 308). It is also possible that depictions of gladiatorial games were also used for the decoration of the graves of the elite. The fragment of a sculptural relief from Chester shows a *retiarius* in combat with a second gladiator, possibly a *secutor* (Jackson 1983). The consumption and display of such images stood not for the valour and prowess of the gladiators themselves, but as a testament to the person who paid for them. In this context, the shame of the gladiator was secondary to the public benefaction of the elite.

However, this is does not account for depiction of gladiators on more everyday artefacts. There are numerous items of portable artefacts decorated with images of gladiators and the arena. Lamps, mirrors, pottery and glass carried images of fights, and lamps and dropper-flasks were made in the form of helmets (Köhne *et al.* 2000). Small statuettes could take the form of a single gladiator in full armour, about to fight in the arena, such as the bone figurine shown (Figure 5.2). These would have had a much wider social distribution, beyond those who produced the games, and so the reasons for possessing these must have been different. It shows that amongst the wider population, gladiators represented a glamorous and popular group rather than being linked with shame. Wiedemann (1992) argues that gladiators were seen in a more positive light because their bravery in the arena was seen as resembling bravery in battle, an important element of Roman concepts of *virtus*. This, associated with the excitement and communal experience of the games themselves, provides an alternative to the ideology of the gladiator as a figure without honour.

This complexity surrounding the identity of gladiator is made more problematic when we consider it from the perspective of the gladiator and his family. Being a gladiator was something he internalised, and became part of his own personal identity. We tend to focus on the day of the actual games, but in reality, it would have been something which was part of his routines outside of the arena, separating him from the rest of the population, and the rest of the servile class. A gladiator would be a member of a gladiatorial school (*ludus*), presumably spending much of his time training with his fellow gladiators. This sense of personal identity was then reinforced as they entered the arena for combat, dressed in their particular forms of armour and carrying their gladiatorial weapons. Their skill and bravery in the games was celebrated in their epitaphs as a source of pride. Hope (1998, 2001) has studied the collection of gladiatorial inscriptions form Nîmes, and has argued that the identification of the deceased as a gladiator took precedence over all other information: in 11 inscriptions out of a total of 14, this information was placed on the first line. Half of the epitaphs also gave the number of appearances in the ring, ranging from three to 37 outings.

Figure 5.2 Bone figure of a gladiator (inv. no. 1856,0701.1309, © Trustees of the British Museum)

It is possible that they were buried in an area reserved for gladiators, to the south of the amphitheatre, reinforcing their membership of the group. We see similar patterns within the tombstones in the Iberian provinces (Gómez-Pantoja 2009). Here there are 19 tombstones for at least 20 gladiators, as here there are instances of inscriptions to more than one person. A number are fragmentary, so we do not always know what was written on the first line, but of the 14 we do, nine give the specialism of the deceased. Of the 20 deceased, 16 give the total number of fights fought, ranging from one to a rather improbable 99. There seems to be a clustering at Cordoba: 15 of the 19 are from here, suggesting a sizable gladiatorial school. This sense of pride in their profession seemingly stands at odds with how they were viewed in the legal codes and by the elite.

The figure of gladiator points to the complexity of identity. Taking the textual sources alone, we are left with the picture of a marginalised and dangerous figure. In literary works, such as the work of Juvenal, the gladiator is a disgraced figure, brutalised by his years of combat, and a shameful figure for the ardour of the elite woman (Juvenal *Sat.* 6). In legal jurists, he is a figure of depravity, subject to certain legal penalties as part of an immoral sub-class (Gardner 1993: 110–54). However, he also stands as the identifiable image of the benefaction of the elite to the community, an important part of their status, and so he is depicted in elite art as a reminder of their social standing, whilst his image is consumed by the non-elite as popular culture. Finally, his specialist fighting skills and his prowess in the ring are features which are celebrated after his death, and presumably during his lifetime. It is these varying attitudes to a single identity group which reveal some of the complexity of reconstructing identity in the past: the contrasts between them warn against accepting the elite view of the non-elites. It points to the possibility of subverting the dominant ideologies, appropriating the elements of identity and twisting the negatives into positives.

Finding rank in the Roman world

Rank within the Roman empire is a fuzzy and tricky concept, which was not fixed, and brought with it the possibility of movement from one level to another. It included elements of legal status, wealth and birth, but also of profession. It tempting to think about rank in terms of a fixed scale, but in reality it was more complex as these various elements intersected. Although the differentiation between elite and non-elite was an important feature of the Roman world, once we begin to investigate this opposition, we begin to see gradations of status, and the potential for sub-groups to form. The most obvious distinction is through legal status, between the free-born and the slave, but even these groups are difficult to see as homogenous. The obvious blurring point is the freedman, whose legal status set him apart from the free-born population, but who, if wealthy, could gain public honour through political service. Mouritsen has recently argued that the development of the various offices of *sevir* and *Augustalis* "offered wealthy freedmen a broader and more direct route to public esteem whilst also integrating them more deeply into municipal life" (Mouritsen 2011: 260). This blurring of absolute categorisation can be extended, with the potential for a hierarchy of specialisms within professional groups, for example.

Reconstructing the identities of the non-elite has generally proved problematic. Initially this was due to the lack of interest on the part of archaeologists and ancient historians. More recently, although there have been multiple calls for research into the subaltern experience of imperialism, there has actually been less research into how their identities were formed and maintained. In part, this is because the power hierarchies of the Roman world rested upon making the non-elite less visible. Consequently we need more critical methodologies for approaching the material culture of the past, such as the idea of entangled spaces, or focusing on production and the archaeology of labour. From such approaches, as demonstrated in this chapter, it is clear that Roman imperialism and the cultural change which followed had the potential to disrupt the existing lives of the non-elite with new elements of daily practice, whether it was using new forms of architecture, learning new skills to respond to the demand for new forms of materials, or enrolling in the Roman military units. These created a disjunction to their lives before the conquest, although this could be of varying intensity, from the new forms of daily work, to the occasional visit to the new urban centres to vote or to attend a gladiatorial spectacle. Trying to reduce the impact of Roman imperialism on rank to a single model is impossible, but this does not negate the significance of the changes.

Chapter 6

Gendering the Provinces

Looking for gender in the Roman provinces

In the previous chapters, we have looked at the ways in which discourses of ethnicity and rank can be, and have been, explored through a combination of evidence. We have seen that identity as an idea and a theoretical paradigm can be used to explore the ways in which people within the Roman empire not only adopted new forms of material culture, but also new forms of thinking about themselves and their roles within society. The changes within the material culture which we can detect within the archaeological record are an expression of that sense of self through new ideas and new routines of everyday living. However, if we turn from rank to ideas of gender and age, it is more difficult to explore these discourses on a similarly broad scale and, as indicated in the opening chapter, this is not a problem of the material record, but of research priorities.

The idea that our reconstruction of the past has been carried out under a male-dominated narrative has been explicitly raised by a series of feminist archaeologists, anthropologists and historians since the 1980s (Nelson 2006). Seminal works such as by Conkey and Spector (1984) and those in Conkey and Gero (1991) have set an agenda for the inclusion of women and gendered approaches into the archaeological narrative. From about the same time, gender and women in particular have been a central topic within the study of Roman literature and art. However, these topics have been largely marginalised within Roman archaeology, as secondary to the supposedly 'big' questions of settlement, imperialism, cultural change and the military (Scott 1995, Culham 1997, Whitehouse 1998). In an A–Z of Gallo-Roman civilisation, women and family are notably absent, although slave, actor and athleticism are present (Pelletier 1993). Perhaps more than other aspects of identity, gender and age together have been dismissed as an 'alternative' form of archaeological discourse (Hill 2001: 12). As theoretical approaches based on identity have become more mainstream, gender has played a somewhat minor part within this. This is not to downplay the work which has been done on gender in the provinces, as there has been some excellent work on appearance and artefact distributions, for example. However, such accounts are still depressingly few in number and generally focus on Roman Britain.

In their manifesto for an engendered archaeology, Conkey and Spector (1984) argued for three distinct stages in the development of feminist approaches (see also Wylie 1991):

1. the critique of male biases in current narratives
2. studies of women's lives
3. studies of relationships between genders and the factors which structure them

Within Roman provincial archaeology, there is now a large literature critiquing the dominance of androcentric narratives (Scott 1993, 1995, Allason-Jones 2001, Hill 2001, Baker 2003, Revell 2010b). There is also a somewhat smaller literature studying the lives of women (Pelletier 1984, Allason-Jones 2005). More encouragingly, within the last ten years, there has been a growing body of literature examining the social ideologies of gender and their material expression. However, these exist as a distinct subfield within Roman provincial archaeology, with the majority of the work being carried out by female archaeologists (although there are some exceptions). We are now at the stage where such studies need to be re-integrated into the wider provincial narratives.

The result of this is that at the moment, it is very difficult to write a coherent account of gender, sexuality or age within the western provinces. We are left with abundant evidence for Rome and the towns of central Italy, but turning outside of this, we are left with snapshots from a small number of isolated case-studies. It could be argued that this is not a problem, as these aspects of identity are something very localised: they are worked through at the local scale, and do not apply to the larger picture of integration into a common ethnic identity. However, if we are to use theories of identity as a way to understand how Roman imperialism impacted on its provinces, and integrate ideas of discrepancy, we need to set aspects such as gender or age back into this (Revell 2010b). We cannot yet start to compare across regions or provinces to begin to understand the regional variability within gender identities. Nor, due to a similar lack of research into Iron Age gender, can we easily understand the impact of imperialism. Nevertheless, although there is still a need for wider studies, we can begin to understand some of the ways in which genders were differentiated, and the way imperialism may have influenced this.

Dress and adornment

One area which formed a focus for research into gender is dress and adornment. The presentation of the body forms a fundamental part of the ways in which an individual person claims their membership of a specific social group (Sørensen 1997, 2000: 124–36, Harlow 2012). It allows them to communicate this membership to a relatively undefined audience without verbal or physical contact. Furthermore, dress and adornment form one way in which the abstractions of identity become embodied and experienced by an individual, and so through which social roles can be learnt and internalised. Dress forms part of the process of socialisation, and the adoption of different modes of dress can indicate the transition from one social group to another. It can be used to signify who was part of a social group, but it can also be used to exclude: those who do not wear it, or who do not understand the significance of the detailing, are not part of the community. In this way, it is not only a symbol of the group, but is used in creating and maintaining its boundaries.

There is a temptation when thinking of dress and social identity to equate this with a uniform. This is a more restricted form of dress, connected with specific groups, such as schoolchildren or particular occupations. Colour, form and decoration can be used to define the group, whilst the requirement to wear it becomes a form of institutional discipline, with punishment for incorrect presentation. However, similar social rules apply to more informal forms of clothing: how we dress is to some extent conditioned by a series of unspoken assumptions of what is appropriate, and so clothing still carries a form of communication. This raises the question of fashion, which Rothe has defined as a rapid, regular and conscious change of forms of clothing (Rothe 2009: 9). It is easy to dismiss the choice of styles of dress and their fittings as 'just fashion', but this is to ignore the specific ideological context of fashion. In contemporary western society, it is part of a rampant conspicuous consumption and the display of disposable income, with tradition and conservatism seen in a negative light. It is questionable how far we can apply this model to the past, and in particular, to the imperial period. Wild has argued that for Belgica, Britain and the German provinces, there were only three distinct ensembles worn by women over a period of four hundred years, "this hardly constitutes a rapid change in style" (Wild 1968: 194). There were changes in dress as part of the wider processes of cultural change, but we should not dismiss this as just part of a change in fashion: this formed part of a series of changes in the message a person was saying about themself to a wider audience.

The clothing of the Roman citizen was explicitly gendered, with the toga standing as the symbol of a political status open only to men (Stone 1994). Women instead wore a tunic, over which was worn a full length slip-like garment (*stola*) belted under the breasts, and over this a rectangular mantle (*palla*) which could be used to cover the head (Olson 2008: 25–39). Literary sources also indicate that she would normally bind her hair with woollen fillets, although these are rarely depicted in iconography. The toga seems to have been adopted by the elite men of provincial communities as part of the reconceptualisation of their social status. We can see this in the togate statues from urban centres, or on funerary portraits of couples, with the man clad in a toga. The toga points to some of the complexity in the relationship between a single item of material culture and multiple aspects of identity. On the one hand, the change in costume is bound up in new ways of expressing social rank, but on the other, and at the same time, it forms part of new ways of expressing gender difference.

The adoption of Roman dress was not universal throughout the provinces, however, and in the north-western provinces in particular, there was an element of continuity of pre-Roman styles. The dominant dress form was the Gallic ensemble, but although there were common elements, the overall ensemble was still clearly gendered (Wild 1968, Rothe 2012). The common element for both men and women was the so-called Gallic coat. This was a wide, flat tunic, with wide sleeves of varying length. It was worn unbelted, and so seems to have fallen from the arms in deep, vertical folds. The male coat was shorter, usually coming to just below the knees, whilst women wore their coats full-length. This may have had implications for the manufacturing process for each. The one complete surviving male example shows that it was woven as a single piece of cloth, with a slit made for the neck, and sewn seams down the side of the body and under the arms. As the female garment was longer, it was probably not made as a single piece. In some regions, women added a fringe to the bottom.

Over the coat, men usually wore a cape and a scarf; it is not clear from the iconographic evidence whether they wore any form of undergarment. This cape was semi-circular in form, with a hood attached to it as a separate item. The two straight edges were brought together at the front, and seem to have usually been sewn together, leaving a vent for the head to go through. It was knee-length, and one or both arms could be rolled up to allow the wearer more movement. Scarves are frequently depicted on reliefs, and were wrapped around the neck, crossed at the front, and the tucked into the cape. In contrast, women wore a cloak over their coat: this was a single rectangular piece, which could be draped across the body in a variety of ways. Some depictions show women wearing another garment under their Gallic cloak: these seem to be some form of shift which is visible at the neck and below the hem of the coat. It is not clear whether they had sleeves or not. Headwear is rare with this ensemble, but not unknown: the women of the Treveri were sometimes depicted wearing a tight-fitting bonnet, for example.

A further difference in the dress of men and women was that whilst the Gallic ensemble seems to have been the only option for men not adopting the toga, for women there were two other variants. One which seems to have had a wide distribution was the outfit termed by Wild as the costume of Menimane, after the woman depicted wearing it on her tombstone (Wild 1968: 199–207). This consisted of a close-fitting bodice with long-sleeves and cuffs. Over this was worn a tunic, made as a single, wide cylinder, which was fastened at each shoulder with a fibula, and sometimes pinned to the bodice at the front. It was usually belted. The cloak seems to have been similar to that in the Gallic ensemble, but there was a further variant in draping, as it could be worn over the left shoulder and under the right arm. This costume seems to have been prevalent in the 1st and possibly the early 2nd century AD, and then seems to stop being worn. The second variant in costume was that of the Ubii, so-called because it seems to have been restricted to their territory. It consisted of a series of tunics, over which was worn a large shawl. This seems to have been half-moon shaped, the main part covering the back, and the two arms hanging down the front and clasped at the waist with a fibula. The most striking feature of this outfit was the large head-dress covering the hair: this was spherical in shape with a smooth surface and a metal tag against one cheek. It is possible that its size depended on the rank of who was wearing it, as the autochthonous Matres are depicted in particularly large examples (Rothe 2009: 37–9).

A second element of personal dress is jewellery, whether the brooches and fibula used to fasten clothing, or the rings and necklaces which adorned the body. Too often, such items have been regarded as women's trinkets, and they have not been subject to the rigorous analysis they merit (Allason-Jones 1995). Not all such items were restricted to a single gender: both men and woman wore brooches and finger rings, both intaglio and simple bands. Nevertheless, there do appear to be certain items which were bound up with the expression of gender. In Roman Britain, ear-rings seem to have been predominantly worn by women (Allason-Jones 2005: 18, Swift 2011); in British cemeteries, no ear-rings have been found unambiguously associated with male skeletons, and in Roman textual sources they were only associated with men from the eastern empire (Allason-Jones 1989: 17). There seems to be a similar restriction of beaded necklaces to women: both men and women were buried with solid torc-style necklaces, but strings of beads seem to be predominantly female. A further element to the gendering of jewellery in Britain is the material from which it was fashioned: jet seems to have been particularly associated with women. Items such as beaded necklaces, armlets, finger-rings and pins were made from the material (Allason-Jones 1996), and these are predominantly found in women's graves.

Associated with the dress and jewellery is the question of the presentation of the body itself. Gender has often been expressed through different attitudes and expectations to the care of the body, and the textual sources reveal that this was the case at Rome (Wyke 1994, Olson 2008). In the *Ars Amatoria*, Ovid's advice to the male and the female lover exemplifies these different attitudes: men were expected to keep themselves clean and tidy, but women were to take care to cultivate their beauty through shaving, make-up and elaborate hair-dos. The distribution of small finds associated with grooming within funerary contexts suggests that there were similar gendered behaviours in Britain and Gaul. General cleanliness was expected for both men and women, as indicated by the lack of a clear gender distribution for toilet instruments such as nail-cleaners and tweezers (Eckardt and Crummy 2008). More elaborate care seems to have been deemed a female occupation, with mirrors and toilet caskets more likely to be found in female burials (Swift 2012). The dressing of the hair is the most visible manifestation of this as women wore their hair long, but arranged into sometimes highly elaborate styles (Bartman 2001). The so-called toilet scene was a common iconographic motif: a woman is depicted seated, often looking at herself in a mirror, whilst a slave dresses her hair. This is reflected archaeologically in the hairpins found associated with women in burial. Rough-fashioned pins are difficult to associate unambiguously with either gender, but the more elaborate, decorated hairpins can be more securely associated with women (Allason-Jones 1995). The relationship between hairpins and women's beauty is reflexively expressed in the figured hairpins which depict Venus emerging from the bath, or women's heads (Cool 1990, group 18A).

It is tempting to take this gendered use of dress and adornment and use it as an absolute: a predictor of gendered behaviour. However, the archaeological record does not produce absolutes, but rather the residue of the practices and discourses through which gender was expressed (Sørensen 2007). This allowed the possibility of a blurring of the boundaries. The fluidity in the meaning of material culture allows it to be used to articulate forms of gender identities which do not fall into the polarity of men and women. This seems to be the case with the so-called Gallus from Catterick in the north of Britain, where there was the instance of an osteologically sexed male skeleton wearing jewellery normally associated with women (Wilson 2002: table 117, grave 951). This was identified as the skeleton of a male, aged 20–5 years. At his neck, he wore a complete jet necklace which would have covered his chest area. On his left arm he wore two bracelets, one of jet and the other of beads, and on his right leg, a copper alloy anklet. He had two pebbles in his mouth, and his grave also contained a fragment from a blue/green glass flask or jug. In her discussion of the small finds, Cool raises the suggestion that he might have been a Gallus, or castrated follower of the goddess Cybele (Cool 2002). Whether this is the case or not, this individual stands between gender boundaries. Although burial cannot be taken as a direct transference of lived experience, this blurring of the grave goods suggests that for whatever reason, in his life he did not fit neatly into either male or female categories. He had been buried wearing not only the jewellery associated with women, but also with two pieces of jet jewellery, also associated predominantly with women.

The Catterick example is something of an extreme case, but it is not unique in Roman Britain. There are other examples of male burials containing jet jewellery. At the roadside settlement at Westhawk Farm, Kent, the richest burial was that of a young adult male (Booth *et al.* 2008: group 5090). He was cremated, and the grave goods included a bracelet of jet and lignate beads, some showing traces of gold leaf, and a copper alloy bracelet, as well as ceramic vessels. His was the only grave containing jewellery. At Brougham, the cremation burial of an adult man contained beads from a jet bracelet (Cool *et al.* 2004: 243–5, 391, 452–3, burial 307.2). Again, this seems to have been a distinctive burial: he seems to have had a richly decorated bier, the ashes were buried in a two-part cist, and as well as the jet bracelet, the grave-goods include two rare types of glass vessel, and loose blue glass beads. In these cases, the jet jewellery was not worn during the cremation itself, but was added to the burial afterwards, and in the case of the Brougham jet, there were not enough beads to form a complete bracelet, suggesting that they had been put in as individual beads. In these cases, it is not only the jet jewellery which makes them stand out, but instead, it forms part of a wider code which marks these individuals out as distinctive. This may be because in life their gender identities were ambiguous or transgressive. However, an alternative explanation may be that in death, gender ideologies were being used as a metaphor for another form of identity difference.

The (re-)construction of the provincial family

Whilst dress and the body provide one important means of gender construction, another is the structure of the family, both the delineation: who was inside and who was outside, but also the relationships between the various members. It is through such intimate relationships that gender roles were learnt and played out on a daily basis. The study of family roles has been an important feature of the study of gender within the last two decades, due largely to the pioneering work of scholars such as Beryl Rawson and Suzanne Dixon (Rawson 1986, 1991, 2011, Dixon 1988, 1992, Rawson and Weaver 1997). However, much of this work has been carried out on Rome, Italy and Roman Egypt where there are plentiful textual sources which can be used to reconstruct relationships and sentiment. Another rich source of information has been the legal codes relating to the family, which have allowed the detailed reconstruction of the power of the paterfamilias, the differences between *in manu* and *sine manu* marriages, and the legal restraints on the ability of wives and sons to assume *potestas* (Gardner 1986). The impression given from these various sources is of the dominance of *paterfamilias*, with literally the power of life and death over the rest of the family.

A fundamental problem for the study of the family within the western provinces is how far we can apply this particular model of patriarchy. Such law codes apply only to Roman citizens, raising the question of what percentage of the population in any provincial community were Roman citizens, whether they adopted this archetypical family structure, and what the family structure was amongst the rest of the population. This can lead to a somewhat pessimistic view of the possibilities of accessing family life in contexts where we are dependent upon archaeological evidence and epigraphy. As Woolf writes in trying to reconstruct family life in the north-west provinces: "there is too little evidence and no reliable means have been found of extrapolating general truths from the few cases we can document" (Woolf 2005: 231–2). Understanding the spread of citizenship and education in Latin cultural values might provide a means to understand the potential adoption of Roman family structures, but awareness is not necessarily the same as adoption. At the core of Woolf's pessimism is the problematic nature of the various forms of evidence. Inscriptions contain few concrete details, and there are different perspectives on its usefulness: Woolf is pessimistic, but others are less so (for example, Edmondson 2005 in the same volume). There have been some attempts to understand family structures from the archaeological evidence of houses and housing (Smith 1978, Guijarro 1997), but the evidence needs to be read with care (see below).

Nevertheless, we can begin to identify regional differences in family structure within the western provinces. One factor in the relationships within the family is the age at first marriage, and the possible age gap between husband and wife. The older partner might expect to be treated with respect, and a much older husband to educate and care for his younger wife. In contrast, an older wife is often regarded with suspicion, leading to the coining of the pejorative terms of 'cougar' and 'toy boy'. It reflects social attitudes to gender roles, and the relationship between the genders.

In situations where the husband was older than the wife, this would impact on the relationship between them. In the case of a patriarchal society, the situation where the husband was significantly older than the wife might be reflect and legitimate an ideology of a woman in need of a male guardian, and being thought less able to act independently than a man. It also affects any active role by the wider family, such as the likelihood of grandparents forming part of the family relations, and taking an active role in activities such as childrearing. However, if the younger wife survived childbirth, she would be more likely to outlive her husband, raising the probability of widowhood and that her role within the family and attitudes towards her might change.

Various studies have attempted to estimate age at first marriage. One of the earliest was that of Harkness (1896), in which he concluded that the average age of marriage in Rome was 24 and 26 for women and men respectively. A later study by Hopkins (1965) using the same material calculated a modal marriage age for women of between 12 and 15 years. However, these studies relied on epitaphs which included both the age at death and the length of marriage, which constitute a small percentage of the whole body of inscriptions: 171 in total used for Hopkins' study, skewed towards Rome and Italy (Shaw 1987). More recently, Saller and Shaw have returned to the question of age at marriage in conjunction with work on family structure in a series of inter-related studies (Saller and Shaw 1984, Saller 1987, 1994, Shaw 1987). Their solution to the low number of epitaphs from which it is possible to definitively calculate age at marriage was to argue that the deceased was commemorated primarily by their parents (the natal family) until marriage, and then by their spouse and children (the conjugal family). By calculating the average age at which the spouse became the more frequent commemorator, it is therefore possible to estimate the average age at marriage. They present a largely homogenous picture for the Gaul and the Danubian provinces. In northern Italy, parents commemorated their daughters until their early 20s, and their sons into their early 30s. In Narbonensis and Aquitania, men seem to marry predominantly between their late 20s and early 30s, and women in their early 20s. In the Danube provinces, women were most frequently commemorated by their husbands from their mid-20s, whereas men were commemorated by wives from their early 30s.

These figures need to be treated with a certain amount of caution: they provide gradients of change rather than abrupt points, and there are associated problems of age at death being variably recorded during the life-course and age-rounding (Saller 1994, Scheidel 1996, Revell 2005). Similarly, they demonstrate the family relations rather than family structure, as shaped through the responsibility to commemorate being in part a legal relationship and ties of emotion and obligation. Nevertheless, allowing for this, the structure of the family in Southern Gaul and the Danubian provinces was shaped by the husband being approximately ten years older than his wife. In some cases, girls married as young as their early teens, possibly providing a greater age asymmetry. It is not known to what extent this represents a change from pre-conquest patterns of marriage, but it does suggest an imbalance between the spouses which was shared with that at Rome. It also suggests the importance of marriage in structuring family ties, and consequently playing an important part within the ideologies of gender roles. Becoming a wife or a husband, with the associated duties and assumptions, played a part in shaping not only the identities of those who had undergone the rite of passage, but also those for whom it was in the future.

However, this normative pattern of the relationship between husband and wife can be questioned. In the Iberian provinces of Baetica and Lusitania the analysis of the epitaphs in the Saller and Shaw survey shows a different pattern of commemoration to that in the more northerly provinces. In these cases, the parents retain a dominant role in commemoration until the age of 40+ for men, and early 30s for women. Saller (1994: 36–7) further argues that the transition is far more gradual than in the other regions, and from this concludes that parents remain the preferred commemorators until their deaths, and that only then do spouses become visible. Their studies also showed that women were far more visible within the funerary record in Iberia than in other provinces, both as commemorators and commemorated. Men and women are equally likely to receive a memorial, the percentages being 50.8% and 49.2% respectively out of a total of 723 relationships recorded. This is supported by my own study of the inscriptions with age-statements from *Conventus Cordubensis*, where women comprise 48.3% of those receiving epitaphs (Revell 2005). Within the Iberian data as a whole, women also take an active role as commemorators: 48.5% of commemorators are female relatives, 44.7% are male relatives, and 6.8% are described as parents (Saller and Shaw 1984). Somewhat surprisingly, mothers are more likely to take on the duty of commemorating their deceased children: of 257 child-parent relationships recorded, 59.1% are child-mother, 21.8% child-father, and 19.1% child-parents.

Saller and Shaw's study looked at the whole of the Iberian provinces as a single group, which had the effect of merging regional variability within the peninsula as a whole. Their work has been followed by studies which have looked at more specific areas, and in particular, Jonathon Edmondson has focussed on Lusitania and using a series of seven case-studies, teases apart some of the differences within the province in terms of family roles in commemoration (Edmondson 2005). Overall, the case-studies reinforce the picture of the nuclear family dominating, but with the birth family retaining an important role in commemoration after marriage. For example, in the town and territory of Olisipo (modern Lisbon) parents commemorated their children up to the age of 50, some of whom were married, and in other case-studies, the younger generation were commemorated by their in-laws. As well as the close relationship between the birth and marriage families, Edmondson's study also shows a more prominent role for women both as commemorators and as those being commemorated, arguing that this is particularly true in areas he describes as 'less Romanized'. The gap between the frequency of commemoration of daughters and sons is lower than in the other western provinces, and in the *Civitas Igaeditanorum*, a greater number of daughters are commemorated, all of which reinforces the picture of women taking a more prominent role within the family in Iberia. Ethnographic writers of the period, such as Strabo and Posidonius, commented on the prominent role women played within Iberian societies, and whilst we are not dealing with a matriarchal society, we are seeing a different picture to that elsewhere in the western provinces and potentially the continuity of pre-conquest gender relations.

A second instance of variation in family structure illustrated by the Saller and Shaw study is in the context of the military. Their study demonstrated a broad civilian pattern of 75–90% of epitaphs recording commemoration by the nuclear family, whether natal or conjugal (spouse, parents, children and siblings). This is in contrast to the commemoration patterns in Britain and Germany, where 75–90% of civilian men were commemorated by their immediate family, in contrast to 30–40% of soldiers. Saller and Shaw argue that this is the product of non-local recruitment, with soldiers separated from their families (Saller and Shaw 1984: 139–45). However, the question of recruitment patterns is more complex, with the likelihood of local recruitment becoming more prominent over time. Furthermore, there is both archaeological and epigraphic evidence for presence of families in and around the forts. Van Driel-Murray (1995) has demonstrated the presence of women and children at Vindolanda and a number of German forts from the early 2nd century AD from the sizes of the leather shoes found, and Allason-Jones' (1999) survey of the epigraphy has supported this for Britain (similarly, Allison 2006).

Objections have been raised to Saller and Shaw's conclusions based on the higher incidence of setting up epitaphs amongst the military than the civilian populations of the frontier provinces. However, these criticisms overlook the fact that this is a comparative study: these factors would impact on the inscriptions recording familial and non-familial commemoration equally. Instead, although the numbers in Britain in particular may be limited, the conclusion must be that amongst the military populations in Britain and Germany, marriages or equivalent attachments between men and women were being formed, with women and any resultant children either living within or in the vicinity of the forts. However, these families had little standing within Roman law due to the ban on soldiers marrying, and so their heirs may have been their fellow-soldiers (Phang 2002). When the soldiers died, they were more likely to be commemorated by their fellow soldiers rather by their relatives. Work looking at the idea of the military community has stressed that for an army to function effectively, there needs to be strong bonds of shared identity between soldiers (Haynes 1999, James 1999). For this reason, it is possible that these relationships took supremacy at the point when the soldier died. It is difficult to believe that this would not have had an impact on the strength of family relationships, the family structure, and consequently gender relationships.

The flipside of the possible disruption to family relations amongst those living in and around the forts is the possible disruption to family structure on the areas from which the soldiers were recruited. One area which was subjected to heavy recruitment of auxiliary troops was Batavia: any numerical figure given to the levels of recruitment must at best be an estimate, but calculations by Willems suggest that in Batavia, each household must have contributed at least one man to military service (Willems 1984). The impact this had on family relationships is difficult to reconstruct, but it must have had the effect of giving women a more prominent role in the family, and van Driel-Murray has argued for family-based agricultural production which ethnographic parallels suggests were often run by women (van Driel-Murray 2002). When their menfolk were discharged from the army, there is evidence that their weapons were hung in the house, as symbolic decorations of honour, promoting a martial ideology as part of male identity. It is possible that these high levels of recruitment led to military families, which supplied forces to the Roman army for a number of generations, and which had a different family structure and gender ideologies to those elsewhere.

Whilst the majority of the studies of family structure have used epigraphic evidence, others have used the layout of houses to argue for different forms of family structure. Smith (1978, 1997) has argued that in Britain and north-western Europe the layout of rural villas points towards a continuation of extended family structures from the Iron Age. He argues that the plan of a house is the product of social organisation, and in particular, the organisation of the family. Using a wide range of examples from Britain and the northern Gallic provinces, he focuses on the villas with a complex plan which seem to contain two or more domestic residences. In some cases these are initially two separate buildings which are later joined together into a single residence. Some lack a single axial approach, with water features or shrines creating two routes of access to the buildings. Another form of modular layout was a single building, with a long, extended plan, lacking a central focus, and occasionally broken into repeated apartments. Smith (1978: 162–4) cites the British estate at Chedworth as an example, which seems of have comprised at least three separate units in its early phase (Figure 6.1). He relates these units to the post-Roman Celtic family structure, which depended on ties of extended kin relations and partible inheritance, arguing that each unit provided living space for a different family group within the extended kin group. If this is the case, then it represents a markedly different family structure to the nuclear family we see in the Roman textual sources. There is a methodological problem with Smith's argument, as it is based on the contested assumption of Celtic continuity from the Iron Age to the early Medieval period when the textual sources date to, and his interpretation of Chedworth, for example, has been rejected by some (Esmonde Cleary 2013: 75–7). Nevertheless, the archaeology may point to different conceptions of the family and family relationships, whether we see it as 'Celtic' or not.

This survey of the variability in the family structures and relationships within the western provinces has seemingly taken us away from gender identities. Nevertheless, gender is implicit within this discussion. Gender identities, as with all aspects of personal identity, are in a constant state of becoming. Relationships within families form an important role in the development of identity, and these differences will have played a part in the transmission of gender roles. Families do not necessarily conform to the western, modern ideal of the nuclear family of two parents and two or three children: they may be formed in different ways, whether nuclear or extended,

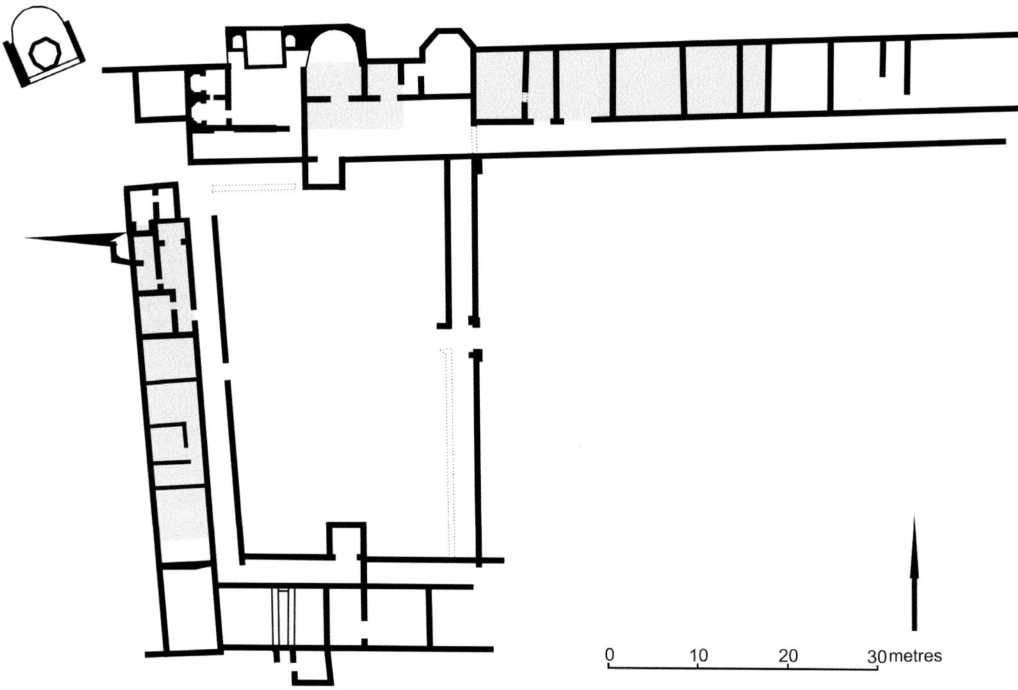

Figure 6.1 Plan of Chedworth villa showing family units proposed by Smith (adapted from Esmonde-Cleary 2013, fig. 4 with additional information from Smith 1978, fig. 54)

and attitudes to the various members and the roles they fulfil culturally determined. Do we see grandmothers as a useful source of knowledge, for example, or a drain on the resources of the family? Similarly, is the raising of children something which is valued? The iconographic evidence from Pannonia demonstrates how this might be regarded in a different light by different parts of the empire (Boatwright 2005). In general, women are rarely depicted breastfeeding in Roman art, and are often shown handing their infants over to wet-nurses. In contrast there is a series of tombstones from Pannonia which depict women nursing their children. These depictions of the role of the mother in the physical well-being of the child suggest that the mother as the nourisher of the new-born infant was seen as an important part of her identity. Its public acknowledgement sends out a message of what it is to be a good mother, and so a good woman. It is involved in the creation of a gender ideal which the viewer should wish to emulate, but which differs from that elsewhere in the empire.

Gendered work

Another way in which we might understand the process of gender differentiation within the western provinces is through ideas of work and labour. In the preceding chapter, I discussed the way in which economic activity could be used in the formulation of non-elite identities. Throughout, the language used to describe the participants was deliberately gender-neutral. However, there is a tendency to think about these activities in gendered terms. When discussing the Snettisham jeweller's hoard, the various contributors to the volume assume that the jeweller was male (Johns 1997: *passim*). Similarly, it could be assumed that those working in the mining industry in Iberia or the sigillata industries in Gaul were also predominantly adult males. However, these are assumptions which need to be questioned. Economic activity can be a powerful way to structure the ideals of gender, both in terms of the activities appropriate for various genders, but also in the ways these activities might be deemed of unequal value to the society, which then feeds into the creation of gender hierarchies.

Understanding the relationship between gender and labour or specific tasks is a somewhat fraught archaeological undertaking. The critique of unspoken assumptions about gendered activities has formed an important part of feminist approaches to prehistory: the narrative of man the hunter and woman the gatherer has dominated palaeolithic archaeology, whilst the agricultural revolution and sedentism were seen to restrict women to the domestic sphere (Gero 1991, Peterson 2006). Questioning both of these assumptions has formed an important part of feminist approaches to prehistory. The attitudes to the economic role of the genders are often the product of essentialist views of labour and work (Wylie 2002: 187): that certain tasks can only be carried out by men because women lacked physical strength, or technical precision, or that because of reproductive differences, man was the economically productive agent, and woman the care-giver. Economic roles would often have been gender-based in the past, as in the present, but these are socially determined, and can be changed through wars, revolutions, and economic developments (for example Frader 2004). A second problem has been the value attributed to various activities: explicitly economic activity has been seen as of value to the wider society, caregiving of limited economic value. As women have been stereotyped as the care-givers, their potential contribution to society has been underestimated, and a corrective to this has been to re-evaluate the contribution of women's roles. For example, an argument against the undervaluing of gathering (characterised as a female activity) as opposed to hunting (a male activity) has been to re-evaluate the contribution gathering food and other supplies made to both the resources for a community, and social development (Zihlman 1998, Dobres 2004).

The relationship between gender and work has not been of great interest to Roman archaeologists, with a few exceptions. Notable is Peacock's arguments for the scale of pottery production, and his model of increasing scale and specialisation of production (Peacock 1982). At the basic level was household production, which he argued was primarily carried out by the women of the family. As ceramic production became increasingly specialised, it was taken over by men. There have been critiques of this model, in part because it is tied in with models of social evolution and essentialist gender roles (Martelle 1999), but this model does at least acknowledge the possibility of gendered labour roles. Other have used grave goods to try to identify gendered activity: at the military cemetery at Brougham, large copper buckets for mixing drinks are associated with female graves, and glass drinking vessels with male graves, suggesting a division between preparation and consumption (Cool *et al.* 2004, Cool 2011). As argued in the previous chapter, incorporation into the Roman empire resulted in considerable changes to the scale and type of economic activity, which had the potential to disrupt existing labour organisations, including those structured along gender lines. In the case of Las Médulas, we saw that as the scale of mining increased, so did the specialisation of activities and jobs. It raises the question of whether the roles of men and women within the production of metals also changed: whether such activities were organised by gender, with either the exclusion of women altogether, or with the restriction of men and women to specific roles within the overall production processes, and furthermore, whether gender activities came to be valued differently, reinforcing existing gender inequalities or creating new ones.

Reconstructing gender roles within such industries may be problematic, but one area where it may be possible is in the agricultural and cloth producing regions of Gallia Belgica. Here, there is a remarkable series of funerary monuments clustering around Trier, Neumagen and Arlon which depict scenes of everyday life, or rather, a somewhat idealised reproduction of daily life. The form of the monuments differs, from large towers to more modest stele, but generally, they are decorated on all sides, sometimes with multiple registers. The front face usually featured the family of the deceased, represented as a spousal couple, sometimes accompanied by children. The rest of the monument might feature other scenes and friezes incorporating mythological scenes, scenes of economic production, and household routines such as dining. The most spectacular extant example of these is the Igel tower (Dragendorff and Krüger 1924, Zahn 1968, Drinkwater 1982), the funerary monument of the Secundinii, a prosperous cloth-producing family. This was decorated on all four sides, with an ascending series of panels from the base, through a main relief, to the upper levels (Figure 6.2). The panels depict the deceased and their family, representations of the cloth-working basis of the family's wealth, and other scenes of daily life, as well as some mythological panels. The lower and attic reliefs are key for the business transactions, depicting the transportation and sale of the bales of cloth; the only scene which possibly depicts the weaving process is badly weathered and difficult to decipher. The smaller upper friezes show more domestic scenes: the serving of a meal, and the kitchen activities associated with it, and the paying of rent by the tenants.

There are clearly activities appropriate to each gender within these scenes. The scenes associated with the cloth business are dominated by men. The lower class labourers associated with the transport of the cloth are all men. Similarly, those involved in the buying and selling of the cloth are also exclusively male. Frustratingly, the only scene which might have hinted at women's work, the scene depicting the weaving of the cloth, has been too badly weathered. This is the lower relief on the

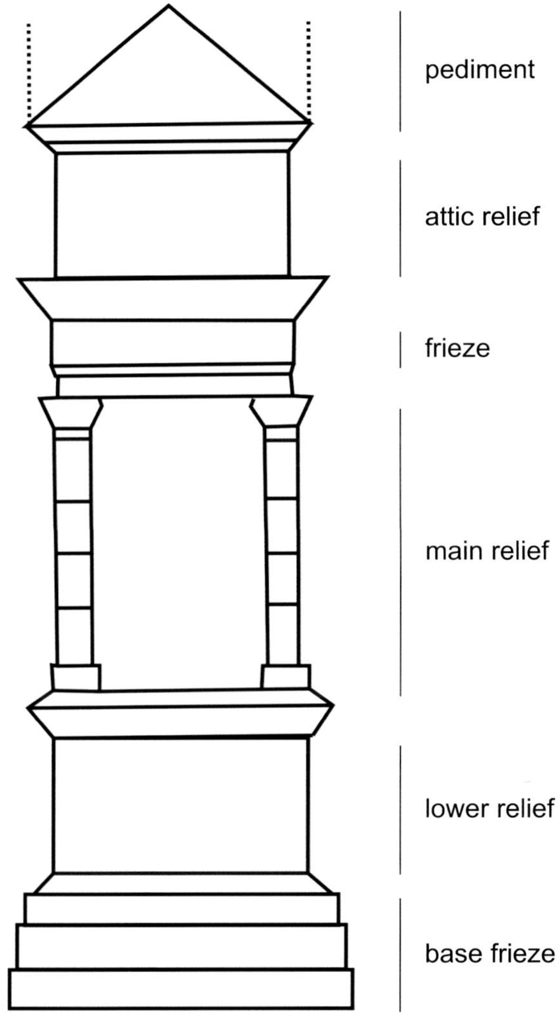

Figure 6.2 Schematic drawing of the Igel Tower, showing main iconographic zones; upper section is not shown (after Cüppers 1990, Abb. 309)

east side, and seems to show two figures, one seated beside an upright post, thought to be the upright of a loom, although this can only be a guess (Zahn 1968: 13). Even if this is correct, the relief is too badly worn to even guess at the gender of the weaver, and whether this was the one activity carried out by women. The scenes of domestic activity on the Igel tower are similarly dominated by active men: two panels relate to the preparation and serving of a meal, but the only woman present is the wife seated at the meal. Those serving the meal or busy in the kitchen, whether servants or slaves, all seem male. Throughout the iconography of the column, in the real-life scenes, the men are depicted in active roles, the women in passive. It is only in the mythological scenes that women are driving the narrative: Thetis dipping Achilles in the river Styx to ensure his immortality, and the nymphs snatching away Hylas.

This stereotype of active male and inactive female roles in repeated throughout the everyday scenes within the region (taken from Espérandieu 1907–81 vols 5 and 6). In these, scenes include cultivating of the soil, collecting agricultural produce, fulling and brick-making. A different social class is represented in a stock scene depicting a man or group of men, clustered around a table or counter which is covered in money. Most of these seem to come from wealthy funerary monuments, and depict the business activities from which the elite derived their wealth, and as such, show both their own labour, and also the labour of others. In terms of gender, the key point is that these activities are almost exclusively carried out by men, whether the agricultural activity of the lower classes, or the accounting transactions of the elite. Women appear predominantly in three forms of scene. The first of these is the main relief showing the family group of spouses with or without children, where the wives stand alongside their husbands, often holding a napkin (a *mappa*) and some type of casket. The other two are domestic scenes: banquets, where they are seated at a table with their husbands, and the toilet scene, where their hair is being dressed by one or more slaves, and they are sometimes looking at their own reflection in a mirror. Thus, as with the Igel tower, we see an idealisation of gender activities: the active male, economically productive (even if for someone else) and the passive woman, consuming that wealth through her leisure.

One objection to this reconstruction of gender activities is that these are idealised representations for a funerary context, generally commissioned by men, and so how representative of reality were they? However, as I argued at the beginning of this section, one problem is that the labour of women is often ignored or trivialised. Within these monuments, we see the erasure of possible women's activities. If women were tilling the fields alongside their men, this is not shown. Similarly, any contribution they make towards cloth production through weaving is not depicted (with the possible exception of the Igel tower); instead, scenes associated with cloth production show the fulling, transport, and selling of the cloth, activities apparently carried out by men. In contrast, women are displayed through their position within the family: they are shown as wives and mothers on the main portrait relief or as part of the family group in the banquet scenes. The alternative depiction is the so-called toilet scene, in reality usually the dressing of the hair. Within both forms of scene, we are seeing the process of downplaying women's labour, either through its erasure (in the case of the economic scenes) or through its trivialising (in the case of the toilet scenes). These images show how different values were placed on men's and women's activities, and a gender ideology which created inequalities. The activities which women were carrying out on a daily basis were presented as less economically important to the well-being of the family. Men were shown using coinage within the iconography, showing the importance attached to their economic activities. This is undoubtedly a dominant male ideology, but regardless of this, it suggests how gender differentiation was negotiated and gender hierarchies legitimised throughout the whole of society.

Gender and status

Whilst we can begin to construct something of the discourses through which gender identities were conceptualised and internalised, there is the danger that we begin to produce absolute categories of 'man' and 'woman'. In reality, such discourses were broadly based, and as gender intersected with other forms of identity, there was the possibility of playing with these discourses. We have already seen this in the case of the Romano-British male burials which included graves goods usually associated with women. Where gender intersected with rank, there were alternative models of self-representation available for women, suggesting different processes and discourses at play. For some less wealthy women, it is possible that the dominant modes of gender expression were not available to them. For example, of 1800 burials from Baldock in Britain, only just over 10% contain artefacts relating to personal adornment (Rosten 2007), so the picture of personal adornment being associated with gender may in reality have been possible to only a small proportion of the population. This does not mean that dress and adornment were not important for the formulation of gender identities for the women buried without jewellery. Rather ideologies and discourses often contain elements of aspiration rather than reality. Such women may have used similar practices, but with material which leaves no archaeological trace. Alternatively, they may have rejected these elements completely, as being only appropriate from women who were not required to contribute economically to the household.

This intersection between gender and rank is most evident in the case of elite women and women of wealth. Political magistracies were reserved for men, with one exception. At Rome, priesthoods were an integral part of a magisterial career, and from the time of the Republic, there were also positions reserved for women (Scheid 1992). The advent of the imperial cult brought with it a new group of priestesses, located outside of Rome in the towns and cities of Italy and the provinces. The evidence for those of the Latin West as a whole has been collected by Hemelrijk, and this has allowed a new perspective on the subject, countering some of the assumptions held about their roles and their religious authority (Hemelrijk 2005, 2006, 2007, 2009). She collected instances of over 250 inscriptions either dedicated to imperial priestesses, or set up by them (258 in Hemelrijk 2005, 260 in Hemelrijk 2006), and from these, argued that these offices were the counterpart of the male priesthoods of the imperial cult. A woman held the office in her own right, rather than as the spouse of a priest of the imperial cult, and seems to have usually officiated over the cult of the female members of the emperor's family. There were priestesses at both municipal and provincial level, although they seem to have been fewer in number than the male priesthoods. In Caesarobriga, for example, a statue was set up to Domitia Proculina the first municipal *flaminica* of Caesarobriga, and also provincial *flaminica* of Lusitania (CIL 2.895). Similarly Flavia Rufina was also *flaminica perpetua* of Merida and provincial priestess of Lusitania, as well as probably the *flaminica* of the local municipium of Salacia, given the location of the inscription (CIL 2.32; Delgado Delgado 1999, Rodríguez Cortés and Salinas de Frías 2010).

As with the male *sacerdotes* and *flamines*, they were elected by the local senate or provincial council, held office for a year (unless they became *perpetua* and held office for the rest of their lives), and were subject to *summa honoria* and benefactions. Hemelrijk also argues that they took an officiating role within cult activities (*contra* Scheid 1992), which probably consisted of offering incense, wine and sacrificial cakes rather than officiating over animal sacrifices. The priestesses were drawn from either the highest ranking families within the community, or from those of wealth. The analysis of the families of the priestesses reveals that when the rank is known, the majority are from decurial rank or above (Table 1). Over 50% do not give a social rank; these are usually assumed to be of elite birth due to the fact that they were elected to the priesthood. However, there is a danger of circularity in this argument, and Hemelrijk questions this:

> To conclude that, because of their priesthood, they must be of a high social rank, is begging the question. On the contrary, in view of the ancient habit of status-display the lack of status-indicators seems to point to a rather modest social standing. (Hemelrijk 2005: 159)

Instead, she proposes that these may be wealthy women who were not from the traditional elite, but who could use the priesthoods as a means of social promotion and prestige.

This ideology of the active male and the passive female can also be questioned for women of lower status. Kampen (1982) has pointed to a small group of reliefs which depict women taking an active role in selling as the main focus of the composition. She uses the example of the relief from Ostia showing a female vegetable vendor centrally placed, framed by the architecture of her shop, and surrounded by the vegetables she is selling. Her simple tunic marks her out as a non-elite woman, whilst her position and her gestures suggest that she is working within the shop rather than buying from it. In this, and other such depictions of saleswomen, the composition of the scene and the depiction of the seller are derived from that of male tradesmen. Here we see the appropriation of traits and behaviours normally gendered as male, but in this case, being used by the woman to emphasise her role as economically active. A similar relief has been discovered at Soulosse in Gallia Belgica (Espérandieu 1907–81: no. 4861): this is a poor quality stele, and shows a woman beside some form of wheeled stall, pointing to her merchandise on sale. The poor quality of the relief and the occupation of the woman suggest that she is not of elite rank. Depicting her professional role as a saleswoman is in marked contrast to the conventional representations of the women

Table 1. Social rank of imperial priestesses (data taken from Hemelrijk 2006, tables 1 and 2)

	municipal priestess	***provincial priestess***
senatorial	13	1
equestrian	24	4
decurial	50	11
lower class/freed family	8	0
unknown	117	8
total	212	24

from this region who, as we have seen, are generally depicted standing passively beside their husbands or having their hair dressed by (female) slaves, whilst absent from scenes of agricultural and cloth production. Although such depictions are rare, they raise questions about the impact of rank on gender roles. Kampen (1982) argues that vendors, male and female, occupied a social rank below the elite, but with more prosperity and autonomy than the poorest members of society since they or their families were able to afford these reliefs. Unlike other occupations at a similar social level, this was the only one where men and women worked together and in the same way, resulting in the job not being gendered in its iconography. It demonstrates a more complex interaction between gender and class which goes beyond elite and non-elite women.

Both the saleswoman and the priestess were able to play with gender ideals, and blur the boundaries as a way to claim social prestige for themselves in a way which was not usually open to women. The normalising ideology was of the active male and passive female, but this masks specific groups who were able to subvert this. This does not mean that other groups of women were not able to do so, and there is a need for work to investigate this. Epigraphic evidence from the city of Rome points to a wider pool of economically active women, many of them slaves and ex-slaves, with occupations largely in domestic service and manufacture (Treggiari 1976, Joshel 1992). This adds a level of complexity to the study of women of the provinces, and breaks apart the ideal of an homogenous construction of gender identities.

Gender and the imperial context

Conquest by Rome had the potential to disrupt gender relations, a topic which has yet to be fully examined from the archaeological evidence (Revell 2010b). Yvonne Marshall (2008) has argued that the examination of cultural change from a gender perspective has the potential to make a wider contribution to feminist scholarship. For example, Wylie has claimed that androcentrism pervades study of the emergence of agriculture, which renders women as passive recipients of change, and men as innovators (Wylie 1992: 22–5), whilst Hastorf (1991) has argued that as pre-Hispanic Andean communities came under Inca control, women's involvement in the production and consumption of certain foodstuffs was reduced, resulting in a diminution of their social authority. This is not to say that women have been totally absent from all accounts of Roman imperialism, and contrasting interpretations of the impact of conquest on their roles have been offered for Roman Britain. Millett argues that as a result of sexual interaction with Roman soldiers, native women could have played an active role in the Romanization of the rest of the society, making them drivers of cultural change (Millett 1990a: 60). In contrast, Mattingly focuses on the possible violence extended towards women, and their potential disempowerment (Mattingly 2011: 94–121). Woolf has acknowledged that conquest and changing cultural discourses had the potential to change ideas of masculinity (Woolf 1998: ix), but without mentioning possible changes for women.

Nevertheless, it is inaccurate to argue that the disruption to gender relations took the same form throughout the western provinces. For example, areas with a high level of army recruitment may have seen the production of different gender relations to those elsewhere in the provinces. We looked at the evidence for Batavia earlier, but this can also be seen in north-western Iberia. It has been estimated that at least 15,180 men were recruited as auxiliary soldiers, and there is also evidence for recruitment from the local towns into the legions and the Praetorian Cohorts (Millett 2001). In contrast to Batavia, there is a strong likelihood that these men never returned home once discharged. If a sizeable proportion of the young men left the area and did not return, this would have impacted on the overall gender make-up of the community. If there was a sizeable number of unmarried women, what was their role and status within their families and the wider society? It may have increased the prominence and authority of women overall, but on the other hand the (presumably) higher incidence of unmarried women may have created a hierarchy between married and unmarried. In instances where women and families accompanied the soldiers, they would have been thrown into a completely new society, with norms of masculinity now based on military action, and potential new models of femininity to carve out.

A further consequence of the impact of imperialism on gender relations may have been that one gender became the keepers of traditional practices within a changing environment. Thus, for example, in Este in northern Italy, women maintained their traditional families names whilst men adopted Roman-style ones (David 1996: 137). David argued that this was part of the rejection of Roman family hierarchies and the overwhelming power of the paterfamilias, and the concept of resistance is repeated in Perego's (2012) study of continuity of the late prehistoric ritual of bone-mingling into the Roman period in the same region. Nevertheless, resistance and conservatism are different phenomenon, and given the adoption of Latin in the inscriptions used as evidence by both authors, we are seeing a more complex form of cultural identification. It is often assumed that women were the keepers of traditional styles and norms, whilst men adopted the new cultural forms, but the work of Rothe (2009) on dress styles in the Rhine region warns against making this assumption. She takes a very localised approach, and demonstrates that it is variable as to whether men or women acted as guardians of tradition. In the rural area of the Treveri territory, women were more likely than men to adopt Roman dress, whereas in the territory of the Ubii, women retained their traditional costume, whilst men adopted the Gallic ensemble. Rothe suggests that this may be the result of different attitudes towards gender between the two areas: whether women acted as conservators of tradition or as displaying the family's status and wealth (*ibid.*: 69–92; see also Rothe 2013). Whether this is the case or not, it warns against making blanket assumptions about the impact of Roman imperialism on the gender relations of subject communities. Instead, we need more local case-studies from a wider range of regions in order to fully understand the relationship between conquest, cultural change and changing discourses of gender.

Chapter 7

Age and Ageing

Introduction

The final category of social identity I want to consider is age. This is probably the most under-studied and under-theorised aspect of identity within archaeology as a whole, and this also holds true for Roman archaeology. It reflects a wider neglect of age within social sciences, where the adult was taken as the norm, the idea of the child unproblematised, and the elderly ignored. Nevertheless, this has changed, largely as a result of the feminist agenda decentring the assumed adult male as the object of study, and consequently, there has been a growing academic literature on childhood (Jenks 1996). At the same time, gerontology has emerged as an important academic discipline due to the changing demographic profile of the west as a result of the aging of the baby boom generation and the questions this has posed for political systems (Arber and Ginn 1995). Archaeology has not been impervious to these changes, and so there has been a growing interest to childhood, and to a lesser extent, the elderly (Moore and Scott 1997, Sofaer Derevenski 2000a).

These developments have also been seen in Roman archaeology and ancient history. As discussed in Chapter 1, the emergence of the family as a key research topic has included work on children and their roles within the family, emotional attachment to them, and their relationships with relatives and other care-givers. There has been less research into age and aging in the western provinces outside of Italy, with epigraphy and iconography providing much of the data. In the last two decades, the analysis of osteological evidence has provided a new avenue into the question of children and age. Much of this work has been explicitly tied into the ideas of age identities. As the wider literature on age has become more sophisticated, and in particular, drawing on ideas from a variety of academic disciplines, the theoretical literature on age has become more questioning. In this chapter, I want to begin with an overview of some of the key ideas within this, and in particular, why we need to talk about age and aging as two different elements within the topic, before exploring this from the archaeological evidence.

Continuum and category

It is tempting to take age as a non-problematic phenomenon. The elapse of time through life can be measured, and from this, a numerical marker appointed signifying the age of an individual. However, identity is rarely this simple, and work on age and aging within the social sciences has demonstrated such complexities. Unlike other aspects of identity, such as gender or ethnicity, age identities are by their very nature expected to change during a person's life. It is this process of transformation which means that there are two complementary approaches to the study of age and aging (Gowland 2006). The first is the study of the life course, that is the movement through different categories of age identities throughout the life of an individual person, the rituals used to mark such transitions and how these might be affected by other aspects of identity, most particularly gender (Sofaer Derevenski 2000b, Harlow and Laurence 2002). The second approach has focused on the age groupings themselves: the categories of age identities within a specific cultural context, and the behaviours and material culture associated with them. Work on age categories has tended to focus on childhood, countering the dominance of the adult (Lillehammer 1996, Scott 1999, Sofaer Derevenski 2000a, Baxter 2005), whilst literature on the elderly is more limited (Appleby 2010). Adulthood has been largely ignored, leaving this stage still considered as normative and not in need of problematizing.

One problem with age is that of definition, and the influence of the tripartite division of chronological, physiological and social age. In the modern world, we generally focus on chronological age as the measurement for a life, that is, the time elapsed from birth, expressed through years, months and days. However, the aging of the body does not always conform to this and physiological age can be culturally variable, such as differences in onset of the menarche. Finally, social attitudes to age do not necessarily agree with either. The linkages between these three aspects has been critiqued by Jo Sofaer, who argues that archaeology has yet to work out how to integrate these various elements (Sofaer 2011). She further argues that these do not encompass the entirety of age categories, as illustrated by the development of the concept of behavioural age in developmental psychology, and functional age in anthropology. As with all other categories of identity, age identities are not universal, and will vary depending on the social context. For example, the age at which a person progresses from childhood at adulthood may not only occur at different points, but may be identified through different types of age. It may be marked by a physiological transition, such as the first shaving of a boy or menarche in a girl, or it might be a social transition, such as marriage or apprenticeship, or chronological, such as 18 years having elapsed since birth.

Whilst initially much of the work on age in archaeology and ancient history focused on specific age categories particularly childhood, in the last two decades the idea of the life course has gained prominence. Spencer (1990) has argued that the life course allows ageing to be seen as a social process, with age becoming a changing and ambiguous element. The life course consists of a series of roles and perspectives appropriate to each age which creates an ideology of correct behaviours. The transformation from one stage to another requires the acquisition of new behaviours and materials, but also the realignment of existing relationships as the individual moves from one age-group to another. Specific rites may mark the transition, making it clear that the individual now has a new social role due to their increased maturity. Archaeology has used this concept as a way to understand age identities: investigating the variation in how different societies divide the life course, and the ways differences in material culture assemblages were used to mark the transitions (Gowland 2006). Of particular interest has been the intersection between age and gender (Sofaer Derevenski 2000b, Gowland 2001), and the point at which a gendered identity becomes apparent. Also relevant, although less studied, is the impact of status or rank on the life-course. Thus we have begun to identify the variability in the social concepts of aging and age transitions.

The life course: (i) the epigraphic evidence

One tantalising form of evidence for understanding the life course in the Roman world is the large collection of written memorials to the dead. With the explicit statement of the (apparent) age of the deceased, they have long been regarded as a key source of evidence in reconstructing the demographic profile of the Roman population, in particular, average ages of marriage and death. In reality, they have proved something of a *faux ami*; as Keith Hopkins has argued, "Roman tombstones provide us with a biassed [*sic*] set of commemorations" (Hopkins 1987: 115). Amongst the forms of bias he identifies is age bias, i.e. that some forms of age are represented more frequently than others. This goes beyond the practice of rounding to numbers ending in five or zero (Duncan-Jones 1977, Duncan-Jones 1990). Hopkins (Hopkins 1966, 1983, 1987) has demonstrated that the profile of ages recorded does not match the profile expected from modern mortality tables, as there are relatively few inscriptions commemorating the very young and the elderly. Furthermore, although the mean age at death seems reasonable, generally between 20 and 30 years old for Rome and Italy, any confidence is undermined by the variation between this and the average recorded in the provinces: in North Africa, for example, age-statements on epitaphs give average age at death as 48.7 years for men and 46.6 for women. Attributing this to the idea of exceptionally healthy living conditions (e.g. Sallust *Jug.* 17.6) is disingenuous. Instead, the commemoration of age on epitaphs is subject to wider social ideologies. The result of this is the widespread agreement that age-statements are not an accurate picture of the age profile of the population.

Whilst epitaphs with age-statements may be of limited use for the study of demography, they are more profitable for the study of identity, as the bias Hopkins complains of can be used to understand ideologies of age. Age is not recorded on the majority of tombstones: Hopkins (1987) gives the figure of 43,000 out of 180,000 epitaphs, whilst Shaw revises this to 55,000 inscriptions (1991). Elsewhere I have argued that this absence of age-statements is the product of age ideology (Revell 2005): age is more likely to be recorded in circumstances where it is believed to be significant by the commemorators. The profile of age-statements does not represent the expected range of age at death, and in a worse case-scenario, may not even be representative of those who receive epitaphs without age-statements. In certain individual cases, age at death may have been recorded because it was of special significance to the family, such as dying at an older age than a parent or sibling. However, over a larger group, the overall trend will reflect the attitudes of the wider community to age. From these trends, we can reconstruct ideologies of the life course, and the specific stages within the life of an individual which were considered of particular consequence. Calculating the 5 or 10 year age stages when age was most likely to be mentioned can allow us to identify which ages were considered particularly important and worthy of commemoration. It is also possible to examine the intersection between age and gender, as separate profiles for men and women can be generated. The gender bias of more men than women receiving epitaphs can be countered by calculating each age stage as a percentage of the total for the particular gender, rather than as a percentage of the assemblage as a whole.

This methodology was tested by analysing the life course in central Italy, and showed a marked profile for both men and women (Figure 7.1). The epitaphs with age statements from *regiones* 4 (Samnium), 5 (Picenum) and 6 (Umbria) demonstrate a clear clustering, with age-statements most likely to be recorded when the deceased was 30 years old or less (83% of the total number of age-statements). There is a slight difference by the gender, with a slightly higher percentage for women than for men (87.7% for women, 80.7% for men). This peak is not accounted for by high infant mortality rates, as the percentage which gives an age at death of 5 years or less is relatively low (10.7%). Instead, the peak in commemoration of age is for those who die between the ages of 15 and 30 years. It should be reiterated that this is unlikely to represent either mortality rates or the distribution of epitaphs as a whole (i.e. including those without age-statements). Instead, it should be taken as demonstrating

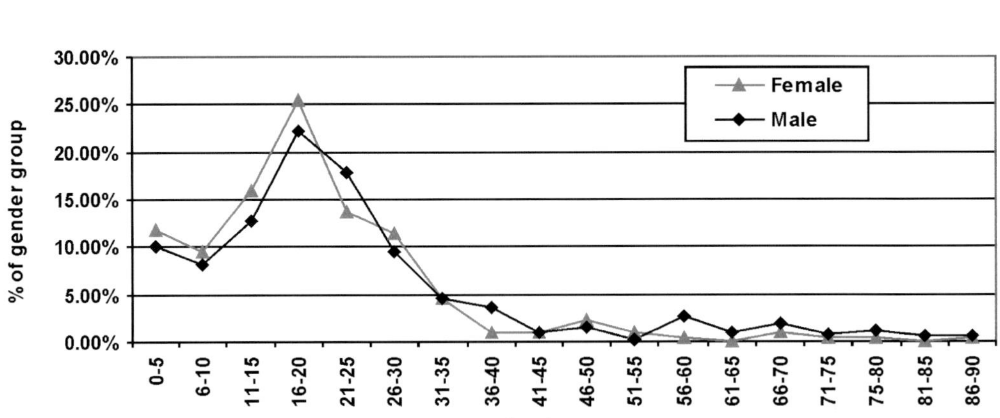

Figure 7.1 Distribution of ages recorded on epitaphs by age group from regiones 4,5 and 6, Italy (n=634; males=414, females=220)

that this is when age at death had particular significance. The profile for men and women is slightly different, with peaks for both in the 16–20 age group, but then a sharper decline for women in their 20s and early 30s.

This profile for central Italy ties in with the textual evidence for the life course, and in particular, the differences in the transition from childhood to adulthood for girls and boys (Wiedemann 1989, Laurence 2000, Harlow and Laurence 2002). The male transition was marked through the staged entry into life as a citizen, with the change in dress from the *toga praetexta* to the *toga virilis* at the age of 14–16 years, and eligibility for military service from the age of 16–18 years. This marked a period of adolescence until the age of 25, when a man was able to take an active role in politics, and would expect to marry. In contrast, a woman's life-course was measured through her role as wife and mother, with the transition from child to adult occurring at marriage in the late teens, and with no intermediate adolescent stage. This suggests that death before the age of 30 years was commemorated as a life which had failed to meet its full potential: that the age of the deceased should be mentioned as more poignant because they had died as or just after they had crossed the transition into adulthood (Martin-Kilcher 2000). The approximately five year difference in this transition for men and women reflects the difference in average age at marriage discussed in the previous chapter. Therefore the slight difference in the age-statement profile for men and women can be explained through the different ages in which men and women would expect to reach full adult status.

The evidence from central Italy demonstrates a very clear profile which can be matched to the evidence we know from Rome itself. This raises the question of whether we see the same ideologies of age being commemorated within the western provinces. We should not necessarily expect this to be the case, as even in central Italy commemoration of age in Etruria and Tarquinia shows different attitudes to age, which may represent continuity from the pre-conquest period. In Etruria overall (*regio* 7), the transition at 30 years is less pronounced, and in the inscriptions from Tarquinia the distribution shows peaks in the late 20s and the 50s (discussed in greater detail in Revell 2005). The profile from Tarquinia matches the pre-conquest Etruscan languages epitaphs (Nielsen 1989), leading to the conclusion that although the mode of commemoration had changed, the underlying age identities had not. Therefore, turning to the evidence from the western provinces, we can expect to see a complex picture of cultural change at play.

Latin epitaphs were adopted as one form of funerary commemoration, demonstrating a change in the social practices associated with the commemoration of the deceased, and the inclusion of age-statements suggests the epitaph may have become a new way of maintaining age identities. However, as we saw with gender, this does not necessarily mean that the underlying structures of the life course followed the patterns seen in central Italy, or indicated through the textual sources. In fact, the evidence from two case studies suggests different reactions to Roman ideas of structuring the life-course. In the case of the province of Narbonensis, we see a similar pattern of age commemoration to that in central Italy (Figure 7.2). There is a marked emphasis on stating the age of those who died under the age of 30 years, with 85.97% of total age statements referring to those 30 years old or less. Again there are subtle differences to the profile from central Italy. As a percentage of the overall distribution, ages are given more frequently for those 10 and under, and we see the continued mention of women's ages into their early 20s. Nevertheless, we can potentially identify similar ideologies of age in southern France to those seen in central Italy, with the death acquiring additional poignancy for those who were either about to, or who had just crossed the threshold into adulthood.

As with gender, we see different patterns of age commemoration emerging in Iberia. In this case, rather than a whole province, data were taken for the *Conventus Cordubensis* in the southern province of Baetica (Figure 7.3). Here, there is not the same concentration on the young adults: the proportion of those aged 30 or under being commemorated with age statements is much lower at 47.55%. There is still an emphasis on age at death of those in their late teens and early 20s, but it is less pronounced than in other cases. Age at death continues to be mentioned throughout the rest of the life, with a slight peak for men in their 50s having age at death included in their epitaph. This points to different attitudes to age, and potentially, the various stages in the life-course being valued differently. This may not be restricted to Baetica, as data from the modern region of Salamanca in Lusitania similarly shows a variation from the pattern in central Italy (data taken from Edmondson 2005). This also shows a less pronounced preference for mentioning the ages of those 30 years and under, and continued commemoration for those older. In this case, there is a second peak

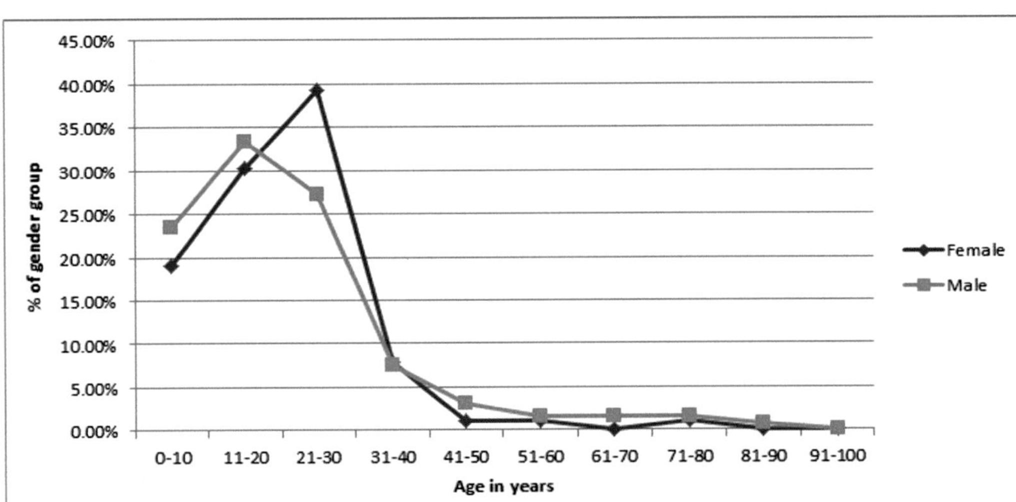

Figure 7.2 Distribution of ages recorded on epitaphs by age group from Narbonensis (n=221; males=132, females=89)

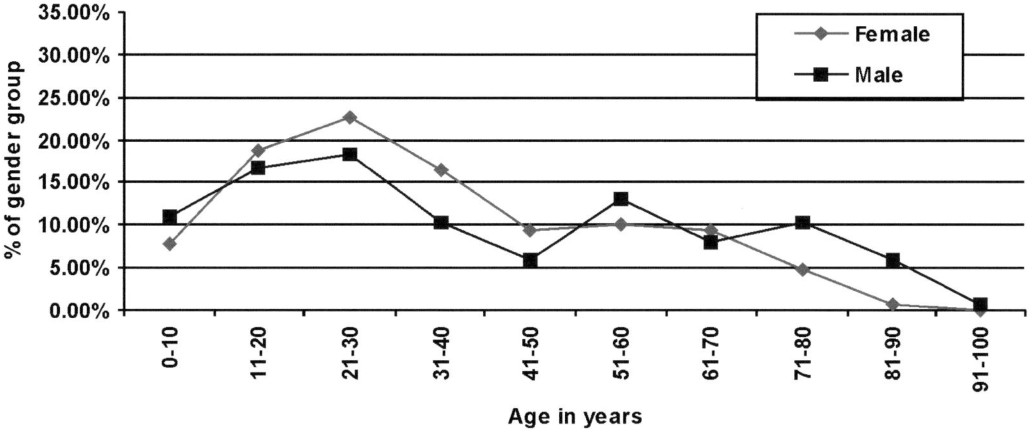

Figure 7.3 Distribution of ages recorded on epitaphs by age group from Conventus Cordobensis, Baetica (n=265; males=137, females=128)

in the inclusion of age for those dying in their 50s, more pronounced than that seen at Cordubensis.

This difference in commemoration of age suggests that a different attitude to those dying at a later stage in the life-course: not only that they were considered worthy of an epitaph, but that the inclusion of their age at death fulfilled some form of social need. It is impossible to know whether this represents a continuity of pre-Roman attitudes to age, as although there are Iberian inscriptions from the pre-conquest period, they are few in number and do not record ages at death. However, it may be connected to the differences in family structures in Iberia which we identified in the previous chapter, with the parental family maintaining a greater significance in the lives of its offspring, and consequently the attitudes to their aging process reflecting this. Nevertheless, these differences do indicate that within the social changes which occurred as part of Roman imperialism, changes in attitudes to age did not necessarily form part of them. It is particularly striking that this is the case for Baetica, usually considered to be one of the more Romanized provinces in the western empire.

The life course: (ii) the burial evidence

A second means used by archaeologists to reconstruct the life-course has been the burial data: that is differences in the treatment and grave goods associated with sexed and aged skeletal remains. As with the case of epitaphs, it relies upon the assumption that as an individual passes through the various stages of the life course, this will be marked by the treatment of the individual at death. In this case, the analysis is generally based on the ageing and sexing of the skeleton or cremated remains, and identifying social differentiation through the differences in, for example, quantity and type of grave goods, or position of the body. While the grave goods are those deposited by the mourners and so show their expectations rather than the realities of the life of the deceased, they do allow us to understand something of the social norms through which identities were formed.

The Roman cemetery at Brougham in the north of England gives some indication of how age and gender might lead to differences in the rituals thought appropriate from the preparation and presentation of the body through to the cremation and act of deposition (Cool *et al.* 2004, in particular 437–62). Most of the bodies seem to have been dressed for the burial, rather than encased in shrouds. Certain items were associated with adults only, most notably shoes as represented by the remains of hob-nails. Children either wore no shoes, or alternatively single piece shoes which required no nails. Also, adults seem to have been carried to the pyre on a bier decorated with bone inlays, as remains of these have been found amongst the pyre debris incorporated within the grave. There is a possibility that the pyres of women and juveniles were constructed of birch, whilst those of adult men of alder, although this interpretation is tentative. Different pyre goods were offered according to the age of the deceased: military equipment, figurines and metal vessels are only found with adults. The lack of animal bone found with children's remains points to different food offerings according to age: children were either not furnished with meat, or were offered different cuts. The final element of age differentiation was the choice of items placed within the grave. Certain vessel types were associated with specific ages: small Samian cups with children under the age of 8 years, deep samian bowls with adults.

This process of differentiating the various stages of the life course can also be seen at the Gallo-Roman cemetery at Champ de l'Image (Allain *et al.* 1992). The dominant ritual for cremation burials was to place the remains within a lidded urn, with one or two other vessels as grave goods. In the case of babies and infants, glass and sigillata vessels were used as the receptacle for the body. This is echoed in the use of glass and sigillata vessels as grave goods for babies and infants. However, in the case of grave goods, the use of these vessels is not restricted to the very young: such vessels are also found in the graves of women, but never in those of men. This overlap in the categories of child and adult females is not an isolated instance, but understanding its significance is more difficult. It raises the question of whether the use of similar forms of grave goods for children and adult women points to them being subject to social ideologies which considered them equivalent. One possibility could be that it signalled the dependence of both groups on the adult male. Alternatively, this could be seen as the normative rite, whilst adult men were marked out through the use of a different vessel form, carinated urns, which were never found in female graves in this cemetery.

An additional means of age differentiation in funerary practices is through the choice of cremation or inhumation for the deceased. As will be discussed below in greater detail, very young children were generally not cremated before burial, and these burials were often further differentiated through the location chosen for the grave. We also see this at Champ de l'Image. The majority of those up to the age of two years were not cremated, unlike the rest of the cemetery population, and instead were buried in the western part of the cemetery. There was a small number of exceptions to this: six infants under the age of 2 years were cremated, and their remains were buried within the adult zone, suggesting that they were deemed to have made the transition from the first stage of the life course. However, there were also two further non-cremated inhumations of older children: one was aged 2–6 years, and the second 10–12 years, both of which were placed in the western part of the cemetery with the infant burials. The rejection of the usual form of funerary treatment for these two individuals suggests that they were seen as being in some way different to the rest of their age cohorts. What this difference might be is unclear: whether it was due to disability, the cause of death, or the intersection with another element of their identity. Nevertheless, the blurring of absolute boundaries at Champ de l'Image points to the complexity of the choices in the deposition of the body, and the way in which the life stages may be used as a metaphor to signal other aspects of identity, as has already seen in the case of gender identities.

Whilst both Brougham and Champ de l'Image point to the importance of age in structuring difference within the burial assemblages, one issue with reconstructing the life-course is how far this is based on predefined life-stages, with the analysis focusing on the means of differentiation rather than the more fundamental question of whether these life-stages were applicable to the society under investigation. Human skeletal reports often give ages as categories, such as infant, child, adult and elderly adult, rather than absolute age at death. Whilst this is in part due to difficulties in accurately aging skeletal remains, it can obscure the cultural variability in the age when the transition from one age category to another takes place (Gowland 2006). To illustrate this problem, Sally Crawford (2000) has argued that in early Anglo-Saxon England, the child-adult transition occurs at the age of 10–12 years rather than in the late teens as usually assumed. In certain cemetery reports, a number of anomalous child burials were identified by the excavators: burials considered to be children under modern categorisation, but which were buried with adult grave goods, such as full-size spearheads. These anomalous burials were aged 10–12 or slightly older, suggesting that the transition from childhood to adulthood occurred at a younger age than assumed. This argument is supported by Anglo-Saxon law codes which regarded 10 year olds as adults under certain circumstances. Understanding age transitions during the life-course is hindered if it is assumed that the age thresholds are the same as those for modern, western societies.

Furthermore, this application of broad, modern categories obscures the possibility of additional age stages within the broader groupings of child and adult. Gowland's (2001) reanalysis of the 4th century cemetery at Lankhills, Winchester points to a greater complexity within the simplistic category of child. She points to differences within the period usually considered as childhood based upon fluctuating numbers of grave goods. At the age of 4 years, there is an increase in the average numbers of grave goods accompanying the body, and gender specific grave goods, such as bracelets and necklaces, also begin to be deposited with the body. This increases until the age of 12 years, when there is a considerable drop in grave goods. Differences in age groupings and the social process of aging between the modern and Roman worlds are also evident in the textual sources. In their study of the life-course in Rome, Harlow and Laurence (2002) argue that childhood had several stages, such as the period of *infantia* up to the age of 7 years (Harlow and Laurence 2002: 35–7), and for boys, there was the additional phase of adolescence between the ages of approximately 17 and 25 (*ibid*.: 65–78). Such sub-groups are rendered invisible when wider categories are used in aging skeletal remains in excavation reports.

The very young – joining the community

While the points of transition, and the variability within them, provide one means to understand the archaeology of age, a second element is the characteristics of the specific age categories: the expected behaviours and the value assigned to them. The first of these is the point when the individual is seen as having a social identity. Within the modern world, this is a fuzzy boundary: the moment of birth is an obvious point, but increasingly, this may be seen as being before birth, whether as a result of parental emotion and attachment to the child, or as a result of religious belief (Hockey and Draper 2005). This fuzziness could be assigned to an uncertainty over the point when a foetus is seen as having either an individuality (be it personality or soul), or a connection with other members of the community, in particular, the parents. These uncertainties are equally present when looking at past societies. The assumption that the individual takes on a social identity and becomes part of the community at birth is problematic: there may be a liminal stage between birth and full integration. In societies with a high infant mortality rate, there is a question of how neonates were considered in respect to the overall community. It has been framed in terms of emotional attachment to very young children (Golden 1988), but this is to impose modern attitudes onto a very different social and demographic context. Furthermore, it potentially misunderstands the nature of the evidence. As we shall see, whilst the very young are not necessarily accorded the wider burial customs, this does not necessarily mean they are less valued. Can we see a different burial custom at play for the very young, and from that can we begin to understand what that means for the social identity of these infants?

This seems to be the case both in elite society at Rome and within the provinces, as demonstrated by both the textual and the archaeological evidence respectively (Pearce 2001, Harlow and Laurence 2002). Within the textual sources, there is an expectation that the treatment of the neonate will be different to that of older infants. There was an idea that a very young child should not receive the same funerary treatment as the rest of society. Both Pliny and Juvenal refer to the belief that they should not be cremated, as was the contemporary custom for the rest of the population, but instead should be buried (Pliny *NH* 7.15.72; Juv. *Sat.* 15.138-40). How long this stage lasted is unclear: Pliny states that the custom extended until the child cut their teeth, whilst Fulgentius, in Late Antiquity, said that the treatment of the body was different until the child was 40 days old (Fulgentius *Expositio sermonum antiquorum* 7). Together these point to the idea of a transition in identity at some point during the first year after birth, but possibly that the point of the transition was somewhat flexible, particularly as Pliny's criterion is tied into a physiological event rather than a chronological age. Fulgentius also refers to the burial places of infants as *suggrandaria*, a term which is problematic to translate, but refers to a domestic context of some kind (Pearce 2001: 126–7). This is in contrast to adult burials in formal cemetery contexts outside the boundaries of the settlement. Thus, we have a situation in the textual evidence of a change in treatment of the body and the place of its deposition at some point very early in the first year of life.

This idea of a differentiation between neonates and other infants can also be seen within the archaeological evidence. We have already seen this in the case of Champ de l'Aude, where the very young were buried in a different way to the rest of the cemetery population, and this can be seen in other cemeteries. However, the most notable characteristic is the general lack of young infants within formal cemeteries. Pearce has analysed the evidence from southern Britain, sampling cemeteries with more than 40 burials (Pearce 2001: 134–6, table 11.2). In late Iron Age and early Roman cemeteries, the dominant rite is cremation. However, the very young are generally inhumed, and are fewer in number than we would expect (typically 1–2%). Numbers increase in the 3rd and 4th centuries AD, but still remain a small proportion. In other places, we find what seem to be infant-only cemeteries, such as at Barton Court Farm, where the excavation of the villa and the surrounding paddock systems produced over 54 infant burials from the Iron Age to the Saxon period (Miles 1984). Of the datable examples, the majority can be attributed to the later Roman empire, when a dedicated infant cemetery was set up in the corner of one of the paddocks. Here there was a group of at least 26 infants, the majority of them new-born. There were no burials on the site of individuals over the age of one year from the Roman period (although there were adult burials from both pre- and post-Roman periods). Instead, the rest of the occupants of the farmstead were probably buried in a small cemetery found 800m away. In addition, there is a further level of differentiation within the infant burials. Three of these burials were found with animal skulls and buried within more substantial graves. It is almost certainly relevant that two of these were slightly older than the rest of the infants in the cemetery, although not older than nine months. A further neonatal infant burial was found in the farmhouse, buried in a stone-lined cist.

The under-representation of the very young in formal, mixed cemeteries is mirrored by the frequency of infant inhumation within domestic contexts, where the burials of older children and adults dating to the Roman period are rarely found. In Britain, for example, the excavation of villas and farmsteads frequently reveals the burial of infants within the settlement boundaries, seeming to contravene the prohibition on burial within settlements (Philpott 1991: 97–102, Moore 2009). A typical example of this is Rockbourne villa, where four infant burials were discovered associated with specific buildings: two within the main house (one of which was associated with a hypocaust), one near a well, and the fourth just outside an agricultural building. Similar patterns can be seen at the roadside settlement of Shiptonthorpe, East Yorkshire (Millett 2006, Millett and Gowland 2015). Here, a group of between 11 and 15 perinatal infants (38–41 weeks gestation age) was excavated from a single, multi-phased property. All were inhumations. Some were associated with the house: one in the centre of the late 2nd–early 3rd century structure, and seven burials representing eight individuals in the later large, hall-like structure. Others were associated with a water hole, gullies and ditches. The lack of inhumations over 41 weeks (gestational age) is notable: the other human remains from the site come from two cremation burials, both containing at least two individuals, and in both cases, one of these was a child. For the people of this community, there was a clear distinction between the burial of infants who were stillborn or died at or just after birth, and older children.

This distinct treatment of very young infants is not confined to Britain, and has been noted in other provinces in the western empire. In Gaul, at the potters' complex at Sallèles-d'Aude, a series of infant inhumations were discovered within the production area (Duday *et al.* 1995). This potters' complex covered 3ha, and represented the activity of a number of families. The lack of non-infant burials within the residential area points to a separation between space for the living and dead, although a formal cemetery has yet to be found. However, a group of 12 infant inhumations were discovered within a building which had been a pottery kiln, but which was no longer used for the purpose, although it may have retained a production role of some kind. The burials were discovered around the edges of a single room built into the original room, and consisted of a simple trench, with all but one partially or completely covered by tile, and the majority without grave goods (Figure 7.4). This group dated to the second half of the 1st century AD. Eleven of the 12 were very young, possibly no more than 3 months old. However, there is one slightly older burial (6–9 months) which was given a different burial rite: the body was placed in a tile box with a relatively rich array of grave goods: a glass vessel, two ceramic vessels, a lamp, and a single bead. This last case points to the complexity of the attitudes towards aged burial: for whatever reason, it was deemed appropriate to bury this child along with the stillborn and very young, but its slightly longer life-span dictated that a different burial style was required.

The archaeological evidence from Britain and Gaul shows the same attitudes as the textual sources from Rome. The analysis of all published burials of infants from domestic contexts in Roman Britain shows that in total, the age range was wider than in these examples: from late foetal infants (29–30 weeks gestation age), to three years (Moore 2009). Nevertheless, it still demonstrated a clear clustering around the first month after birth. This points to a level of differentiation for the very young, and that childhood or even infancy did not form a single, uniform age group. For stillborn

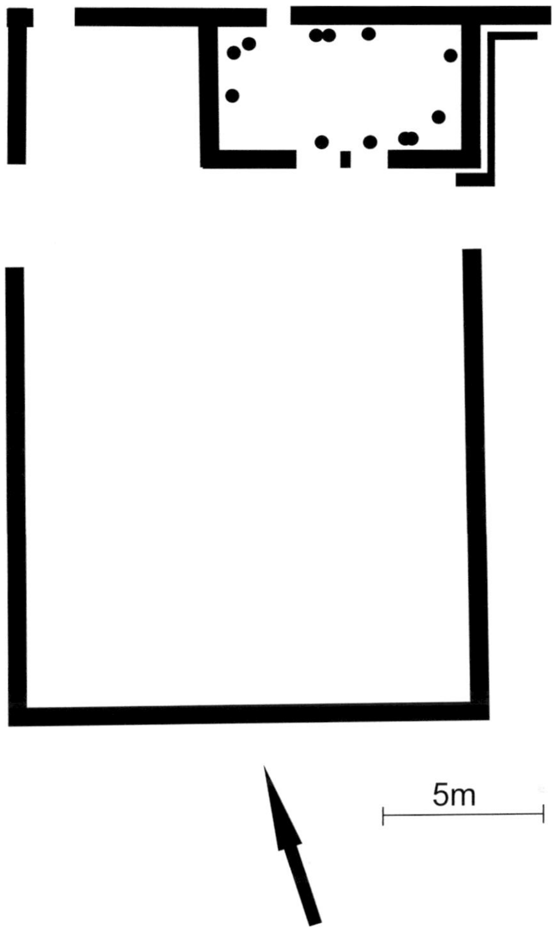

Figure 7.4 Approximate location of neonatal and infant burials, building 3, phase 2, Sallèles d'Aude; position of burials indicated by circles (adapted from Duday et al. 1995, fig. 8)

infants and those who died in the first months after birth, the difference in burial rite was part of the construction of their social difference. The idea that it was not taboo to bury them within a settlement, unlike the treatment for the rest of society, was part of the way in which their difference was reaffirmed. For most, after the first month after birth, they passed into a different social category, at which point the dominant burial custom became the norm. However, the older individuals suggest that for some reason they did not make the transition, or that due to another aspect of their identity, or some event in their life-course, it was considered more appropriate to bury them in the same way as the very young.

Whilst identifying this age-group within the archaeological record is relatively unproblematic, the same cannot be said for understanding the way in which this group was viewed. In early accounts of phenomenon there was a tendency to see their burial as the discarding of unwanted children, whether due to illegitimacy or the lowly social status of the mother. This has then led to the question of infanticide: whether these infants died of natural causes, or were killed (Mays 1993, Faerman *et al.* 1998, Mays 2000, Scott 2001, Gowland and Chamberlain 2002, Lewis 2011). This has proved a problematic and controversial interpretation of these unusual burials. Mays (1993) has proposed a methodology of identifying groups of infanticide burials through the analysis of the age profile. Based on ethnographic and anthropological parallels, he advocates the hypothesis that if the age profile clusters at the 40 week gestation period, then the death was the result of infanticide, whereas a wider age-profile was the product of natural deaths. However there has been some debate about the osteological and statistical techniques involved in the aging of the skeletal remains (Gowland and Chamberlain 2002), and a re-evaluation of the same material has argued for a wider range profile. The re-examination of the Hambledon infants using multiple techniques has led to conclusion that this was the product of infanticide (Mays and Eyers 2011). However, this is a very unusual group: the number of bodies collected together is very large, and the clustering at the time of birth, if accurate, is unusual. Whether the interpretation of this one group can then be applied to all infant burials is dubious: although some of these infant burials may have been due to infanticide, it does not necessarily explain all of them.

Alternative interpretations of this phenomenon in Roman Britain have rejected the idea of infanticide and instead focussed on associations between children and spiritual belief. Eleanor Scott (1991), for example, has argued that similarities between the burial of the very young and the deposition of animal burials points to an association with wider ritual practices which date back to the pre-conquest period. She argues that the burial of the very young forms part of a revitalization of pre-conquest religion, and that the connection between the burials and places of agricultural production (such as malting floors and corn driers) symbolises an association with fertility. She sees these rituals as controlled by women, and part of fourth century shifts in gender relations with women using such rituals as part of an attempt to gain greater control of agricultural production. Watts (1989) also argues for a religious interpretation as the explanation for an apparent greater visibility of the very young in 4th century cemeteries, but instead attributes it to the rise of Christianity and a greater reverence for children. In contrast, Moore (2009) argues that the lack of unity in the precise detail of the infant burial makes any single interpretation impossible. Instead, she focusses on the very early age as the common denominator: that these were infants on the cusp of life, and as such, were transitional beings. This allowed them to be used to negotiate ambiguous elements of life, moments which could be subject to danger. An association with fire (through hearths and bath-houses) could make them either benign or dangerous, and their association with liminal places similarly points to a potential uncertainty over their power. This special ritualised treatment of these infants warns against seeing them as unwanted, as in many cases there is evidence for care being taken over the burial. The uniformity over time in how they were to be treated in death suggests this was part of the wider social idea that they were seen as different, and that this difference could be used as a means to negotiate other aspects of life and its uncertainties.

Childhood

Following this period of very young infancy, the next identifiable age-group within an individual's life-course was that of the child. Archaeological interest in childhood developed in the 1990s, with the publication of a group of edited volumes containing a series of significant papers (Moore and Scott 1997, Sofaer Derevenski 2000a), as well as the influential work of Lillehammer (Lillehammer 1996). To state that there were children in the archaeological past seems self-evident and yet, until this new body of literature, there was little mention of them, and they were largely invisible. Generally, children were only mentioned in contexts where their presence could be identified beyond doubt, such as in cemetery reports, or in cases such as the fortress baths at Caerleon, where a milk tooth was found in the main baths drain (Zienkiewicz 1986). They were presented as passive members of society, and there was limited discussion of their use of material culture or spaces, unless it was in connection with items dedicated to children, such as toys or feeding vessels (Harlow 2014). There is a stronger tradition of work relating to the iconography of childhood in Roman sculpture, which has examined both the representation of children as a means of reconstructing ideals of childhood, and the ways in which children were used as an iconographical metaphor (Currie 1996, Huskinson 1996). Archaeological work on childhood has concentrated on firstly applying the growing work on childhood from other disciplines to archaeology, and secondly, developing methodologies for understanding childhood as a social institution from the material evidence. This work has been carried out by a small, multi-period group of researchers (predominantly women), which has arguably led to its limited impact on wider period studies. This is as true for the Roman period as for others, and consequently material approaches to Roman children are poorly served; the one exception to this is the analysis of the cemetery evidence.

One avenue for research is the spatial context of childhood. Differences between the age groups can be expressed through access to and use of spaces, even the same space (Holloway and Valentine 2000). Changes in these can be used in the construction of identity: do children have access to specific places, or are they banned from them? Within modern, western societies, there is an idea of specific areas for children: areas within the home or schools and playgrounds. This could be related to the stereotype of the Victorian nursery, predominantly an elite or middling class phenomenon. More recently, there is a concentration on the idea of the child's own room. The study of a late twentieth century, British house inhabited by a mother and her two young children demonstrates the way on which child-adult differences were constructed through the spatial layout of the house (Buchli and Lucas 2000). That a room was allocated as the children's room is clear from the concentration of children's artefacts (clothing and toys), and the complete absence of adult related material. The walls were decorated differently from the rest of the house, with wallpaper depicting scenes from children's cartoons. Similar studies of artefact distribution within houses for the Roman period have failed to identify specific zones for various family members, and instead, it has been argued that the Roman house was structured around the differentiation of status (Wallace-Hadrill 1994). In this case, we are looking at spaces arguably allocated and potentially shaped by adults. However, children are able to create their own spaces, as a venue for interaction with children of their own age cohort. These might be removed from the watch (or surveillance) of adults, in somewhat remote places within an area. For example, Wilkie (2000) has argued that children created secret places for themselves in derelict houses in the Riverlake plantation, Louisiana, as demonstrated by the clusters of marbles found wedged into brick surfaces which had once supported chimneys. In this case, the children's use of the space involves the subversion of adult norms: to an adult, these are abandoned places, but to the child, it is a place of activity and importance.

Whilst we might struggle to identify such child-specific places, we can begin to think about how geographical difference might impact upon the practices of childhood (Revell 2010a). For a child growing up within the context of the town, places for play might have been the porticoes associated with public spaces in the town. These would have been populated by the rest of the community, and so there would have been elements of interaction with other age-groups, and supervision from adults (whether related or not). Alternatively, in towns such as those of Roman Britain where areas within the walls seem to have been left vacant, these potentially overgrown areas would have provided a place for children to meet and socialise away from the watch of adults. Another alternative may be the elaborate necropoleis on the outskirts of the towns, with elaborate funerary monuments providing an architectural setting for their interaction. There is evidence for teachers and the process of learning, notoriously in Tacitus' *Agricola* where the children of the elite are educated in the new Roman customs (Tac. *Agr.* 21), although the epigraphic attestations of schoolteachers is variable, with none attested in Britain, Germania, Noricum or Raetia (Laes 2007). However, we do not know where this education took place. During the Medieval period, the parish church would be used as a place for schooling, warning against associating children's learning with a dedicated space. The public spaces of the town, in particular the porticoes of public buildings, may have acted as the location for such activities, as suggested by the placement of graffiti alphabets in Pompeii, where the porticoes of the Large Palaestra were the site of a marked concentration and may have been the location of a school (Laurence 2013).

For children in more rural locations, the geographical setting of their childhood would be different. There would be opportunities to congregate on the outskirts of the settlement, or in out of the way areas of a villa estate. The many outbuildings associated with the usual farm or villa estate could have been used, not only by the children of the villa owner, but also by the wider community of children. For the children of military families, their areas of interaction may well have been the fort itself, or the surrounding *vicus*. The question of where the families of the soldiers resided is controversial: whether they lived within the fort or fortress itself, or if they left each night to dwellings in the associated settlement. Regardless of this debate, the fort and its surrounding settlement would have provided a setting for any learning and play, providing a familiarity with military life and material culture quite different to children in non-military zones. Did the large granaries provide a tantalising place to hide away from adults? Or was there some form of school within the *principia*? We may never be able to answer these questions, but their use of either space would be different to that of the adult population of the community, thus structuring the differences which made them children.

However, focusing on the spaces for play and education runs the risk of imposing western attitudes to childhood onto the past, and in particular ignores their experience of such places as workers. During the 19th and 20th centuries, the eradication of child labour became a symbol of modernity and progress, and scandals over, for example, the use of child labour in garment production have become a powerful critique of capitalism. In pre-industrial societies, the work of children had the potential to make an important contribution to the household economy, and this is particularly true of household industries, such as farming. In chapter 5, we saw the different levels of ceramic production, and in the household level of the production of Malvern ware, for example, the children of the family may have taken on some of the less specialist tasks, such as collecting firewood for the kilns. They may also have begun to work outside the house, either bringing money into the family if freeborn or freed, or proving their economic worth if a slave.

In this area, problems with reading the evidence are exacerbated by issues of presentism, as demonstrated by the differing conclusions drawn from the tombstone of Q. Artulus (CIL 2.3258; an alternative reading of his name is Q[u]artulus). The text reads that he died aged 4, but in the iconography, he is depicted as a miner. The usual reading of this form of tombstone would be that the deceased was a miner, with the consequence that this provides evidence for child labour in the Iberian mines (Edmondson 1987). However, disquiet over the possibility of child labour has led to the alternative interpretation that Artulus was the son of a miner (Domergue 1990: 352). This is not an isolated instance of a working child, and other inscriptions from Iberia give ages at death of ten and eleven years for miners (*ibid.*: 339–40, table 17). Furthermore, evidence from epitaphs for child labour at the city of Rome includes two 9-year-old girls who worked as a gold-embroiderer and a hair-dresser, a 4-year-old boy who was an infant athlete, and an 11-year-old dancer (Sigismund-Nielsen 2007), whilst from Iberia an epitaph commemorates a silver engraver who died aged 11 years old (CIL 2.2243).

This evidence for child labour is supported by contracts for apprentices from Roman Egypt (Bradley 1991: 103–24), which show children being apprenticed predominantly into the textile industry, but also into building, copper smithing and nail making. These contracts were made by their parents, and interestingly there are examples where parents apprentice their child into the same trade as their own, but with a different workshop. We do not have equivalent evidence for the western provinces, but it does raise the possibility of child mobility, particularly for boys. They might leave their own families for an extended period (the longest apprenticeship contract cited by Bradley is for 6 years) during which time they would learn a specialist trade amongst a different family group. We have already seen a potential case of an apprentice with the Snettisham jeweller in chapter 5, and it is possible that many of the craft workshops in the urban centres may have had an apprentice within the household. This did not mean these children had crossed the threshold into adulthood: the fact that these contracts were taken out by their parents shows that they were still not considered as adults.

Being adult: the second and third ages

The focus on childhood within age studies has tended to overshadow the other aspects of age identity, and the transition to adulthood has almost seemed to herald a lack of interest amongst modern scholars. One notable exception to this is Mary Harlow and Ray Laurence's book on the life-course at Rome and Italy (Harlow and Laurence 2002), in which they explicitly consider the adult stage for men and women separately, and the category of the elderly. In considering the identity of the adult within the western provinces, much of the material presented in the previous chapters about use of space, work identities and family structures in reality also applies here. For example, we saw in the sections on the life-course that for women, the transition to adulthood seems to occur at roughly the point of marriage and motherhood, and these roles formed important elements of the definition of the adult woman. Nevertheless, just as childhood in reality encompasses a series of stages, so adulthood also can be fragmented. In particular, the process of growing old can lead to a separate category of the elderly, and it is this group I propose to focus on in this section.

Any search for literature on the elderly, whether in ancient history or archaeology, would produce a distinctly depressing list of studies. It is possible that the focus on the average age at death of 20–30 years has rendered those older than this less visible, and there are problems with the various forms of evidence we might use. The ageing of the skeletal evidence of the elderly is difficult due to problems of preservation and lack of precise diagnostic features, generally producing a date of 50+ (Gowland 2007). Similarly, the evidence of epitaphs for the very old warrants some scepticism given the claims for those over 100 in the African provinces and the overall lack of age-statements over the age of 30 in most regions. Finally, the iconographic evidence contains its own series of stereotypical conventions. Nevertheless, the work on the elderly in Rome itself has established that this did exist as a discrete age-grouping, subject to both respect but also a certain amount of revulsion (Cokayne 2003, Parkin 2003). The challenge is how to explore old age within the context of the provinces.

We have already seen that there were regional differences towards the elderly in the Iberian provinces. The life-course profile from the Conventus Codubensis demonstrates a concentration of age-statements for those in their 50s and 60s, particularly for men. This is likely to be tied into their children as the preferred commemoration group, both trends running contrary to those in other provinces, and as I argued earlier, suggests a difference in family structure. These distinctive family ties brought the older members of the family into greater prominence, giving them more status and authority within society as a whole. This may contrast with the situation elsewhere in the western provinces, and may be the reason for the inflation of age at death: the oldest person given an age in *Conventus Cordubensis* was a man from Cordoba, apparently 98 years old (CIL 2.7.348).

The analysis of the cemetery evidence reinforces this picture of variability. As stated earlier, it is difficult to be precise about skeletal age after about the age of 50 years, and so we can only talk of the elderly in general terms. However, studies of the burial of the elderly in southern Britain warn against expecting uniformity in attitudes towards them. Moore (2010) analysed the funerary treatment of 677 individuals aged 30+ from Gloucester, Cirencester and the surrounding rural region. Those 50+ showed some differences in treatment from those aged 30–49 in terms of the burial ritual (i.e. use of coffin, etc.) and grave goods. Of particular note was the difference in aging between the urban and the rural burials: the transition was more marked within rural contexts, suggesting that the ageing process caused greater disruption in the countryside. This may have been the product of the agricultural economy. As Moore suggests (*ibid.*: 112) increasing ill-health would have impacted on their economic productivity, potentially reducing their status amongst the rest of the family. Amongst women, the dominant form of grave good shifts from being coinage in their 40s to jewellery both amongst the urban and the rural populations. This may represent an increased independence: the difference in age at marriage between men and women meant they were likely to have been widows, and if they bore their children in their 20s, their role in raising their own children would be less important, although they may been involved in providing childcare for their grandchildren. Gowland's study of the burial of the elderly in Winchester and Colchester similarly shows the different burial practices for those who died over the age of 50 years, with few grave goods found with individuals of this age (Gowland 2007). She also noted changes in the types of grave goods at in the 30s and 40s, such as men over the age of 35 years, and usually older, being associated with cross-bow brooches in Winchester, possibly indicating the authority and power derived from age.

Whilst both Gowland and Moore's studies rely on the physiological age of the skeleton, this approach has been questioned by Appleby (Appleby 2010). She argues that one issue is how we identify someone as old: the usual technique is to amalgamate the osteological indicators to give an average physiological age. She argues that instead, the focus should be on individual indicators such as a loss of teeth or postural change, which would allow an understanding of age as a process of senescence, but also how the burial evidence might differ for different pathologies, and so how those of an apparent similar averaged skeletal age might be accorded a different burial treatment. Her analysis of a Bronze Age cemetery in Austria demonstrated that the degeneration of the body had an impact on the formulation of an elderly identity. This alternative technique for investigating the idea of old age has the potential to further explore the difference between urban and rural treatment of the elderly identified by Moore.

Conclusion

As archaeologists and Roman historians have argued, age is the neglected category of identities. Whilst interest in the family has gone some way to remedy this amongst historians, this is still the case for archaeology more widely, and Roman provincial archaeology in particular. A small number of studies are beginning to emerge which have demonstrated the potential of the funerary evidence to provide a window into the topic. Whether using a life course approach or focussing on a specific age stage, we are beginning to understand something of the age identities in the Roman provinces. One issue which has hampered the critical analysis has been assumptions about age stages, and the behaviour and material appropriate for each, such as play and toys for children. These new studies have demonstrated that our modern assumptions cannot be imposed onto the past. Instead, we see different attitudes towards, for example, the very young, but also to children and child labour. There is also the indication that as with gender, we should expect regional variability, and that using the picture of age stages drawn from the textual sources from Rome as an interpretive tool for the provincial evidence needs to be undertaken with great care.

One issue which has emerged is that the study of age identities is dominated by the funerary evidence, whether this is epitaphs or the burial data. This is because the nature of the remains allow us to derive an approximate age at death with relative confidence (although neither source is without its problems). However, other sources of evidence have been less explored for their potential. Work on age in other periods has demonstrated that it is possible to devise methodologies for other forms of material culture which allow an insight into, for example, childhood (for example, papers in Sofaer Derevenski 2000a). We need to move beyond the stage where we envisage the assumed producer and consumer of material culture being only adults; the idea of entangled objects and spaces allows us to envisage how these may have been used by other age categories. It is only as we begin to develop new methodologies for approaching the evidence from the past that we can understand age identities.

Chapter 8

Conclusions

This book arose from the premise that identity in the Roman provinces has been underexplored within archaeology. In the past, this was caused by presentist arguments that the Romans were just like us, but it was also the product of an undervaluing of social archaeology in preference to other topics such as cultural change or economics, or a pessimistic view of what archaeological analysis can actually achieve. Whilst there have been a number corrective research projects, much of this research is still marginal, in particular the work on gender and age identities. There is still an androcentric bias within Roman archaeology, with too many studies still assuming an empire populated by adult men, sometimes but not always elite. I have not claimed to be comprehensive in my coverage: my aim was to demonstrate that a social archaeology of the western provinces is possible, and to propose some ways of undertaking its study. It has inevitably focused on the forms of material I specialise in (buildings and inscriptions), and the regions I am more familiar with (Iberia and Britain). Furthermore, not all aspects of identity have been covered here: religious identities, military identities and disability are three examples which have not featured. Nevertheless, in the preceding chapters, I have demonstrated the ways in which we can understand the process of identity formation and maintenance, and methodologies which can be applied to different identities and different regions.

A key theme throughout has been that there is no direct on-to-one relationship between specific items of material culture and aspects of identity. The theoretical approach taken here has been based upon ideas of social practice: that identity is both internalised and communicated through the actions of daily living. Secondly, that there needs to be a contextual reading of the data as far as possible, although in certain cases analogy is needed. Thirdly, that identity rests on the creation of difference, both from the real 'other' with whom the groups interact, but also the imaginary other. Throughout, my focus has been on the group discourses, rather than search for the individual experience. This is not to deny that it is possible to use the idea of the individual as a successful heuristic tool to explore wider questions of identity (for example Carroll 2012). However, such studies rely on the wider discourses of identity to understand the individual.

This raises the important question of the relationship between the individual and the group. An individual is socialised into the group discourses from infancy, learning the behaviours and attitudes expected of them, and furthermore, the new identities they might acquire as they move through the life-course. Any individual's identity cannot be reduced to a single aspect, but in reality forms a point within the intersecting and at times conflicting discourses of the varying components and the sub-groups they belong to within a particular society. This concept of multiple aspects of identity has led to an element of disquiet about its academic study: if we investigate 'Roman' as an ethnic identity, which Romans are we looking at and where; does this apply to the non-elite, or to the non-elite woman? As the various and at times contradictory elements of any single person's identity are built up, any idea of homogeneity breaks down, whilst the sense of the group remains. Roman archaeology is not unique in this questioning, and it has formed an important part of the feminist critique of identity, such as the work of Judith Butler on lesbian identities within gendered identities (Butler 1999). The solution advocated here has been to investigate the discourses and ideologies of the identity group in order to understand the wider concepts and practices through which a sense of self is created. This shifts the balance from the individual to the discourses. It responds to arguments that identity is never a completed project, with any person in a constant state of becoming rather than being. It allows the ambiguity and fuzziness of the lived experience to be recreated from the static nature of the archaeological record.

The study of identity is in general the study of the mundane and the banal. However, there are times when a group comes under pressure, particularly in moments of social change. At a specific moment, a single aspect of identity may come to the fore, and be dominant in the experience of the individual. As an established discourse of identity comes under threat, it becomes more important to the individual, and its demonstration may take precedence over other aspects, with the policing of the boundaries between 'us' and 'them' becoming subject to greater vigilance. Within the Roman west, conquest by Rome led to a threat to ethnic identities. For the first generations post-conquest, their ethnic identities potentially came to the forefront, but as familiarity grew with the new imperial authorities, and the division between conquered and conqueror began to break down, this may have ceased to be the most contested aspect of identity, and others have come to the foreground.

However, conquest did not only impact upon ethnic identities, and as demonstrated, changes which came with incorporation into empire, such as political activity, organisation of economic activities, or new laws of inheritance, all had the potential to disrupt further elements of an individual's identity such as their rank, profession, age or gender. Thus Roman imperialism had the potential to cause wider social shifts and to have a more profound impact on identity than just on ethnicity. This did not take a single trajectory. In some cases we see new ideas of particular forms of identity, such as the shift to elite rank through urban magistracies, or non-elite ranks through economic specialisms. In other cases we see the adoption of new materials and practices, but the underlying identities unchanged, as in Iberia where it is possible that aspects of gender relationships (in particular as articulated through family roles) retained aspects of their pre-conquest form, but came to be expressed through the practice of erecting memorials on stone to the deceased in Latin.

It is this complexity which reveals the next step needed in the study of identity in the western provinces. Much of the existing archaeological work has focused on Roman Britain, and ethnicity has tended to dominate. Similarly, burial evidence has formed a popular means of answering such questions, particularly in the cases of gender and age, where the intersection between the body and the grave goods has been used as a methodology for understanding the process of differentiation (although generally tempered with caveats). Such studies tend to be highly focused, concentrating on a small number of sites, or a particular aspect of identity. This is not to dismiss them, as this book would have been impossible without them. However, we need to build upon these. The danger is that without more comparative material, the reality of the variability of identity and the complexity of the dynamics are lost: the particular characteristics of the small scale studies become assessed against an imagined homogeneity of a 'Roman' ideal, usually drawn from the textual sources. Further localised, detailed studies, using a wider range of archaeological materials, from more regions and provinces, coupled with more synthetic and comparative works will allow us to investigate whether we can in fact talk about 'typical' identities, and if so, what form they took and how they were expressed. Alternatively, we will be able to identify the regional differentiation in all elements of identity as part of the wider variability within Roman imperialism, and the complex responses to a changing world.

References

AA.VV. 1991. *La casa urbana hispanorromana: ponencias y comunicaciones*. Zaragoza Institución Fernando el Católico.

Adams, J. N. 2003. *Bilingualism and the Latin Language*. Cambridge, Cambridge University Press.

Alföldy, G. 1985. *The Social History of Rome*. London, Croom Helm.

Alföldy, G. 1998. *Inscriptiones Hispaniae Latinae: Conventus Astigitanus*. Editio altera. Berlin, New York, de Gruyter.

Allain, J., I. Fauduet and M. Tuffreau-Libre 1992. *La nécropole gallo-romaine du Champ de l'Image à Argentomagus (Saint-Marcel, Indre)*. Saint-Marcel, Musée d'Argentomagus.

Allason-Jones, L. 1989. *Ear-rings in Roman Britain*. Oxford, British Archaeological Report 201.

Allason-Jones, L. 1995. 'Sexing' small finds. In P. Rush, (ed.) *Theoretical Roman Archaeology: second conference proceedings*. Aldershot, Avebury: 22–32.

Allason-Jones, L. 1996. *Roman Jet in the Yorkshire Museum*. York, Yorkshire Museum.

Allason-Jones, L. 1999. Women and the Roman army in Britain. In A. Goldsworthy and I. P. Haynes (eds) *The Roman Army as a Community*. Portsmouth, R. I., *Journal of Roman Archaeology* Supplementary Series 34: 41–51.

Allason-Jones, L. 2001. Material culture and identity. In S. James and M. Millett (eds) *Britons and Romans: advancing an archaeological agenda*. York, Council for British Archaeology Research Report 125: 19–25.

Allason-Jones, L. 2005. *Women in Roman Britain*. New ed. York, Council for British Archaeology.

Allen, J. R. L. 2013. Some potters of samian ware at La Graufesenque. In M. Fulford and E. Durham (eds) *Seeing Red: new economic and social perspective on Gallo-Roman terra sigillata*. London, Institute of Classical Studies: 49–65.

Allison, P. 2001. Using the material and written sources: turn of the millennium approaches to Roman domestic space. *American Journal of Archaeology* 105: 181–208.

Allison, P. M. 2006. Mapping for gender. Interpreting artefact distribution inside 1st- and 2nd-century AD forts in Roman Germany. *Archaeological Dialogues* 13: 1–20.

Antonaccio, C. M. 2010. (Re)defining ethnicity: culture, material culture and identity. In S. Hales and T. Hodos (eds) *Material Culture and Social Identities in the Ancient World*. Cambridge, Cambridge University Press: 32–53.

Appleby, J. E. P. 2010. Why we need an archaeology of old age, and a suggested approach. *Norwegian Archaeological Review* 43.2: 145–68.

Aquilué, X., P. Castanyer, M. Santos and J. Tremoleda 2006. The Greek city of Emporion and its relationship to the Roman Republican city of Empúries. In L. Abad Casal, S. J. Keay and S. Ramallo Asensio (eds) *Early Roman towns in Hispania Tarraconensis*. Portsmouth, R. I. *Journal of Roman Archaeology* Supplementary Series 62: 18–32.

Aranegui Gascó, C. 1992. Evolución del área cívica saguntina. *Journal of Roman Archaeology* 5: 56–68.

Aranegui Gascó, C. 2006. From Arse to Saguntum. In L. Abad Casal, S. J. Keay and S. Ramallo Asensio (eds) *Early Roman towns in Hispania Tarraconensis*. Portsmouth, R. I., *Journal of Roman Archaeology* Supplementary Series 62: 63–74.

Arber, S. and J. Ginn 1995. 'Only connect': gender relations and ageing. In S. Arber and J. Ginn (eds) *Connecting Gender and Ageing: a sociological approach*. Buckingham, Open University Press, 1–14.

Archer, L. J., S. Fischler and M. Wyke (eds) 1994. *Women in Ancient Societies: an illusion of the night.* Basingstoke, Macmillan.
Ariès, P. 1962. *Centuries of Childhood: a social history of family life.* London, Cape.
Arnold, B. 1990. The past as propaganda: totalitarian archaeology in Nazi Germany. *Antiquity* 244: 464–78.
Ashby, T. 1906. Excavations at Caerwent, Monmouthshire, on the site of the Romano-British city of Venta Silurum, in the year 1905. *Archaeologia* 60.1: 111–30.
Bailey, D. M. 1963. *Greek and Roman Pottery Lamps.* London, British Museum Press.
Baker, P. 2003. A brief comment on the TRAC session dedicated to the interdisciplinary approaches to the study of Roman women. In G. Carr, E. Swift and J. Weekes (eds) *TRAC2002. Proceedings of the twelfth annual Theoretical Roman Archaeology Conference.* Oxford, Oxbow Books: 140–46.
Balsdon, J. P. V. D. 1962. *Roman Women: their history and habits.* London, Bodley Head.
Barrett, J. C. 1988. Fields of discourse: reconstituting a social archaeology. *Critique of Anthropology* 7.3: 5–16.
Barrett, J. C. 1989. Afterword: render unto Caesar ... In J. C. Barrett, A. P. Fitzpatrick and L. Macinnes (eds) *Barbarians and Romans in North-west Europe from the Later Republic to Late Antiquity.* Oxford, British Archaeological Report S571:235–39.
Barrett, J. C. 1994. *Fragments from Antiquity. An Archaeology of Social Life in Britain, 2900–1200BC.* Oxford, Blackwells.
Barrett, J. C. 1997. Theorising Roman archaeology. In K. Meadows, C. Lemke and J. Heron (eds) *TRAC98. Proceeding of the sixth annual Theoretical Roman Archaeology Conference.* Oxford, Oxbow Books: 1–7.
Barth, F. 1969. Introduction. In F. Barth (ed.) *Ethnic Groups and Boundaries. The Social Organization of Cultural Difference.* Oslo, Universitetsforlaget: 9–38.
Bartlett, R. 1994. *The Making of Modern Europe. Conquest, Colonization and Cultural Change.* Harmondsworth, Penguin.
Bartman, E. 2001. Hair and the artifice of Roman female adornment. *American Journal of Archaeology* 105.1: 1–25.
Baxter, J. E. 2005. *The Archaeology of Childhood: Children, Gender and Material Culture.* Walnut Creek, CA, Altamira Press.
Beard, M. and M. Crawford 1999. *Rome in the Late Republic: problems and interpretations.* 2nd ed. London, Duckworth.
Bedon, R., R. Chevallier and P. Pinon 1988. *Architecture et urbanisme en Gaule romaine.* Paris, Errance.
Bell, A. J. E. 1997. Cicero and the spectacle of power. *Journal of Roman Studies* 87: 1–22.
Bénabou, M. 1976. *La résistance africaine à la romanization.* Paris, F. Maspero.
Bendala Galán, M. 1993. *The Hispano-Roman Town.* Barcelona, Ministerio of Cultura: Àmbit Servicios Editoriales.
Bender, B. 1992. Theorising landscapes, and the prehistoric landscapes of Stonehenge. *Man* 27: 735–55.
Bhabha, H. K. 1994. *The Location of Culture.* London, Routledge.
Billig, M. 1995. *Banal Nationalism.* London, Sage.
Bird, M. 2000. The wall-plaster. In M. Fulford and J. Timby (eds) *Late Iron Age and Roman Silchester: excavations in the site of the forum basilica.* London, Society for the Promotion of Roman Studies: 100–15.
Birley, A. R. 2008. Cives Galli de(ae) Galliae concordesque Britanni: a dedication at Vindolanda. *L'Antiquité Classique*: 171–87.
Blagg, T. F. C. 1990. Architectural munificence on Britain: the evidence of the inscriptions. *Britannia* 21: 13–31.
Blanco Freijeiro, A. 1978. *Mosaicos romanos de Italica.* Madrid, Instituto Español de Arqueología "Rodrigo Caro" del Consejo Superior de Investigaciones Científicas.

Boatwright, M. T. 2005. Children and parents on the tombstones of Pannonia. In M. George (ed.) *The Roman Family in the Empire: Rome, Italy and beyond*. Oxford, Oxford University Press: 287–318.

Bonneville, J.-N. l., S. Dardaine and P. Le Roux 1988. *Belo V. L'épigrafie: les inscriptions romaines de Baelo Claudia*. Madrid, Casa de Velázquez.

Booth, P., A.-M. Bingham and S. Lawrence 2008. *The Roman Roadside Settlement at Westhawk Farm, Ashford, Kent: excavations 1998–9*. Oxford, Oxford Archaeology.

Bost, J.-P. and G. Fabre 2001. *Inscriptions Latines d'Aquitaine: Pétrucores*. Pessac, Ausonius.

Bourdieu, P. 1977. *Outline of a Theory of Practice*. Cambridge, Cambridge University Press.

Bowman, A. K. and A. Wilson. 2009. *Quantifying the Roman economy: methods and problems*. Oxford: Oxford University Press.

Bradley, K. R. 1991. *Discovering the Roman Family: studies in Roman social history*. Oxford, Oxford University Press.

Brewer, R. J. 1993. Caerwent – Venta Silurum: a civitas capital. In S. J. Greep (ed.) *Roman Towns: the Wheeler inheritance. A review of fifty years research*. York, Council for British Archaeology Research Report 93: 56–65.

Brewer, R. J. 2006. *Caerwent Roman Town*. Cardiff, Cadw.

Brigham, T. 1992. Civic centre redevelopment: forum and basilica reassessed. In G. Milne (ed.) *From Roman Basilica to Medieval Market*. London, HMSO: 81–95.

Brown, P. 1992. *Power and Persuasion in Late Antiquity: towards a Christian empire*. Madison, WI; London, University of Wisconsin Press.

Brown, S. 1997. "Ways of seeing" women in antiquity. An introduction to feminism in classical archaeology and ancient art history. In A. O. Koloski-Ostrow and C. L. Lyons (eds.) *Naked Truths: women, sexuality and gender in classical art and archaeology*. London, Routledge: 12–42.

Buchli, V. and G. Lucas 2000. Children, gender and the material culture of domestic abandonment in the late twentieth century. In J. Sofaer Derevenski (ed.) *Children and Material Culture*. Cambridge, Cambridge University Press: 131–38.

Burnett, A. 1997. The coins. In C. Johns (ed.) *The Snettisham Roman Jeweller's Hoard*. London, British Museum Press: 16–19.

Butler, J. 1993. *Bodies that Matter: on the discursive limits of sex*. London, Routledge.

Butler, J. 1999. *Gender Trouble: feminism and the subversion of identity*. 10th anniversary ed. New York, London, Routledge.

Carandini, A. and M. R. Filippi 1985. *Settefinestre: una villa schiavistica nell'Etruria romana*. Modena, Panini.

Carreté, J.-M., S. J. Keay and M. Millett 1995. *A Roman Provincial Capital and its Hinterland: the survey of the territory of Tarragona, Spain, 1985–90*. Ann Arbor, *Journal of Roman Archaeology* Supplementary Series 15.

Carroll, M. 2002. Measuring time and inventing histories in the early empire: Roman and Germanic perspectives. In M. Carruthers, C. van Driel-Murray, A. Gardner and J. Lucas (eds) *TRAC2001. Proceedings of the eleventh annual Theoretical Roman Archaeology Conference*. Oxford, Oxbow Books: 104–12.

Carroll, M. 2012. The insignia of women. Dress, gender and identity on the Roman funerary monument of Regina from Arbeia. *Archaeological Journal* 169: 281–311.

Childe, V. G. 1929. *The Danube in Prehistory*. Oxford, Clarendon Press.

Childe, V. G. 1930. *The Bronze Age*. Cambridge, Cambridge University Press.

Cokayne, K. 2003. *Experiencing Old Age in Ancient Rome*. London, Routledge.

Collingwood, R. G. 1932. *Roman Britain*. Oxford, Clarendon Press.

Conkey, M. W. and J. D. Spector 1984. Archaeology and the study of gender. *Advances in Archaeological Method and Theory* 7: 1–38.

Cool, H. E. M. 1990. Roman metal hair pins from Southern Britain. *Archaeological Journal* 147: 148–82.

Cool, H. E. M. 2002. An overview of the small finds from Catterick. In P. R. Wilson (ed.) *Cataractonium: Roman Catterick and its hinterland. Excavations and research, 1958–97, Part II*. York, Council for British Archaeology Research Report 129: 24–43.

Cool, H. E. M. 2011. Funerary contexts. In L. Allason-Jones (ed.) *Artefacts in Roman Britain: their purpose and use*. Cambridge, Cambridge University Press: 293–312.

Cool, H. E. M., J. Bond and L. Allason-Jones 2004. *The Roman Cemetery at Brougham, Cumbria: excavations 1966–67*. London, Society for the Promotion of Roman Studies.

Cooley, A. E. 2002. The survival of Oscan in Roman Pompeii. In A. E. Cooley (ed.) *Becoming Roman, Writing Latin? Literacy and Epigraphy in the Roman West*. Portsmouth, R. I., *Journal of Roman Archaeology* Supplementary Series 48, 77–86.

Cotton, M. A. and R. E. M. Wheeler 1953. Verulamium 1949. *Transactions of the St Albans and Hertfordshire Architectural and Archaeological Society* 1953: 13–97.

Crawford, M. 1996. *Roman Statutes*. London, *Bulletin of the Institute of Classical Studies* 64.

Crawford, S. 2000. Children, grave goods and social status in Early Anglo-Sasxon England. In J. Sofaer Derevenski (ed.) *Children and Material Culture*. London, Routledge: 169–79.

Crielaard, J. P. 2009. The Ionians in the Archaic period. Shifting identities in a changing world. In T. Derks and N. Roymans (eds) *Ethnic Constructs in Antiquity. The Role of Power and Tradition*. Amsterdam, Amsterdam University Press: 37–84.

Crone, P. 1989. *Pre-industrial Societies*. Oxford, Blackwell.

Culham, P. 1997. Did Roman women have an empire? In G. Golden and P. Toohey (eds) *Inventing Ancient Culture: historicism, periodization, and the ancient world*. London, Routledge: 192–204.

Cüppers, H. 1990. *Die Römer in Rheinland-Pfalz*. Stuttgart, Theiss.

Currie, S. 1996. The empire of adults: the representation of children on Trajan's arch at Beneventum. In J. Elsner (ed.) *Art and Text in Roman Culture*. Cambridge, Cambridge University Press:153–81.

Dasen, V. and T. Späth 2010. *Children, Memory, and Family Identity in Roman Culture*. Oxford, Oxford University Press.

Davey, N. and R. Ling 1982. *Wall-Painting in Roman Britain*. London, Society for the Promotion of Roman Studies.

David, J.-M. 1996. *The Roman Conquest of Italy*. Oxford, Blackwell.

Delgado Delgado, J. 1999. Flamines Provinciae Lusitania. *Gerión. Revista de Historia Antigua* 17: 433–61.

Dench, E. 2005. *Romulus's Asylum*. Oxford, Oxford University Press.

Derks, T. 1998. *Gods, Temples and Ritual Practices. The Transformation of Religious Ideas and Values in Roman Gaul*. Amsterdam, Amsterdam University Press.

Derks, T. 2009a. Ethnic identity in the Roman frontier. The epigraphy of Batavi and other Lower Rhine tribes. In T. Derks and N. Roymans (eds) *Ethnic Constructs in Antiquity*. Amsterdam, Amsterdam University Press: 239–82.

Derks, T. 2009b. Ethnic identity in the Roman frontier. The epigraphy of Batavi and the other Lower Rhine tribes. In T. Derks and N. Roymans (eds) *Ethnic Constructs in Antiquity. The Role of Power and Tradition*. Amsterdam, Amsterday University Press: 239–82.

Derks, T. and N. Roymans 2009. Introduction. In T. Derks and N. Roymans (eds) *Ethnic Constructs in Antiquity. The Role of Power and Tradition*. Amsterdam, Amsterdam University Press: 1–9.

Dixon, S. 1988. *The Roman Mother*. London, Routledge.

Dixon, S. 1992. *The Roman Family*. Baltimore, Johns Hopkins University Press.

Dobres, M.-A. 2004. Digging up gender in the earliest human societies. In T. A. Meade and M. E. Wiesner-Hanks (eds) *A Companion to Gender History*. Oxford, Blackwell.

Dobres, M.-A. and J. E. Robb 2000. *Agency in Archaeology*. London, Routledge.

Domergue, C. 1983. *La mine antique d'Aljustrel (Portugal) et les tables de bronze de Vipasca*. Paris, Boccard.

Domergue, C. 1990. *Les mines de la Péninsule Ibérique dans l'antiquité romaine*. Rome, Ecole française de Rome.

Dragendorff, H. and E. Krüger 1924. *Das Grabmal von Igel*. Trier, J. Lintz.
Drinkwater, J. F. 1979. A note on local careers in the three Gauls under the early Empire. *Britannia* 10: 89–100.
Drinkwater, J. F. 1982. The wool textile industry of Gallia Belgica and the Secundinii of Igel: questions and hypotheses. *Textile History* 13.1: 111–28.
Duday, H., F. Laubenheimer and S. Tillier 1995. *Sallèles d'Aude: nouveau-nés et nourrissons gallo-romains*. Paris, Belles Lettres.
Duncan-Jones, R. 1982. *The Economy of the Roman Empire: quantitative studies*. 2nd ed. Cambridge, Cambridge University Press.
Duncan-Jones, R. P. 1977. Age-rounding, illiteracy and social differentiation in the Roman empire. *Chiron* 7: 333–53.
Duncan-Jones, R. P. 1990. *Structure and Scale in the Roman Economy*. Cambridge, Cambridge University Press.
Dyson, S. L. 2008. *In Pursuit of Ancient Pasts: a history of classical archaeology in the nineteenth and twentieth centuries*. New Haven, Yale University Press.
Eck, W. 1984. Senatorial representation: developments in the Augustan period. In F. Millar and E. Segal (eds) *Caesar Augustus: seven aspects*. Oxford, Clarendon Press: 129–67.
Eckardt, H. 2002. *Illuminating Roman Britain*. Montagnac, Editions Monique Mergoil.
Eckardt, H. (ed.) 2010. *Roman Diasporas: archaeological approaches to mobility and diversity in the Roman empire*. Portsmouth, R. I., *Journal of Roman Archaeology* Supplementary Series 78.
Eckardt, H. and N. Crummy 2008. *Styling the Body in Late Iron Age and Roman Britain: a contextual approach to toilet instruments*. Montagnac, Editions Monique Mergoil.
Edmondson, J. 2005. Family relations in Roman Lusitania: social change in a Roman province. In M. George, (ed.) *The Roman Family in the Empire: Rome, Italy and beyond*. Oxford, Oxford University Press: 183–229.
Edmondson, J. C. 1987. *Two Industries in Roman Lusitania: mining and garum production*. Oxford, British Archaeological Report S362.
Edwards, C. 1993. *The Politics of Immorality in ancient Rome*. Cambridge, Cambridge University Press.
Edwards, C. 1997. Unspeakable professions: public performance and prostitution in ancient Rome. In J. P. Hallett and M. B. Skinner (eds) *Roman Sexualities*. Princeton, Princeton University Press: 66–95.
Ellis, S. P. 1991. Power, architecture, and decor: how the Late Roman aristocrat appeared to his guests. In E. K. Gazda (ed.) *Roman Art in the Private Sphere: new perspectives on the architecture and decor of the domus, villa, and insula*. Ann Arbor, University of Michigan Press: 117–34.
Elsner, J. 1998. *Imperial Rome and Christian Triumph. The Art of the Roman Empire AD100-450*. Oxford, Oxford University Press.
Eriksen, T. H. 1991. Ethnicity versus nationalism. *Journal of Peace Research* 28.3: 263–78.
Eriksen, T. H. 1993. *Ethnicity and Nationalism: anthropological perspectives*. London, Pluto.
Eriksen, T. H. 2001. *Small Places, Large Issues: an introduction to social and cultural anthropology*. 2nd ed. London, Pluto.
Esmonde Cleary, A. S. 2013. *Chedworth: life in a Roman villa*. Stroud, History Press.
Espérandieu, E. 1907–81. *Recueil général des bas-reliefs de la Gaule romaine*. Paris, Imprimerie nationale.
Euzennat, M. 1994. *Principia* militaires et forum civils. In X. Dupré i Raventós (ed.) *La ciudad en el mundo romano*. Tarragona, Consejo Superior de Investigaciones Científicas: 197–203.
Faerman, M., G. Bar-Gal, D. Filon, C. Greenblatt, L. Stager, A. Oppenheim and P. Smith 1998. Determining the sex of infanticide victims from the late Roman era through ancient DNA analysis. *Journal of Archaeological Science* 25: 861–65.
Farland, H. S. Jr. 1990. Geographical mobility in Roman Lusitania: an epigraphical perspective. *Zeitschrift für Papyrologie und Epigraphik* 82: 249–69.

Farney, G. D. 2007. *Ethnic Identity and Aristocratic Competition in Republican Rome*. Cambridge, Cambridge University Press.

Fear, A. T. 1996. *Rome and Baetica: urbanization in southern Spain c.50BC–AD150*. Oxford, Clarendon.

Ferguson, L. 1992. *Uncommon Ground: archaeology and early African America, 1650–1800*. Washington, DC, Smithsonian Institution Press.

Foucault, M. 1979. *The History of Sexuality. Volume 1: An introduction*. London, Allen Lane.

Foucault, M. 1985. *The History of Sexuality volume 2: The use of pleasure*. New York, Random House.

Foucault, M. 1986. *The History of Sexuality volume 3: the care of the self*. New York, Pantheon.

Foxhall, L. and J. Salmon (eds) 1998a. *Thanking Men: masculinity and its self-representation in the classical tradition*. London, Routledge.

Foxhall, L. and J. Salmon (eds) 1998b. *When Men were Men: power and identity in classical antiquity*. London, Routledge.

Frader, L. L. 2004. Gender and labor in world history. In T. A. Meade and M. E. Wiesner-Hanks (eds) *A Companion to Gender History*. Oxford, Blackwell.

Freeman, P. W. M. 1997. Mommsen through to Haverfield: the origins of Romanization in late 19th-century Britain. In D. Mattingly (ed.) *Dialogues in Roman Imperialism: power, discourse and discrepant experience in the Roman empire*. Portsmouth, R. I., *Journal of Roman Archaeology* Supplementary Series 23, 27–50.

Frere, S. S. 1971. The forum and baths at Caistor by Norwich. *Britannia* 2: 1–26.

Frere, S. S. 1983. *Verulamium Excavations II*. London, Society of Antiquaries of London.

Frere, S. S. 1991. Roman Britain in 1990. 1. Sites explored. *Britannia* 22: 222–92.

Fulford, M. and J. Timby 2000. *Late Iron Age and Roman Silchester: excavations on the site of the forum-basilica 1977, 1980–86*. London, Society from the Promotion of Roman Studies.

García y Bellido, A. 1960. *Colonia Aelia Augusta Italica*. Madrid, Consejo Superior de Investigaciones Científicas

Gardner, A. 2002. Social identity and the duality of structure in late Roman-period Britain. *Journal of Social Archaeology* 2.3: 323–51.

Gardner, A. 2013. Thinking about Roman imperialism: postcolonialism, globalisation and beyond? *Britannia* 44: 1–25.

Gardner, J. 1993. *Being a Roman Citizen*. London, Routledge.

Gardner, J. F. 1986. *Women in Roman Law and Society*. London, Croom Helm.

Gardner, J. F. 2011. Slavery and Roman law. In K. Bradley and P. Cartledge (eds) *Cambridge World History of Slavery: the Ancient World*. Cambridge. Cambridge University Press: 414–37.

Garriguet, J. 2004. Grupos estatuarios imperiales de la Bética: la evidencia escultórica y epigráfica. In T. N. Bassarate and L. J. Gonçalves (eds) *IV Reunión sobre escultura romana en Hispania, Madrid*. Madrid, Ministerio de Cultura: 67–101.

Gazda, E. K., (ed.) 1991. *Roman Art in the Private Sphere. New Perspectives on the Architecture and Decor of the Domus, Villa, and Insula*. Ann Arbor, University of Michigan Press.

Geary, P. 1983. Ethnic identity as a situational construct in the early middle ages. *Mitteilungen der Anthropoligischen Gesellschaft in Wien* 133: 15–26.

Geary, P. 1994. *Phantoms of Remembrance: memory and oblivion at the end of the first millenium*. Princeton, Princeton University Press.

Gehrke, H.-J. 2009. From Athenian identity to European ethnicity – the cultural biography of the myth of Marathon. In T. Derks and N. Roymans (eds) *Ethnic Constructs in Antiquity: the Role of Power and Tradition*. Amsterdam, Amsterdam University Press: 85–99.

George, M., (ed.) 2005. *The Roman Family in the Empire: Rome, Italy and beyond*. Oxford, Oxford University Press.

Gero, J. M. 1991. Genderlithics: women's roles in stone tool production. In J. M. Gero and M. Conkey (eds) *Engendering Archaeology: women and prehistory*. Oxford, Blackwell: 163–93.

Gero, J. M. and M. W. Conkey 1991. *Engendering Archaeology: women and prehistory.* Oxford, Blackwell.
Giddens, A. 1984. *The Constitution of Society. Outline of a Theory of Structuration.* Oxford, Blackwells.
Gleason, M. W. 1995. *Making Men. Sophists and Self-representation in Ancient Rome.* Princeton NJ, Princeton University Press.
Goffmann, E. 1959. *The Presentation of the Self in Everyday Life.* New York, Doubleday.
Golden, M. 1988. Did the ancients care when their children died? *Greece & Rome* 35.2: 152–63.
Golvin, J.-C. 1988. *L'amphithêatre romain: essai sur la théorisation de sa forme et des ses fonctions.* Paris, Boccard.
Gómez-Pantoja, J. 2009. *Epigrafia anfiteatrale dell'Occidente Romano. Vol. VII: Baetica, Tarraconensis, Lusitania.* Roma, Quasar.
González, J. 1986. The lex Irnitana: a new copy of the Flavian municipal law. *Journal of Roman Studies* 76: 147–243.
Goodchild, R. G. 1946. The origins of the Romano-British forum. *Antiquity* 20: 70–7.
Gordon, R. 1990. Religion in the Roman empire: the civic compromise and its limits. In M. Beard and J. North (eds) *Pagan Priests: religion and power in the ancient world.* London, Duckworth: 233–55.
Goudineau, C. 1979. *Les Fouilles de la Maison au Dauphin. Recherches sur la Romanization de Vaison-la-Romaine. Gallia* Supplement 37.
Goudineau, C. and Y. d. Kisch 1999. *Vaison-la-Romaine.* Paris, Ministère de la Culture.
Gowland, R. 2001. Playing dead: implications of mortuary evidence for the social construction of childhood in Roman Britain. In G. Davies, A. Gardner and K. Lockyer (eds) *TRAC 2000. Proceedings of the tenth annual Theoretical Roman Archaeology Conference.* Oxford, Oxbow Books: 152–68.
Gowland, R. 2006. Aging in the past: examining age identity from funerary evidence. In R. Gowland and C. Knüsel (eds) *Social Archaeology of Funerary Remains.* Oxford, Oxbow Books: 143–54.
Gowland, R. 2007. Age, ageism, and osteological bias: the evidence from Late Roman Britain. In M. Harlow and R. Laurence (eds) *Age and Aging in the Roman Empire.* Portsmough, RI, *Journal of Roman Archaeology* Supplementary Series 65: 153–69.
Gowland, R. L. and A. T. Chamberlain 2002. A Bayesian approach to ageing perinatal skeletal material from archaeological sites: implications for the evidence for infanticide in Roman Britain. *Journal of Archaeological Science* 29.6: 677–85.
Gratton, J., S. Huxlet, L. A. Karak, H. Toland, D. Gilbertson, B. Pyatt and Z. Saad 2002. 'Death ... more desirable than life'? The human skeletal record and toxicological implications of ancient copper mining and smelting in Wadi Faynan, southwestern Jordan. *Toxicology and Industrial Health* 18: 297–307.
Gros, P. 1996. *L'architecture romaine.* Paris, les Manuels d'Art et d'Archeologie Antiques.
Gruen, E. S. 1992. *Culture and national identity in Republican Rome.* New York, Cornell University Press.
Gruen, E. S. 2011. *Rethinking the other in Antiquity.* Princeton, Princeton University Press.
Guijarro, S. 1997. The family in first century Galilee. In H. Moxnes,(ed.) *Constructing Early Christian Families: family as social reality and metaphor.* London, Routledge, 42–65.
Hajnal, J. 1965. European marriage patterns in perspective. In D. V. Glass and D. E. C. Eversley (eds) *Population in History: essays in historical demography.* London, Edward Arnold: 101–43.
Hales, S. 2000. At home with Cicero. *Greece and Rome* 47.1: 44–55.
Hales, S. 2009. Freedmen's cribs: domestic vulgarity on the Bay of Naples. In J. Prag and I. Repath (eds) *Petronius: a handbook.* Chichester, Wiley-Blackwell: 161–80.
Hall, J. M. 1997. *Ethnic Identity in Greek Antiquity.* Cambridge, Cambridge University Press.
Hammond, M. 1957. Composition of the senate, AD 68–225. *Journal of Roman Studies* 47: 74–81.
Hanson, W. S. 1997. Forces of change and methods of control. In D. Mattingly, (ed.) *Dialogues in Roman Imperialism. Power, Discourse and Discrepant Experience in the Roman Empire.* Portsmouth, R.I., *Journal of Roman Archaeology* Supplementary Series 23: 76–80.

Harkness, A. G. 1896. Age and marriage at death in the Roman empire. *Transactions of the American Philological Association* 27: 35–72.

Harlow, M. 2012. Dress and identity: an introduction. In M. Harlow (ed.) *Dress and Identity*. British Archaeological Report S2356, 1–5.

Harlow, M. 2014. Toys, dolls and the material culture of chidhood. In J. Evans Grubbs, T. Parkin and R. Bell (eds) *Oxford Handbook of Childhood and Education in the Classical World*. Oxford, Oxford University Press: 322–240.

Harlow, M. and R. Laurence 2002. *Growing Up and Growing Old in Ancient Rome*. London, Routledge.

Harlow, M. and R. Laurence 2007. Age and aging in the Roman empire. In M. Harlow and R. Laurence (eds) *Age and Aging in the Roman Empire*. Portsmouth, RI, *Journal of Roman Archaeology* Supplementary Series 65, 11–24.

Harris, W. V. 1980. Roman terracotta lamps: the organization of an industry. *Journal of Roman Studies* 70: 126–45.

Harris, W. V. 1989. *Ancient Literacy*. Cambridge, Mass., Harvard University Press.

Hartley, B. R. 2002. Associations of potters on stamps from la Graufesenque. In M. Genin and A. Vernhet (eds) *Céramiques de la Graufesenque et autres productions d'époque romaine. Nouvelles recherches*. Montagnac, Éditions Monique Mergoil: 133–38.

Hartog, F. 1988. *The Mirror of Herodotus: the representation of the other in the writing of history*. Berkeley CA, University of California Press.

Haselberger, L. 2007. *Urbem adornare: Rome's urban metamorphosis under Augustus*. Portsmouth, R. I., *Journal of Roman Archaeology* Supplementary Series 64.

Hastorf, C. A. 1991. Gender, space and food in prehistory. In J. M. Gero and M. W. Conkey (eds) *Engendering Archaeology: women and prehistory*. Oxford, Blackwells: 132–59.

Haverfield, F. and G. MacDonald 1923. *The Romanization of Roman Britain*. 4th ed. (rev. G. Macdonald). Oxford, Clarendon Press.

Hawley, R. and B. Levick (eds) 1995. *Women in Antiquity: new assessments*. London, Routledge.

Haynes, I. P. 1999. Military service and cultural identity in the auxilia. In A. Goldsworthy and I. P. Haynes (eds) *The Roman Army as a Community*. Portsmouth, R. I., *Journal of Roman Archaeology* Supplementary Series 34, 165–74.

Hemelrijk, E. A. 2005. Priestesses of the imperial cult in the Latin West: titles and function. *L'Antiquité Classique* 74: 137–70.

Hemelrijk, E. A. 2006. Priestesses of the imperial cult in the Latin west: benefactions and public honour. *L'Antiquité Classique* 75: 85–117.

Hemelrijk, E. A. 2007. Local empresses: priestesses of the Imperial cult in the cities of the Latin west. *Phoenix* 61.3/4: 318–49.

Hemelrijk, E. A. 2009. Women and sacrifice in the Roman empire. In O. Hekster, S. Schmidt-Hofner and C. Witschel (eds) *Ritual Dynamics and Religious Change in the Roman Empire*. Leiden, Brill: 253–67.

Henig, M. 2007. *A Corpus of Roman Engraved Gemstones from British Sites*. 3rd ed. Oxford, British Archaeological Report 8.

Hill, J. D. 1997. The end of one kind of body and the beginning of another kind of body? Toilet instruments and 'Romanization' in southern England during the first century AD. In A. Gwilt and C. C. Haselgrove (eds) *Reconstructing Iron Age Societies*. Oxford, Oxbow Books: 96–107.

Hill, J. D. 2001. Romanization, gender and class: recent approaches to identity in Britain and their possible consequences. In S. James and M. Millett (eds) *Britons and Romans: advancing an archaeological agenda*. York, Council of British Archaeology Research Report 125: 12–18.

Hingley, R. 1997. Resistance and domination: social change in Roman Britain. In D. Mattingly (ed.) *Dialogues in Roman Imperialism: power, discourse and discrepant experience in the Roman empire*. Portsmouth, R. I., *Journal of Roman Archaeology* Supplementary Series 23: 81–100.

Hingley, R. 2000. *Roman Officers and English Gentlemen*. London, Routledge.
Hingley, R. 2005. *Globalizing Roman Culture: unity, diversity and empire*. London, Routledge.
Hobsbawm, E. J. and T. O. Ranger 1983. *The Invention of Tradition*. Cambridge, Cambridge University Press
Hockey, J. and J. Draper 2005. Beyond the womb and the tomb: identity, (dis)embodiment and the life course. *Body & Society* 11.2: 41–57.
Hodder, I. 1982. *Symbols in Action: ethnoarchaeological studies of material culture*. Cambridge, Cambridge University Press.
Hodder, I. 1986. *Reading the Past: current approaches to interpretation in archaeology*. Cambridge, Cambridge University Press.
Holloway, S. L. and G. Valentine 2000. Children's geographies and the new social studies of childhood. In S. L. Holloway and G. Valentine (eds) *Children's Geographies: playing, living and learning*. London, Routledge, 1–26.
Hope, V. 1998. Negotiating identity and status: the gladiators of Roman Nîmes. In R. Laurence and J. Berry (eds) *Cultural Identity in the Roman Empire*. London, Routledge: 179–95.
Hope, V. 2001. *Constructing Identity: the Roman funerary monuments of Aquileia, Mainz and Nimes*. Oxford, British Archaeological Report S960.
Hopkins, K. 1965. The age of Roman girls at marriage. *Population Studies* 20: 309–27.
Hopkins, K. 1966. On the probable age structure of the Roman population. *Population Studies* 20: 245–64.
Hopkins, K. 1980. Taxes and trade in the Roman Empire (200 BC–AD 400). *Journal of Roman Studies* 70: 101–25.
Hopkins, K. 1983. *Death and Renewal*. Cambridge, Cambridge University Press.
Hopkins, K. 1987. Graveyard for historians. In F. Hinard (ed.) *La mort, les mortes et l'au-delà dans le monde romain*. Caen, Centre de publications de l'Université de Caen: 113–26.
Huskinson, J. 1996. *Roman Children's Sarcophagi. Their Decoration and its Social Significance*. Oxford, Clarendon Press.
Jackson, R. 1983. The Chester gladiator rediscovered. *Britannia* 14: 87–95.
James, S. 1999. The community of soldiers: a major identity and centre of power in the Roman empire. In P. Baker, C. Forcey, S. Jundi and R. Witcher (eds) *TRAC98. Proceedings of the eighth annual Theoretical Roman Archaeology Conference*. Oxford, Oxbow Books: 14–25.
James, S. 2001a. 'Romanization' and the peoples of Britain. In S. Keay and N. Terrenato (eds) *Italy and the West: comparative issues in Romanization*. Oxford, Oxbow Books: 187–209.
James, S. 2001b. Soldiers and civilians: identity and interaction in Roman Britain. In S. James and M. Millett (eds) *Britons and Romans: advancing an archaeological agenda*. York, Council for British Archaeology Research Report 125: 77–89.
James, S. and M. Millett 2001. Introduction. In S. James and M. Millett (eds) *Britons and Romans: advancing an archaeological agenda*. York, Council for British Archaeology Research Report 125: 1–3.
Jenks, C. 1996. *Childhood*. London, Routledge.
Jiménez, A. 2011. Pure hybridism: late Iron Age sculpture in southern Iberia. *World Archaeology* 43.1: 102–23.
Johns, C. 1997. *The Snettisham Roman Jeweller's Hoard*. London, British Museum Press.
Johnson, M. 1999. *Archaeological Theory: an introduction*. Oxford, Blackwell Publishers.
Johnson, M. H. 1989. Conceptions of agency in archaeological interpretation. *Journal of Anthropological Archaeology* 8.2: 189–211.
Jones, S. 1997. *The Archaeology of Ethnicity*. London, Routledge.
Joshel, S. R. 1992. *Work, Identity, and Legal Status at Rome: a study of the occupational inscriptions*. Norman, University of Oklahoma Press.
Joshel, S. R. 2010. *Slavery in the Roman World*. Cambridge, Cambridge University Press.

Joshel, S. R. 2013. Geographies of slave containment and movement. In *Roman Slavery and Roman Material Culture*. Toronto, University of Toronto Press: 99–128.

Joshel, S. R. and S. Murnaghan 1998. *Women and Slaves in Greco-Roman Culture: differential equations*. London, Routledge.

Kampen, N. B. 1982. Social status and gender in Roman art: the case of the saleswoman. In N. Broude and M. D. Garrard (eds) *Feminism and Art History: questioning the litany*. New York, Harper and Row: 62–77.

Keay, S. 2013. Were the Iberians Hellenised? In J. Prag and J. C. Quinn (eds) *The Hellenistic West: rethinking the ancient Mediterranean*. Cambridge, Cambridge University Press: 300–19.

Keay, S. J. 1995. Innovation and adaptation the contribution of Rome to urbanism in Iberia. In B. W. Cunliffe and S. J. Keay (eds) *Social Complexity and the Development of Towns in Iberia*. London, *Proceedings of the British Academy* 86: 291–337.

Keay, S. J. 1997. Early Roman Italica and the Romanization of western Baetica. In A. Caballos and P. Léon (eds) *Itálica MMCC. Actas de las jornadas del 2.200 aniversario de la fundación de Italica*. Seville, Consejería de Cultura: 21–47.

Kimes, T., C. Haselgrove and I. Hodder 1982. A method for the identification of the location of regional cultural boundaries. *Journal of Anthropological Archaeology* 1.2: 113–31.

King, A. C. 1990. *Roman Gaul and Germany*. London, British Museum Press.

King, A. C. 2001. The Romanization of diet in the western empire: comparative archaeozoological studies. In S. J. Keay and N. Terrenato (eds) *Italy and the West: comparative issues in Romanization*. Oxford, Oxbow Books: 210–23.

Kleibrink, M. 1997. The style and technique of the engraved gems. In C. Johns (ed.) *The Snettisham Roman Jeweller's Hoard*. London, British Museum Press, 25–33.

Kleiner, D. E. and S. B. Matheson 1996. *I, Claudia: women in ancient Rome*. New Haven, Yale University Art Gallery.

Köhne, E., C. Ewigleben and R. Jackson 2000. *Gladiators and Caesars: the power of spectacle in ancient Rome*. London, British Museum.

Kolendo, J. 1981. La répartition des places aux spectacles et la stratification sociale dans l'Empire Romain: à propos des inscriptions sur les gradins des amphithéâtres et théâtres. *Ktema* 6: 301–13.

Konstan, D. 2001. To Hellenikon ethnos: ethnicity and the construction of ancient Greek identitiy. In I. Malkin, (ed.) *Ancient Perceptions of Greek Ethnicity*. Cambridge MA, Harvard University Press: 29–50.

Laes, C. 2007. School-teachers in the Roman empire: a survey of the epigraphical evidence. *Acta Classica: Proceedings of the Classical Association of South Africa* 50: 109–207.

Lago, D. and C. Katsari 2008. *Slave Systems: ancient and modern*. Cambridge, Cambridge University Press.

Laurence, R. 1998. Territory, ethnonyms and geography: the construction of identity in Roman Italy. In R. Laurence and J. Berry (eds) *Cultural Identity in the Roman Empire*. London, Routledge: 95–110.

Laurence, R. 1999. Review: Theoretical Roman Archaeology. *Britannia* 30: 387–90.

Laurence, R. 2000. Metaphors, monuments and texts: the life course in Roman culture. *World Archaeology* 31.3: 442–55.

Laurence, R. 2006. *Roman Pompeii: space and society*. 2nd ed. London, Routledge.

Laurence, R. 2013. Writing in public space from child to adult: the meaning of graffiti. In G. Sears, P. Keegan and R. Laurence (eds) *Written Space in the Latin West, 200BC to AD300*. London, Bloomsbury: 123–34.

Lefebvre, S. 2004. Espace et pouvoir local dans les provinces occidentales: quelques remarques. In C. Auliard and L. Bodiou (eds) *Au jardin des Hespérides: histoire, société et épigraphie des mondes anciens. Mélanges offerts à Alain Tranoy*. Rennes, Presses Universitaires de Rennes: 379–406.

Lewis, M. 2011. The osteology of infancy and childhood: misconceptions and potential. In M. Lally and A. Moore (eds) *(Re)thinking the Little Ancester: new perspectives on the archaeology of infancy and childhood*. Oxford. British Archaeological Report S2271: 1–13.

Lillehammer, G. 1996. A child is born: the world of the child in an archaeological perspective. *Norwegian Archaeological Review* 22.2: 89–105.

Linduff, K. M. 1979. Epona: a Celt among the Romans. *Latomus* 38.4: 817–37.

Lintott, A. 1993. *Imperium Romanum: politics and administration*. London, Routledge.

Liu, J. 2009. *Collegia centonariorum: the guilds of textile dealers in the Roman West*. Leiden, Brill.

Lucy, S. 2000. *The Anglo-Saxon Way of Death: burial rites in early England*. Stroud, Sutton.

Lucy, S. 2005. Ethnic and cultural identities. In M. Diaz-Andreu, S. Lucy, S. Babic and D. N. Edwards (eds) *The Archaeology of Identity. Approaches to gender, age, status, ethnicity and religion*. London, Routledge: 86–109.

Macias Solé, J. M., I. Fiz Fernández, L. Piñol Masgoret, M. T. Miró i Alaix and J. Guitart i Duran 2007. *Planimetria arqueològica de Tàrraco*. Tarragona, Institut Català d'Arqueologia Clàssica.

Mackie, N. 1990. Urban munificence and the growth of urban consciousness in Roman Spain. In T. F. C. Blagg and M. Millett (eds) *The Early Roman Empire in the West*. Oxford, Oxbow Books: 179–91.

MacMullen, R. 1982. The epigraphic habit in the Roman empire. *American Journal of Philology* 103: 233–46.

Malkin, I. 1994. *Myth and territory in the Spartan Mediterranean*. Cambridge, Cambridge University Press.

Malkin, I. 1998. *The returns of Odysseus: colonization and ethnicity*. Berkeley; London, University of California Press.

Malkin, I. 2001. Introduction. In I. Malkin, (ed.) *Ancient perceptions of Greek ethnicity*. Cambridge, Mass., Harvard University Press.

Mañas Romero, I. 2010. *Pavimentos decorativos de Itálica (Santiponce, Sevilla). Un estudio arqueológico*.

Mann, J. C. 1983. *Legionary recruitment and military settlement during the Principate*. London, Institute of Archaeology.

Marichal, R. 1988. *Les graffites de la Graufesenque*. Paris, Éditions du Centre national de la Recherche scientifique.

Marshall, Y. 2008. Archaeological possibilities for feminist theories of transition and transformation. *Feminist Theory* 9.1: 25–45.

Martelle, H. 1999. Redefining craft specialisation: women's labor and pottery production – an Iroquoian example. In B. Arnold and N. Wicker (eds) *From the Ground Up: beyond gender theory in archaeology*. Oxford, British Archaeological Report S812: 133–42.

Martin-Kilcher, S. 2000. *Mors immatura* in the Roman world – a mirror of society and tradition. In J. Pearce, M. Millett and M. Struck (eds) *Burial, Society and Context in the Roman world*. Oxford, Oxbow Books: 63–77.

Mattingly, D. 2004. Becoming Roman: expressing identity in a provincial setting. *Journal of Roman Archaeology* 17: 5–25.

Mattingly, D. 2006. *Britain: an imperial possession*. London, Allen Lane.

Mattingly, D. J. 1996. From one colonialism to another: imperialism and the Maghreb. In J. Webster and N. Cooper (eds) *Roman Imperialism: post-colonial perspectives*. Leicester, Leicester Archaeology Monographs: 49–69.

Mattingly, D. J. 2011. *Imperialism, Power, and Identity: experiencing the Roman empire*. Princeton, Princeton University Press.

Maurin, L., M. Theuré and F. Tassaux 1994. *Inscriptions latine d'Aquitaine, Santons*. Bordeaux, Centre Pierre Paris.

Mays, S. 1993. Infanticide in Roman Britain. *Antiquity* 67: 883–88.

Mays, S. 2000. The archaeology and history of infanticide, and its occurrence in earlier British populations. In J. Sofaer Derevenski (ed.) *Children and Material Culture*. London, Routledge: 180–90.
Mays, S. and J. Eyers 2011. Perinatal infant death at the Roman villa site at Hambleden, Buckinghamshire, England. *Journal of Archaeological Science* 38.8: 1931–38.
McDonnell, M. A. 2006. *Roman Manliness: virtus and the Roman republic*. Cambridge, Cambridge University Press.
Meskell, L. 2007. Archaeologies of identity. In T. Insoll (ed.) *The archaeology of identity: a reader*. London, Routledge: 23–43.
Meyer, E. A. 1990. Explaining the epigraphic habit in the Roman empire: the evidence of the epitaphs. *Journal of Roman Studies* 80: 74–96.
Meyer, K. A. 1999. Axial peristyle houses in the western empire. *Journal of Roman Archaeology* 12: 101–21.
Miles, D. 1984. *Archaeology at Barton Court Farm, Abingdon, Oxon: an investigation of late Neolithic, Iron Age, Romano-British, and Saxon settlements*. London, Council for British Archaeology Research Report 50.
Miller, D. and C. Tilley 1984. Ideology, power and prehistory: an introduction. In D. Miller and C. Tilley (eds) *Ideology, Power and Prehistory*. Cambridge, Cambridge University Press: 1–15.
Millett, M. 1990a. *The Romanization of Britain: an essay in archaeological interpretation*. Cambridge, Cambridge University Press.
Millett, M. 1990b. Romanization: historical issues and archaeological interpretations. In T. F. C. Blagg and M. Millett (eds) *The Early Roman Empire in the West*. Oxford, Oxbow Books: 35–41.
Millett, M. 2001. Roman interaction in north-western Iberia. *Oxford Journal of Archaeology* 20.2: 157–70.
Millett, M. 2003/04. The Romanization of Britain: changing perspectives. *Kodai: Journal of Ancient History* 13/14: 169–73.
Millett, M. (ed.) 2006. *Shiptonthorpe, East Yorkshire: archaeological studies of a Romano-British roadside settlement*. Leeds, Yorkshire Archaeological Report 5.
Millett, M. and R. Gowland 2015. Infant and child burial rites in Roman Britain: a study from East Yorkshire. *Britannia* 45, available on CJO2015. doi:10.1017/S0068113X15000100.
Mirza, M. N. and D. Dungworth 1995. The potential misuse of genetic analyses and the social construction of 'race' and 'ethnicity'. *Oxford Journal of Archaeology* 14.3: 345–54.
Moore, A. 2009. Hearth and home: the burial of infants within Romano-British contexts. *Childhood in the Past* 2: 33–54.
Moore, A. 2010. Age and identity in funerary contexts: the elderly in southern Roman Britain. In A. Moore, G. Taylor, E. Harris, P. Girdwood and L. Shipley (eds) *TRAC2009. Proceedings of the nineteenth annual Theoretical Roman Archaeology Conference*. Oxford, Oxbow Books: 105–19.
Moore, H. 1986. *Space, Text and Gender. An Anthropological Study of the Marakwet of Kenya*. Cambridge, Cambridge University Press.
Moore, J. and E. Scott 1997. *Invisible People and Processes: writing gender and childhood into European archaeology*. London, Leicester University Press.
Morris, I. 2001. Remaining invisible: the archaeology of the excluded in Classical Athens. In S. R. Joshel (ed.) *Women and Slaves in Greco-Roman Culture: differential equations*. London, Routledge: 193–220.
Morris, I. 2011. Archaeology and Greek slavery. In K. Bradley and P. Cartledge (eds) *The Cambridge World History of Slavery: the ancient Mediterranean world*. Cambridge, Cambridge University Press: 176–93.
Mouritsen, H. 2011. *The Freedman in the Roman World*. Cambridge, Cambridge : Cambridge University Press.
Mullen, A. and P. James 2012. *Multilingualism in the Graeco-Roman Worlds*. Cambridge, Cambridge University Press.

Nash, M. 1989. *The Cauldron of Ethnicity in the Modern World.* Chicago, University of Chicago Press.

Neal, D. S. and S. R. Cosh 2009. *Roman Mosaics of Britain. Volume 3 South-east Britain. Part 2.* London, Society of Antiquaries.

Nelson, S. M. 2006. Introduction: archaeological perspectives on gender. In S. M. Nelson (ed.) *Handbook of Gender Archaeology.* Berkeley CA, AltaMira Press: 1–27.

Nevett, L. 1997. Perceptions of domestic space in Roman Italy. In B. Rawson and P. Weaver (eds) *The Roman Family in Italy: status, sentiment, space.* Oxford, Clarendon Press: 281–98.

Niblett, R. 2001. *Verulamium. The Roman city of St Albans.* Stroud, Tempus.

Nicolay, J. 2002. The use and significance of military equipment and horse gear from non-military contexts in the Batavian area: continuity from the Late Iron Age to the Early Roman period. In T. Grünewald and S. Seibel (eds) *Kontinuität und Diskontinuität. Germania inferior am Beginn und am Ende der römischen Herrschaft.* Berlin, Walter de Gruyter: 345–73.

Nicolet, C. 1980. *The World of the Citizen in Republican Rome.* London, Batsford.

Nicolet, C. 1991. *Space, Geography and Politics in the Early Roman Empire.* Ann Arbor, University of Michigan Press.

Nielsen, M. 1989. Women and family in a changing society: a quantitative approach to late Etruscan burials. *Analecta Romana Instituti Danici* 17–18: 53–98.

Noreña, C. F. 2011. *Imperial Ideals in the Roman West: representation, circulation, power.* Cambridge, Cambridge University Press.

Noy, D. 2010. Epigraphic evidence for immigrants at Rome and in Roman Britain. In H. Eckardt (ed.) *Roman Diasporas: archaeological approaches to mobility and diversity in the Roman empire.* Portsmouth, R. I., *Journal of Roman Archaeology* Supplementary Series 78, 13–26.

Oliver, J. H. 1953. The ruling power: a study of the Roman empire in the second century after Christ through the Roman oration of Aelius Aristides. *Transactions of the American Philosophical Association* 53: 871–1003.

Olson, K. 2008. *Dress and the Roman Woman: self-presentation and society.* London, Routledge.

Orejas, A. and F. J. Sánchez-Palencia 2002. Mines, territorial organization, and social structure in Roman Iberia: Carthago Noua and the Peninsular northwest. *American Journal of Archaeology* 106.4: 581–99.

Painter, B. 2005. *Mussolini's Rome: Rebuilding the Eternal City.* New York, Macmillan.

Parkin, T. 2003. *Old Age in the Roman World: a cultural and social history.* Baltimore, John Hopkins University Press.

Patterson, C. B. 1998. *The Family in Greek History.* Cambridge MA, Harvard University Press.

Patterson, J. 2000. *Political Life in the City of Rome.* Bristol, Bristol Classical Press.

Peacock, D. P. S. 1982. *Pottery in the Roman World: an ethnoarchaeological approach.* London, Longman.

Pearce, J. 2001. Infants, cemetaries and communities in the Roman provinces. In G. Davies, A. Gardner and K. Lockyer (eds.) *TRAC 2000. Proceedings of the tenth annual Theoretical Roman Archaeology Conference.* Oxford, Oxbow Books: 125–43.

Peers, L. 1999. 'Many tender ties': the shifting contexts and meanings of the S BLACK Bag. *World Archaeology* 31.2: 288–302.

Pelletier, A. 1984. *La femme dans la société gallo-romaine.* Paris, Picard.

Pelletier, A. 1993. *La civilisation gallo-romaine de A à Z.* Lyon, Presses universitaires de Lyon.

Perego, E. 2012. Family relations in Late Bronze Age, Iron Age and Early Roman Veneto (Italy): preliminary considerations on the basis of osteological analysis and epigraphy. In R. Laurence and A. Strömberg (eds) *Families in the Graeco-Roman World.* London, Continuum Books: 121–42.

Perring, D. 2002. *The Roman House in Britain.* London, Routledge.

Peterson, J. D. 2006. Gender and early farming societies. In S. M. Nelson (ed.) *Handbook of Gender Archaeology.* Berkeley CA, AltaMira: 537–70.

Phang, S. A. 2002. The families of Roman soldiers (first and second centuries A.D.): culture, law and practice. *Journal of Family History* 27: 352–73.
Philpott, R. 1991. *Burial Practices in Roman Britain: a survey of grave treatment and furnishing AD43–410.* Oxford, British Archaeological Report 210.
Pitts, M. 2007. The Emperor's New Clothes? The utility of identity in Roman archaeology. *American Journal of Archaeology* 111.4: 693–713.
Pomeroy, S. B. 1975. *Goddesses, Whores, Wives and Slaves.* New York, Schocken Books.
Pomeroy, S. B. 1997. *Families in Classical and Hellenistic Greece: representations and realities.* Oxford, Clarendon Press.
Prag, J. R. W. 2002. Epigraphy by numbers: Latin and the epigraphic culture in Sicily. In A. E. Cooley (ed.) *Becoming Roman, Writing Latin? Literacy and epigraphy in the Roman West.* Portsmouth, R. I., *Journal of Roman Archaeology* Supplementary Series 48: 14–31.
Pugsley 2003. *Roman Domestic Wood.* Oxford, British Archaeological Report S1118.
Purcell, N. 1995. The Roman *Villa* and the Landscape of Production. In T. J. Cornell and K. Lomas (eds) *Urban Society in Roman Italy.* London, UCL Press, 151–79.
Quinnell, H. 1986. Cornwall during the Iron Age and the Roman period. *Cornish Archaeology* 25: 111–34.
Rawson, B. (ed.) 1986. *The Family in Ancient Rome: new perspectives.* London, Croom Helm.
Rawson, B. (ed.) 1991. *Marriage, Divorce and Children in Ancient Rome.* Oxford, Clarendon Press.
Rawson, B. 2005. The future of childhood studies. In K. Mustakallio, J. Hanska, H.-L. Sainio and V. Vuolanto (eds) *Hoping for Continuity: childhood, education and death in Antiquity and the Middle Ages.* Rome, Institutum Romanum Finlandiae.
Rawson, B. 2011. *A Companion to Families in the Greek and Roman Worlds.* Chichester, Wiley-Blackwell.
Rawson, B. and P. R. C. Weaver (eds) 1997. *The Roman Family: status, sentiment and space.* Oxford, Clarendon Press.
Rawson, E. 1987. Discrimina ordinum: the lex Iulia theatralis. *Papers of the British School at Rome* 55: 83–114.
Reece, R. 1995. Models in collision; east and west in Roman Britain. *Oxford Journal of Archaeology* 14.1: 113–15.
Revell, L. 2000. The creation of multiple identities in Roman Italica. In G. Fincham, G. Harrison, R. Holland and L. Revell (eds) *TRAC99. Proceedings of the ninth annual Theoretical Roman Archaeology Conference.* Oxford, Oxbow Books: 1–7.
Revell, L. 2005. The Roman life-course: a view from the inscriptions. *European Journal of Archaeology* 8.1: 43–63.
Revell, L. 2007. Architecture, power and politics: the forum-basilica in Roman Britain. In J. Sofaer (ed.) *Projecting Identities.* London, Blackwells.
Revell, L. 2009. *Roman Imperialism and Local Identities.* Cambridge Cambridge University Press.
Revell, L. 2010a. Geography and environment. In M. Harlow and R. Laurence (eds) *The History of Children and the Family Volume 1: Antiquity (500 BCE–800 CE).* Oxford, Berg: 61–78.
Revell, L. 2010b. Romanization: a feminist critique. In P. Girdwood, E. Harris, A. Moore, T. Moore, L. Shipley, and G. Taylor (eds) *TRAC 2010. Proceedings of the nineteenth annual Theoretical Roman Archaeology Conference.* Oxford, Oxbow Books: 1–10.
Revell, L. 2013. The written city: political inscriptions from Roman Baetica. In G. Sears, P. Keegan and R. Laurence (eds) *Written Space in the Latin West: 200BC–AD300.* London, Bloomsbury: 231–45.
Richardson, J. 2008. *The Language of Empire: Rome and the idea of empire from the third century BC to the second century AD.* Cambridge, Cambridge University Press.
Rodgers, R. 1995. Women underfoot in life and art: female representations in fourth-century Romano-British mosaics. *Journal of European Archaeology* 3.1: 177–87.

Rodríguez Cortés, J. and M. Salinas de Frías 2010. Las élites femeninas en la provincia romana de Lusitania. *Historia Antigua* 18: 243–55.
Rodríguez Gutiérrez, O. 2004. *El teatro romano de Itálica: estudio arqueoarquitectónico*. Madrid, Servicio de Publicaciones de la Universidad Autónoma de Madrid, Fundación Pastor de Estudios Clásicos, Diputación de Sevilla.
Rodríguez Hidalgo, J. M. 1991. Dos ejemplos domésticos en la Traianopolis (Itálica): las Casas de los Pájaros y de la Exedra. In AA.VV (ed.) *La casa urbana*: 303–11.
Rodríguez Hidalgo, J. M. and S. J. Keay 1995. Recent work in Italica. In B. W. Cunliffe and S. J. Keay (eds) *Social Complexity and the Development of Towns in Iberia from the Copper Age to the Second Century AD*. Oxford, Oxford University Press: 395–420.
Roldán Gómez, L. 1994. El anfiteatro de Itálica. Técnicas y materiales de construcción. In AA.VV (ed.) *Bimilenario del anfiteatro Romano de Mérida. El anfiteatro en la Hispania Romana*. Badajoz, Junta de Extremadura: 213–38.
Rosten, J. 2007. Identities in life and death in Roman Britain: the case of Baldock. In B. Croxford, N. Ray, R. Roth and N. White (eds) *TRAC2006. Proceedings of the sixteenth annual Theoretical Roman Archaeology Conference*. Oxford, Oxbow Books: 172–82.
Roth, U. 2011. Men without hope. *Papers of the British School at Rome* 79: 71–94.
Rothe, U. 2009. *Dress and Cultural Identity in the Rhine-Moselle Region of the Roman Empire*. Oxford, British Archaeological Report S2038.
Rothe, U. 2012. The "Third Way": Treveran women's dress and the "Gallic ensemble". *American Journal of Archaeology* 116.2: 235–52.
Rothe, U. 2013. Whose fashion? Men. women and Roman culture as reflected in dress in the cities of the Roman north-west. In E. A. Hemelrijk and G. Woolf (eds) *Women and the Roman City in the Latin West*. Leiden, Brill: 243–68.
Roymans, N. 1996. The sword or the plough. Regional dynamics in the romanization of Belgic Gaul and the Rhineland area. In N. Roymans (ed.) *From the Sword to the Plough. Three Studies on the Earliest Romanization of Northern Gaul*. Amsterdam, Amsterdam University Press: 9–126.
Roymans, N. 2004. *Ethnic Identity and Imperial Power*. Amsterdam, Amsterdam University Press.
Rueda Roigé, F.-J. 2002–3. El mosaico de las Estaciones de Casa de Hilas, en Itálica. *Locus Amoenus* 6: 7–20.
Ruiz de Arbulo, J. 2006. *Scipionum opus* and something more: an Iberian reading of the provincial capital (2nd–1st c. B.C.). In L. Abad Casal, S. Keay and S. Ramallo Asensio (eds) *Early Roman Towns in Hispania Tarraconensis*. Portsmouth, R. I., *Journal of Roman Archaeology* Supplementary Series 62. 62: 32–50.
Rüpke, J. 2006. Religion in the *lex Ursonensis*. In C. Ando and J. Rüpke (eds) *Religion and Law in Classical and Christian Rome*. Stuttgart, Franz Steiner Verlag: 34–46.
Said, E. 1979. *Orientalism*. London, Routledge.
Said, E. W. 1993. *Culture and Imperialism*. London, Random House.
Saller, R. P. 1987. Men's age at marriage and its consequences in the Roman family. *Classical Philology* 82: 21–34.
Saller, R. P. 1994. *Patriarchy, Property, and Death in the Roman Family*. Cambridge, Cambridge University Press.
Saller, R. P. and B. D. Shaw 1984. Tombstones and Roman family relations in the Principate: civilians, soldiers and slaves. *Journal of Roman Studies* 74: 124–56.
Sánchez-Palencia, F. J. and M. D. Fernández-Posse 2000. *Las Médulas, León: un paisaje cultural en la Asturia augustana*. León Spain, Instituto Leonés de Cultura, Diputación Provincial de León.
Scheid, J. 1992. The religious roles of women. In P. Schmitt Patel, (ed.) *A history of women in the west. Volume 1. From ancient goddess to Christian saints*. Cambridge MA, Harvard University Press: 377–408.

Scheidel, W. 1996. *Measuring Sex, Age and Death in the Roman Empire.* Ann Arbor, *Journal of Roman Archaeology Supplementary Series* 21.
Scheidel, W. 2003. The archaeology of ancient slavery (review of L. Schumacher *Slaverei in der Antike: Alltag und Schicksal der Unfreien*). *Journal of Roman Archaeology* 16: 577–81.
Scheidel, W. 2011. The Roman slave supply. In K. Bradley and P. Cartledge (eds) *The Cambridge World History of Slavery: the ancient Mediterranean World.* Cambridge, Cambridge University Press: 287–310.
Scott, E. 1991. Animal and infant burials in Romano-British villas: a revitalization movement. In P. Garwood, D. Jennings, R. Skeates and J. Toms (eds) *Sacred and Profane: proceedings of a conference on archaeology, ritual and religion, Oxford 1989.* Oxford, Oxford University Committee for Archaeology: 115–21.
Scott, E. 1993. Introduction: TRAC (Theoretical Roman Archaeology Conference) 1991. In E. Scott (ed.) *Theoretical Roman Archaeology: first conference proceedings.* Aldershot, Avebury: 1–4.
Scott, E. 1995. Women and gender relations in the Roman empire. In P. Rush (ed.) *Theoretical Roman Archaeology: second conference proceedings.* Aldershot, Avebury: 174–89.
Scott, E. 1999. *The Archaeology of Infancy and Infant Death.* Oxford, British Archaeological Report S819.
Scott, E. 2001. Unpicking a myth: the infanticide of female and disabled infants in antiquity. In G. Davies, A. Gardner and K. Lockyer (eds) *TRAC 2000. Proceedings of the tenth annual Theoretical Roman Archaeology Conference.* Oxford, Oxbow Books: 143–51.
Scott, S. 2000. *Art and Society in Fourth-century Britain: villa mosaics in context.* Oxford, Oxford University School of Archaeology.
Scott, S. 2003. Provincial art and Roman imperialism: an overview. In S. Scott and J. Webster (eds) *Roman Imperialism and Provincial Art.* Cambridge, Cambridge University Press: 1–7.
Sear, F. 2006. *Roman Theatres: an architectural study.* Oxford, Oxford University Press.
Shanks, M. and C. Tilley 1982. Ideology, symbolic power and ritual communication: a reinterpretation of Neolithic mortuary practices. In I. Hodder (ed.) *Symbolic and Structural Archaeology.* Cambridge, Cambridge University Press: 129–54.
Shanks, M. and C. Tilley 1992. *Reconstructing Archaeology: theory and practice.* 2nd ed. London, Routledge.
Shaw, B. D. 1987. The age of Roman girls at marriage: some reconsiderations. *Journal of Roman Studies* 77: 30–46.
Shaw, B. D. 1991. The cultural meaning of death: age and gender in the Roman family. In D. I. Kertzer and R. P. Saller (eds) *The Family in Italy: from antiquity to present.* New Haven, Yale University Press: 66–90.
Shennan, S. J. 1989. Introduction: archaeological approaches to cultural identity. In S. J. Shennan (ed.) *Archaeological Approaches to Cultural Identity.* London, Unwin Hyman: 1–32.
Sherwin-White, A. N. 1973. *The Roman Citizenship.* 2nd ed. Oxford, Clarendon Press.
Sigismund-Nielsen, H. 2007. Children for profit and pleasure. In M. Harlow and R. Laurence (eds) *Age and Aging in the Roman Empire.* Portsmouth, R. I., *Journal of Roman Archaeology* Supplementary Series 65, 39–54.
Sillières, P. 1995. *Baelo Claudia: une cité romaine de Bétique.* Madrid, Casa de Velázquez.
Silliman, S. W. 2001. Theoretical perspectives on labor and colonialism: reconsidering the California missions. *Journal of Anthropological Archaeology* 20.4: 379–407.
Silliman, S. W. 2010. Indigenous traces in colonial spaces: archaeologies of ambiguity, origin and practice. *Journal of Social Archaeology* 10.1: 28–58.
Slofstra, J. 1983. An anthropological approach to the study of Romanization processes. In R. Brandt and J. Slofstra (eds) *Roman and Native in the Low Countries: spheres of interaction.* Oxford, British Archaeological Report S184: 71–104.
Smith, A. D. 1986. *The Ethnic Origins of Nations.* Oxford, Blackwells.
Smith, J. M. H. 2005. *Europe after Rome: a new cultural history 500–1000.* Oxford, Oxford University Press.

Smith, J. T. 1978. Villas as a key to social structure. In M. Todd (ed.) *Studies in the Romano-British Villa*. Leicester, Leicester University Press: 149–86.

Smith, J. T. 1997. *Roman Villas: a study in social structure*. London, Routledge.

Sofaer Derevenski, J. (ed.) 2000a. *Children and Material Culture*. London, Routledge.

Sofaer Derevenski, J. 2000b. Rings of life: the role of early metalwork in mediating the gendered life course. *World Archaeology* 31.3: 389–406.

Sofaer, J. R. 2011. Towards a social bioarchaeology of age. In S. C. Agarwal and B. A. Glencross (eds) *Social Bioarchaeology*. Oxford, Wiley–Blackwell: 285–311.

Sørensen, M. L. S. 1997. Reading dress: the construction of social categories and identities in Bronze Age Europe. *Journal of European Archaeology* 5.1: 93–114.

Sørensen, M. L. S. 2000. *Gender Archaeology*. Malden MA, Polity Press.

Sørensen, M. L. S. 2007. On gender negotiation and its materiality. In S. Hamilton, R. Whitehouse and K. I. Wright (eds) *Archaeology and Women: ancient and modern issues*. Walnut Creek, CA, Left Coast Press: 41–51.

Spencer, P. 1990. The riddle of the Sphinx: theories of age and its transformations. In P. Spencer (ed.) *Anthropology and the Riddle of the Sphinx*. London, Routledge: 1–34.

Stern, H., M. Blanchard-Lemée, J.-P. Darmon, H. Lavagne, J. Lancha and C. Balmelle 1957. *Recueil général des mosaïques de la Gaule*. Paris, Centre national de la recherche scientifique.

Stewart, P. 2003. *Statues in Roman Society*. Oxford, Oxford University Press.

Stewart, P. 2009. *Totenmahl* reliefs in the northern provinces: a case-study in imperial sculpture. *Journal of Roman Archaeology* 22: 253–74.

Stewart, P. 2010. Geographies of provincialism in Roman sculpture. *RIHA Journal* 5.

Stone, S. 1994. The toga: from national to ceremonial costume. In J. L. Sebasta and L. Bonfante (eds) *The World of Roman Costume*. Madison WI, University of Wisconsin Press: 13–45.

Swan, V. G. 1992. Legio VI and its men: African legionaries in Britain. *Journal of Roman Pottery Studies* 5: 1–33.

Swan, V. G. 2009. *Ethnicity, Conquest, and Recruitment: two case studies from the northern military provinces*. Portsmouth, R. I., *Journal of Roman Archaeology* Supplementary Series 72.

Swift, E. 2011. Personal adornment. In L. Allason-Jones (ed.) *Artefacts in Roman Britain: their purpose and use*. Cambridge, Cambridge University Press: 194–218.

Swift, E. 2012. The archaeology of adornment and the toilet in Roman Britain and Gaul. In M. Harlow and A. Strömberg (eds) *Dress and Identity*. Oxford, British Archaeological Reports S2356: 47–57.

Talbert, R. J. A. 2004. Rome's provinces as framework for world-view. In L. de Ligt, E. A. Hemelrijk and H. W. Singor (eds) *Roman Rule and Civic Life: local and regional perspectives*. Amsterdam, J. C. Gieben: 21–37.

Terrenato, N. 1998. The Romanization of Italy: global acculturation or cultural bricolage. In C. Forcey, J. Hawthorne and R. Witcher (eds) *TRAC97. Proceedings of the seventh annual Theoretical Roman Archaeology Conference*. Oxford, Oxbow Books: 20–7.

Terrenato, N. 2005. The deceptive archetype: Roman colonialism in Italy and postcolonial thought. In H. Hurst and S. Owens (eds) *Ancient Colonizations: analogy, similarity and difference*. London, Duckworth: 59–72.

Thébert, Y. 1993. Private and public spaces: the components of the *domus*. In E. D'Ambra, (ed.) *Roman Art in Context: an anthology*. Englewood Cliffs NJ, Prentice-Hall: 213–37.

Thomas, J. 1998. *Time, Culture and Identity: an interpretive archaeology*. New York, Routledge.

Thomas, N. 1991. *Entangled Objects: exchange, material culture, and colonialism in the Pacific*. Cambridge MA, Harvard University Press.

Thompson, F. H. 2003. *The archaeology of Greek and Roman slavery*. London, Duckworth.

Tomlin, R. S. O. 2003. 'The girl in question': a new text from Roman London. *Britannia* 34: 41–51.

Treggiari, S. 1976. Jobs for women. *American Journal of Ancient History* 1: 76–104.

Trigger, B. 1989. *A History of Archaeological Thought*. Cambridge, Cambridge University Press.
Trigger, B. G. 2006. *A History of Archaeological Thought*. 2nd ed. Cambridge, Cambridge University Press.
Trillmich, W. and P. Zanker (eds) 1990. *Staftbild und Ideologie. Die Monumentalisierung hispanischer Städte zwischen Republik und Kaiserzeit. Kolloquium in Madrid vom 19. bis 23. Oktober 1987*. Munich, Verlag der Bayerischen Akademie der Wissenschaften.
Tronchetti, C. and P. Van Dommelen 2005. Entangled objects and hybrid practices: colonial contacts and elite connections at Monte Prama, Sardinia. *Journal of Mediterranean Archaeology* 18.2: 183–208.
Trow, S., S. James and T. Moore 2009. *Becoming Roman, Being Gallic, Staying British: research and excavations at Ditches 'hillfort' and villa 1984-2006*. Oxford, Oxbow Books.
Trümper, M. 2009. *Graeco-Roman Slave Markets: fact or fiction?* Oxford, Oxbow Books.
Upex, S. 2008. *The Romans in the East of England: Settlement and Landscape in the Lower Nene Valley*. Stroud, Tempus.
van Driel-Murray, C. 1995. Gender in question. In P. Rush (ed.) *Theoretical Roman Archaeology: second conference proceedings*. Aldershot, Avebury: 3–21.
van Driel-Murray, C. 2002. Ethnic soldiers: the experience of the Lower Rhine tribes. In T. Grünewald and T. Seibel (eds) *Kontinuität und Diskontinuität. Germania inferior um Geginn und am Ende der römischen Herrschaft. Beiträge des deutsch-niederländischen Kolloquiums in der Katholieke Universiteit Nijmegen (27. bis 30.06.2001)*. Berlin, Walter de Gruyter: 200–17.
Versluys, M. J. 2002. *Aegyptiaca Romana. Nilotic Scenes and Roman View of Egypt*. Leiden, Brill.
Versluys, M. J. 2014. Understanding objects in motion. An archaeological dialogue on Romanization. *Archaeological Dialogues* 21.01: 1–20.
Veyne, P. 1993. Humanitas: Romans and non-Romans. In A. Giardina (ed.) *The Romans*. Chicago, University of Chicago Press: 342–69.
Wacher, J. S. 1995. *The Towns of Roman Britain*. 2nd ed. London, Batsford.
Wallace-Hadrill, A. 1990. Roman arches and Greek honours: the language of power at Rome. *Proceedings of the Cambridge Philological Society* 36: 143–81.
Wallace-Hadrill, A. 1994. *Houses and Society in Pompeii and Herculaneum*. Princeton, Princeton University Press.
Wallace-Hadrill, A. 2008. *Rome's Cultural Revolution*. Cambridge, Cambridge University Press.
Ward-Perkins, J. B. 1970. From republic to empire: reflections on the early provincial architecture of the Roman west. *Journal of Roman Studies* 60: 1–19.
Watts, D. J. 1989. Infant burials and Romano-British Christianity. *Archaeological Journal* 46: 372–83.
Weaver, P. R. C. 1972. *Familia Caesaris: a social study of the Emperor's freedmen and slaves*. Cambridge, Cambridge University Press.
Weber, M. 1968 [1956]. *Economy and Society. An Outline of Interpretive Sociology*. New York: Bedminster Press.
Webster, J. 1995. Interpretatio: Roman word power and the Celtic gods. *Britannia* 26: 153–61.
Webster, J. 1996. Roman imperialism and the 'post-imperial' age. In J. Webster and N. Cooper (eds) *Roman Imperialism: post-colonial perspectives*. Leicester, Leicester University Press.
Webster, J. 1997. A negotiated syncretism: readings on the development of Romano-Celtic religion. In D. Mattingly (ed.) *Dialogues in Roman Imperialism: power, discourse and discrepant experience in the Roman empire*. Portsmouth, R. I., *Journal of Roman Archaeology* Supplementary Series 23: 165–84.
Webster, J. 2001. Creolizing the Roman provinces. *American Journal of Archaeology* 105.2: 209–25.
Webster, J. 2003. Art as resistance and negotiation. In S. Scott and J. Webster (eds) *Roman Imperialism and Provincial Art*. Cambridge, Cambridge University Press: 24–51.
Webster, J. 2005. Archaeologies of slavery and servitude: bringing 'New World' perspectives to Roman Britain. *Journal of Roman Archaeology* 18: 161–79.
Webster, J. 2008. Less beloved. Roman archaeology, slavery and the failure to compare. *Archaeological Dialogues* 15.2: 103–23.

Whitehouse, R. 1998. Introduction. In R. Whitehouse (ed.) *Gender and Italian Archaeology: challenging the stereotypes.* London, Accordia Research Institute and Institute of Archaeology: 1–8.

Wiedemann, T. 1989. *Adults and Children in the Roman Empire.* London, Routledge.

Wiedemann, T. 1992. *Emperors and Gladiators.* London, Routledge.

Wild, J. P. 1968. Clothing in the north-west provinces of the Roman empire. *Bonner Jahrbücker* 168: 166–240.

Wilkie, L. 2000. Not merely child's play: creating a historical archaeology of children and childhood. In J. Sofaer Derevenski (ed.) *Children and Material Culture.* Cambridge, Cambridge University Press: 100–13.

Willems, W. H. J. 1984. Romans and Batavians: a regional study in the Dutch East River Area II. *Berichten van de Rijksdienst voor het Oudheidkundig Bodemonderzoek* 34: 39–331.

Wilmott, T. 2007. *The Roman Amphitheatre in Britain.* Stroud, Tempus.

Wilson, P. R. 2002. *Cataractonium: Roman Catterick and its hinterland; excavations and research, 1958–97; part II.* York, Council for British Archaeology Research Report 129.

Wiseman, T. P. 1994. *Conspicui postes tectaque digno deo*: the public image of aristocratic and imperial houses in the Late Republic and Early Empire. In T. P. Wiseman (ed.) *Historiography and Imagination: eight essays on Roman culture.* Exeter, Exeter University Press: 98–115.

Woolf, G. 1992. Imperialism, empire and the integration of the Roman economy. *World Archaeology* 23.3: 283–93.

Woolf, G. 1994. Power and the spread of writing in the West. In A. K. Bowman and G. Woolf (eds) *Literacy and Power in the Ancient World.* Cambridge, Cambridge University Press: 84–98.

Woolf, G. 1995. The formation of Roman provincial cultures. In J. Metzler, M. Millett, N. Roymans and J. Slofstra (eds) *Integration in the Early Roman West. The role of culture and ideology.* Luxembourg, Dossiers d'Archeologie du Musee National d'Histoire et d'Art IV, 9–18.

Woolf, G. 1996. Monumental writing and the expansion of Roman society in the early empire. *Journal of Roman Studies* 86: 22–39.

Woolf, G. 1998. *Becoming Roman: the origins of provincial civilization in Gaul.* Cambridge Cambridge University Press.

Woolf, G. 2001. Representation as cult: the case of the Jupiter columns. In W. Spickermann, H. Cancik and J. Rüpke (eds) *Religion in den germanischen Provinzen Roms.* Tubingen, Mohr Siebeck: 117–34.

Woolf, G. 2003. Seeing Apollo in Roman Gaul and Germany. In S. Scott and J. Webster (eds) *Roman Imperialism and Provincial Art.* Cambridge, Cambridge University Press: 139–52.

Woolf, G. 2005. Family history in the Roman north-west. In M. George (ed.) *The Roman Family in the Empire: Rome, Italy and beyond.* Oxford, Oxford University Press: 231–54.

Woolf, G. 2009. Cruptorix and his kind. Talking ethnicity on the middle ground. In T. Derks and N. Roymans (eds) *Ethnic Constructs in Antiquity: the role of power and tradition.* Amsterdam, Amsterdam University Press: 207–17.

Wuilleumier, P. 1963. *Inscriptions latines des trois Gaules (France).* Paris, Centre national de la recherche scientifique.

Wyke, M. 1994. Women in the mirror: the rhetoric of adornment in the Roman world. In L. J. Archer, S. Fischler and M. Wyke (eds) *Women in Ancient Societies: an illusion of the night.* London, Macmillan: 134–51.

Wylie, A. 1991. Gender theory and the archaeological record: why is there no archaeology of gender. In M. W. Conkey and J. M. Gero (eds) *Engendering Archaeology: women in prehistory.* Oxford, Blackwells: 31–56.

Wylie, A. 1992. The interplay of evidential constraints and political interests: recent archaeological research on gender. *American Antiquity* 57.1: 15–35.

Wylie, A. 2002. *Thinking from Things: essays in the philosophy of archaeology.* Berkeley CA, University of California Press.

Zahn, E. 1968. *Die Igeler Säule bei Trier*. Cologne, Rheinischer Verein für Denkmalpflege und Heimatschutz.

Zanker, P. 1988. *The Power of Images in the Age of Augustus*. Ann Arbor, University of Michigan Press.

Zanker, P. 1998. *Pompeii. Public and Private Life*. Cambridge MA, Harvard University Press.

Zienkiewicz, J. D. 1986. *The Legionary Fortress Baths at Caerleon. Volume 2: the finds*. Cardiff, National Museum of Wales and Cadw.

Zihlman, A. L. 1998. Woman the gatherer: the role of women in early hominid evolution. In K. Hays-Gilpin and D. S. Whitley (eds) *Reader in Gender Archaeology*. London and New York, Routledge: 91–105.

Zoll 1995. A view through inscriptions: the epigraphic evidence for religion at Hadrian's Wall. In J. Metzler, M. Millett, N. Roymans and J. Slofstra (eds) *Integration in the Early Roman West: the role of culture and ideology*. Luxenbourg: 129–37.

Index